THE
CONSUMER'S
BRAND-NAME
GUIDE TO
HOUSEHOLD
PRODUCTS

Other books by the author:

The Dictionary of Medical Folklore
Cosmetics: What the Ads Don't Tell You
🔴 The Book of Chocolate

THE CONSUMER'S BRAND-NAME GUIDE TO HOUSEHOLD PRODUCTS

by Carol Ann Rinzler

LIPPINCOTT & CROWELL, PUBLISHERS   NEW YORK

FIRST EDITION

Designed by Ginger Legato

U.S. Library of Congress Cataloging in Publication Data

Rinzler, Carol Ann.
    The consumer's brand-name guide to household products.

    Includes index.
    1. Consumer education. 2. Household supplies.
3. Branded merchandise—United States. I. Title.
TX335.R49   640.73   79–27842
ISBN 0–690–01762–6
ISBN 0–690–01913–0 pbk.

---

80 81 82 83 84 10 9 8 7 6 5 4 3 2 1

For Perry
for all the usual reasons,
and a couple of others, too

CONTENTS

ACKNOWLEDGMENTS

I really could not have put this book together without the help of a number of people, all of whom were kind enough to lend me their time and expertise. Abel Banov of the *Paints and Coatings Handbook,* Henry C. Jadow of Krazy Glue, and William Seitz of the Neighborhood Cleaners Association were each of invaluable assistance in reading a portion of the manuscript. The gentleman who checked the toxicological material prefers his anonymity, but I appreciate his patient efforts nonetheless.

Anyone who has ever written to a large corporation and then waited for an answer will understand why I also appreciate the help of the following people, each of whom answered my questions about specific products quickly and completely: Cathy Anderson (Airwick), Celia Baros (American Cyanamid), Clem Lay (Amway), Patrick L. Weidner (Armour-Dial), Dona Fundis (Beecham Products), Betty L. Tisher (Bissell), Peter S. Columbus (Borden, Inc.), Lin C. Flachmeier (Clorox), J. E. Miller (CPC), J. D. Bonfiglio (DAP), Robert McKellar (Dow Chemical), James P. Reynolds and Richard B. Ward (DuPont), Frederick C. Binter (Independence Chemical), K. D. Vos (S. C. Johnson), Abe Goldman (Knomark), Helmut L. Melzer (Lehn & Fink), L. Bradford Armstrong (Miller-Morton), R. F. Cruickshank (NIP-CO), Edward M. Jackson (Noxell), D. G. Sarvadi (Sherwin-Williams), David L. Licht (Testors), James E. Long (3M), Larry W. Gambill (Topco), W. G. Whitehead (Union Carbide), William Schmidt (West Chemical), Bonnie Benhayon and Patrick Hurd (National Paint and Coatings Association), and Mark Thorn (Consumer Products Safety Commission).

Congressman Henry A. Waxman and New York State Assemblyman Arthur J. Kremer were kind enough to forward to me copies of bills they had introduced and hearings they had held regarding product safety labeling.

Finally, I am indebted to Russell Luntz, who clued me in to the intricacies of cat-box litter; to Alan Lieberman, who may well be the only man in the world who can photograph household products so that they look sexy; and to Donald Bernstein, who may be the only one who can photograph me so that I look like I'm enjoying it. I appreciate Andrea Rosen's maddening but invaluable questions about all the nasty little details in the manuscript, and Arnold Dolin and Phyllis Westberg's touching faith in the fact that I would eventually finish the book.

One way or another, all these people made this book possible.

C. R.

THE
CONSUMER'S
BRAND-NAME
GUIDE TO
HOUSEHOLD
PRODUCTS

How To Use This Book

I hate a mystery. Give me a book about a master detective unraveling some complicated plot thread by thread, and I will read the last page first every time.

I've been known to sneak into movie theaters in the forbidden last minutes of suspense films, too. Once I know what's going on, I can relax and sit through the whole thing to see how what's happening happened.

I have come to feel much the same way about many of the more mundane mysteries of modern life: for example, the labels on the household products we are all used to stashing away around the house.

You know the products I mean, all those cleaners and scrubbers in the bottles, jars, and boxes under the kitchen sink or in the dark closet in the back hall that I swear I'm going to clean out this year.

Of course, the only time I really get to move anything out of the closet is when I'm about to do the laundry or wash the windows or scrub down the kitchen cabinets and I reach in for some bleach or ammonia or such to help get the job done.

There was a time when I did most of my reaching automatically, without worrying about what was in the cleaner I pulled out of the closet (only checking the label to be certain I'd gotten the right one, of course). Not any more.

In the past few years, a rising consumer consciousness has produced a lot of consumer-oriented laws and regulations. Of them all, perhaps the most important, from an individual consumer's point of view, have been those requiring *full-disclosure ingredient labeling.*

A full-disclosure label is one on which you can find a complete list of all the ingredients in the product, listed in order of their prominence in the mix. A really good label may even have a one- or two-word explanation of what each ingredient does. All foods and cosmetics have labels like that, but most household products (those cleaners and scrubbers in my dark hall closet) do not.

I bet that comes as a surprise to you.

If so, you're definitely not alone. Most people think that household

1

products already have full-disclosure labels, probably because there are so many words on them.

All household products, for example, must have the name and address of the manufacturer or distributor on the label. They must have a list of any major hazardous ingredients, as well as the word DANGER or WARNING where it is appropriate, a phrase describing the particular danger the product poses (FLAMMABLE or IRRITANT, for example), special instructions as to handling or storing the product (such as "keep away from open flame" or "store in a cool place"), antidotes to use if you accidentally swallow the product or spill it on your skin, and, sometimes, a warning to keep the stuff out of the reach of children.

All that information is required by the provisions of the federal Hazardous Substances Act, as amended in 1977 and administered by the Consumer Product Safety Commission. And the impression such labels give is that you're being told all you need to know about the product.

But there are some catches.

Problem number one: only those ingredients that the federal government regards as "hazardous" have to be listed on most household product labels. There are some ingredients, like lye, on which everyone agrees. Lye *is* hazardous. But what about colors and dyes? It now appears that a lot of them may turn out to be carcinogenic, but they are not yet officially recognized as hazardous, so they don't have to be listed on the label, even when the product is something you soak your hands in, like dishwashing liquid.

Problem number two: So far, no one has come up with a standardized list of names for the individual chemicals that are listed on the product labels. Since any one of the thousands of chemicals used in household products may go by as many as six or seven or even twenty different trade and/or scientific names, amateurs like you and me have the Devil's own time trying to compare products. How can we succeed, when the ingredients in them may appear under different names on different labels?

Problem number three, the most important one, is that it now appears to many poison control experts that the antidotes listed on a number of household products may be incomplete, out-of-date, or even dangerously wrong. For example, virtually any antidote listed on the label of a caustic drain cleaner will be ineffective in the long run if the cleaner is swallowed. Giving someone who has swallowed a caustic poison two glasses of milk may slow down the corrosive action of the chemical by diluting it and giving it a protein-and-fat substance other than body tissue to work on. But the milk will not repair any damage that has already been done. Nothing except surgical treatment can do that, and in many cases even a skilled surgeon may be unable to repair major injury to internal tissues. To put that on a label would certainly put a damper on sales, but it would be the truth, and sooner or later it is going to have to be said—even by the people who sell cleaners.

Alas, it may be a lot later than sooner. Federal agencies such as the Environmental Protection Agency (EPA) and the Consumer Product Safety Commission (CPSC) do not seem to be in any special hurry to reevaluate antidote labeling on the products they regulate (the EPA has jurisdiction over household insecticides; the CPSC over most other household products). In fact, it has been estimated that if they continue to reevaluate these labels at the rate they have been going, it may take something like two hundred years to get the job done.

So for the foreseeable future, anyone who cleans a house, does the laundry, goes after a roach, paints a wall, or lives with someone who does any of these things is living around a lot of relatively mysterious, potentially dangerous products.

This being the case, it is only sensible to pick up all the information you can about what's in the products you use and what these things in them can do to you.

That is what this book is all about. On the following pages, you will find product descriptions for everything from air fresheners to laundry detergents to mothproofers to wallpaper cleaners. Under each listing, there are five separate categories of information: *Safety rating, What's in it, How it works, What it can do to you,* and *What's better, safer, or cheaper.* Here's what each category is intended to offer you:

Safety rating: I hope you'll never have to use this section of the product description, because it's meant to let you see at a glance whether or not you've got an emergency on your hands if someone in your house has swallowed one of the products listed in this book.*

It is unfortunate but true that this kind of accident happens all the time. In 1976, for example, the National Poison Control Center at Pittsburgh Children's Hospital reported that more than 90,000 children under the age of five had been involved in accidental poisonings

---

* Other possible problems relating to contact with or misuse of a product are listed under **What it can do to you.**

caused by chemicals found around the home. And it has been estimated that for every such poisoning reported to a poison control center, hospital, or family doctor, another six probably happen without anyone outside the family's being told about it. The total, therefore, may be closer to 630,000 such accidental poisonings every year.

Not all household products are deadly, even if swallowed. Therefore, the Safety Ratings describe four general classes of toxicity, with—naturally—lots of room for individual variation. These classes are:

1. Products that are nontoxic and generally assumed to be nonpoisonous even if swallowed. Example: laundry starch.

2. Products that may be toxic (a) if swallowed in quantity or (b) if they contain certain optional ingredients. Example: laundry detergents.

3. Products that are assumed to be harmful if swallowed even in small amounts. Example: anything (a furniture polish, an insecticide) containing a petroleum distillate.

4. Products that are so harmful if swallowed that they require immediate medical attention. Example: caustic drain cleaners and certain rat poisons.

There are no antidotes listed in this book for any of these categories. I thought about including some, but after speaking with many poison control authorities, I came to the conclusion that no one should ever administer an antidote without checking with an expert first. Administering an antidote on your own can be dangerous. For example, following label directions that tell you to give an acid (fruit juice) to neutralize an alkali (drain cleaner) can cause a chemical reaction that heats up the contents of the stomach, sometimes making them hot enough to burn a hole right through the stomach walls. And giving an alkali (soapy water) to neutralize an acid (hydrochloric acid toilet bowl cleaner) can create carbon dioxide, a gas that can swell the stomach, sometimes severely enough to rupture it.

Perhaps the single exception would be two glasses of milk for someone who's swallowed a caustic poison. But poison experts stress that as soon as the milk has been swallowed the victim should be taken directly to a hospital emergency room for further treatment.

And, in general, the fact is that even milk may not be a perfectly safe antidote. For example, there is some evidence that the fat in it can increase the body's absorption of fat-soluble poisons like the petroleum distillates. If you give milk to someone who has swallowed a wood polish containing a petroleum distillate solvent such as naphtha, you may actually increase the toxicity of the polish.

In short, your best bet is always to call the poison control center. Have the container from which the poison came in your hand when you call, so you can answer any questions the expert at the center may have. You might also want to keep a small (one-ounce) bottle of syrup of ipecac in your first-aid cabinet in case you are told to make the person who has swallowed a poison vomit it up, *but you should never administer the ipecac without being specifically told to do so.* In some cases, as with caustic poisons, causing someone who has swallowed a poison to vomit it up may increase the chance of injury.

Note: The reason for calling your poison control center rather than your family doctor is that the people at the center are more likely to have the extensive files required to stay up-to-date on the poisons in commercial products. In many cases your doctor may have to call poison control to check out the information. By calling directly you can save precious time. To make it easy to get the right number, I've included a list of major poison control centers across the nation on page 215.

What's in it: The law says that a manufacturer has to let you know if there's something in a product which the government considers hazardous. For example, nobody can package a cleaner containing potassium hydroxide (lye) or ammonia without putting that information on the label.

But the government's idea of what's hazardous is rather narrow. As already noted, coloring agents don't make the list, and neither do emulsifiers. You may be allergic to them, and they may be hazardous to you, but the government doesn't take this possibility into consideration, so they don't have to be listed on the label.

As a result, when it comes to ingredients, the amount of information you can get from the label generally depends on what product you're talking about *and,* sometimes, on how serious a manufacturer is about treating you as an intelligent consumer.

Paint labels, for example, are usually terrific. They tell you everything: what the pigments or coloring agents are, what the vehicle or solvent is, what's used as a filler or inert ingredient to bulk up the paint.

Labels for cleaners like household ammonia or detergents are rarely as good. The law will get you the big stuff listed on the label—ammonia, sodium carbonate—but will the manufacturer also tell you if his ammonia contains a detergent, a color, a perfume, or a clarifier? And if so, which one? Maybe.

Labels for products that don't contain any truly lethal ingredients are the worst. Pick up a package of a solid air freshener to see what I mean. There's probably not one single ingredient listed on the label. No mention of perfume. Or emulsifiers. Or dyes. Or preservatives.

That being the case, it's exciting to see that sometimes (and more often nowadays than, say, just five years ago) manufacturers will simply refuse to take advantage of the legal loopholes that permit them to get away with worthless labels and will go ahead and give you informative ones anyway. Both Armour-Dial and Procter & Gamble are examples of companies that have done that. All their labels, or at least all the ones I've seen, list the ingredients in the products plus, where needed, a short one- or two-word explanation of what the ingredient does. I hold no brief for either company and not a single share of stock, so I feel perfectly free to say that I think it makes sense to support these and any others who make it easy to see what you're buying.

Some manufacturers, however, are noticeably shy about letting you know what's in the household products they are selling. That is why under each product listing you will find a listing of the ingredients most likely to be found in the product (i.e., laundry starch, spot removers, and the like). And just to make sure we are all talking about the same type of product (does anyone other than the people who make it really know what a "detergent booster" is?), I have included brand-name examples.

If there are two basic ways to make any one product—laundry bleaches, for example, may be based either on a chlorine bleach source or on a peroxy (sodium perborate) bleach—there will also be a brand-name list to show which active ingredients the popular brands are based on.

The ingredients may be listed by class name, such as "emulsifiers," or by chemical name, such as "carboxymethyl cellulose." Either way, if the word looks like Greek to you, you can look it up in the Glossary of Ingredients and Label Terms, which begins on page 167. There, the listings include handy bits of information such as how toxic an ingredient may be, whether it's flammable or irritating or allergenic, where it comes from, what other ingredients it is related to, and what kinds of products you are likely to find it in.

How it works: Did you know that a fabric softener works by making fabric more absorbent so that it retains moisture, which serves as a conductor and dissipates static electricity? Or that "instant" glues hold things together by actually combining their molecules with the molecules of the surfaces to which they are applied?

I didn't—not until I started working on this book. But I have always found this kind of household chemistry fascinating, and I hope you will, too. The explanations in this section of the product description, therefore, are full of the kind of technical minutiae that can help you understand why and how the product you're using does what it is supposed to do.

What it can do to you: The Safety Rating at the head of each product listing is meant for fast reference, the only kind you're likely to have time for when someone accidentally swallows some of that enticingly lemon-scented liquid you keep under the kitchen sink. This section, however, is meant for more leisurely reading. It spells out in detail all the possible side effects of household products: what can go wrong if you misuse the product, as well as what can go wrong even when you follow all the directions on the label to the letter.

You can get a large hint of possible problems simply by scanning the label copy. If there's a real danger, the Hazardous Substances Act requires some kind of warning. Among the words you may find as warnings are:

- TOXIC/HIGHLY TOXIC. These words describe ingredients or products that are poisonous or injurious if you eat them, inhale them, or absorb them through your skin. A highly toxic substance is simply one that does its dirty work faster than a plain toxic substance when tested on laboratory rats.
- EXTREMELY FLAMMABLE/FLAMMABLE/COMBUSTIBLE. All these words mean "this can catch fire." The difference among them is the degree of flammability they describe. Extremely flammable liquids, for example, are liquids whose vapors will "flash" (ignite, but not continue to burn) at a lower temperature than the vapors of flammable or combustible liquids.

Solids are considered extremely flammable if they ignite and burn when exposed to friction or to an electrical spark at temperatures lower than 80 degrees Fahrenheit. They are flammable if they ignite and burn when sprayed through a candle flame in a laboratory setting.

Aerosols are extremely flammable if the spray ignites and produces a "flashback" (a flame traveling back into the can) when they are spritzed through a candle flame. Flammable aerosols are those whose spray either ignites and causes a flashback or simply burns with an eighteen-inch flame.

• CORROSIVE. This is a caustic substance, a poison that literally eats away animal or plant tissues. Potassium hydroxide (lye) is the perfect example.

• IRRITANT. This is a substance that, while it isn't corrosive, can cause inflammation of your skin or mucous membranes. The irritation may occur the first time the ingredient falls on your skin, or it may take repeated exposure to cause the reaction. Laundry detergents are examples of products that fall into this category.

• STRONG SENSITIZER. This is an ingredient that may either provoke an allergic reaction itself or make you more sensitive to an allergic reaction caused by some other material. Some strong sensitizers are *photosensitizers,* which means that they make your skin more sensitive to light. If you put a photosensitizer (such as lime oil) on your skin and go out in the sun, your skin may be severely sunburned.

The word DANGER on the label means that you're dealing with a product that is extremely flammable or corrosive or highly toxic. WARNING or CAUTION is used on products that are hazardous but, in the opinion of the Consumer Product Safety Commission, less so than products marked DANGER.

All this is fine if you can read. Unfortunately, the person most likely to become a victim of accidental poisonings is a child under the age of five who is just beginning to explore the house and to make decisions on his or her own.

Children swallow household products for all kinds of reasons. The most common ones seem to be curiosity and hunger. The solids and liquids children swallow often look and smell like food. You may not realize it, but many of the ingredients that you instinctively regard as distasteful because you know they are dangerous actually smell or taste good. Many are sweetish or fruity, even without the added lemon or lime perfumes that are so popular today. Packaging makes them even more attractive and acceptable.

Because so many children have made the connection between "it looks good" and "it will taste good," I have included in this part of the product description the probable lethal dose for each product listed. This dose can be, but is not necessarily, fatal. It is figured in terms of a child who weighs 22 pounds or, for those of you dealing in metrics, 10 kilograms. To get the probable lethal dose for an adult, you would ordinarily multiply by seven. Exceptions are given.*

As noted, except for the commonsense advice to flush or brush the chemical off your skin or out of your eyes as quickly as possible, you won't find any antidotes listed here. Once again, that's because it can be dangerous to give an antidote to someone who has swallowed poison, unless specifically directed to do so by a doctor or a member of the staff at the poison control center.

What *can* you do?

Prevention is the word. Prevention. The neatest way to deal with accidental poisonings is to prevent them from happening in the first place. That is so axiomatic you would think everyone with a toddler in the house would store dangerous things like drugs and cosmetics and household products in places where no child could ever reach them.

Alas, few people take such simple precautions. And even those who do are sometimes tripped up by an adventurous and inventive child. That's why one of the best things that has ever happened to poisonous products has been the invention of child-proof caps. These caps are now required by law on a whole range of cleaners, including those that contain 10 percent or more petroleum distillates (furniture polish, for example); those containing 4 percent or more methanol, or wood alcohol; those containing 10 percent or more sulfuric acid; those containing 10 percent or more ethylene glycol; dry products, like drain cleaners, containing 10 percent or more unneutralized lye; and any other liquid or solid product containing 2 percent or more unneutralized lye. It is difficult for a small child to get a lethal dose of most products from an aerosol can because operating the push button requires muscular coordination which may be beyond the child's skill. Therefore, these rules do not apply to any aerosol containers except those containing lye (even a little bit of lye may be too much).

As good as all this sounds, it is somewhat arbitrary. Who's to say, for example, that a cleaner containing 9 percent petroleum distillates is less dangerous than one containing 10 percent? The child-proof cap is helpful, but it cannot eliminate all problems. When you are dealing with things as potentially disastrous as furniture polishes, paints, and

---

* These figures are based upon ratings provided in *The Clinical Toxicology of Commercial Products* (see Sources, page 221). The ratings describe toxicity for entire classes of products and are based upon standard formulae. Obviously, some individual products may vary from these formulae and may thus be more, or less, toxic than others. These probable lethal doses, therefore, are guidelines only. For specific products, your best source is your local poison control center.

drain cleaners, the thing to keep firmly in mind is Murphy's Law: Anything that can go wrong will go wrong. Your job is to anticipate and prevent it.

What's better, safer, or cheaper: I'm not about to tell you that you can whip up a safe alternative for every one of the things you use to clean the house, or that you can replace all the products in your house with just one small bottle of something like ammonia or chlorine bleach.

Alas, the simple fact is that there are some products that just can't be duplicated at home, unless home is a well-equipped chemistry lab. For example, if your aim is to paint the house, nothing but house paint will do the job. The same thing goes for adhesives (glues and pastes), cold-water soaps meant to be used for hand-washables, dishwasher detergents, dishwasher rinse aids, fabric softeners, floor and furniture polishes, insecticides, paint solvents and strippers, rat poisons, rust-preventive coatings, putty and spackling compounds, and waterproofing sprays.

Sometimes there is an alternative, but it either costs more than the ready-made commercial product or it's so difficult or dangerous to work with at home that it's hardly worth the bother. The example that comes most quickly to mind is wood polish. To make that at home, you're often told to boil a flammable oil. Frankly, I'd rather pay more for mine at the supermarket.

Despite the pitfalls, there are some products for which cheap, safe, and sensible alternatives exist. Sometimes you can whip up the alternative by combining a little of this with a little of that. When that's the case, I'll list the this and that for you to try.

Of course, the easiest way to save money on household products is to use one product for more than one job. The people who make these things would have us believe that we need one special formula for cleaning sinks, one for tubs, one for tile, and so on. That's nonsense: most of the cleaners in our cabinets can do double, triple, even quadruple duty. For example:

If You Have This . . .	*. . . You May Not Need to Buy This*
Ammonia	Copper cleaner
	Glass/window cleaner
	Some jewelry cleaners
	Liquid household detergents
	Some stain removers

Ammonia and soap	Glass wax
Chlorine bleach	Disinfectant cleaner
	Mildew-stain remover
	Mildew preventive
	Toilet bowl cleaner
	Tub and tile cleaner
Cooking oil	Nonstick cooking spray
Cornstarch	Laundry-starch powder
	Carpet and rug shampoo
	Some stain removers
General-purpose household cleaner	Floor-polish remover
(powder)	Scouring powder
	Tub and tile cleaner
	Oven cleaner
Laundry detergent	Laundry presoak
Mineral oil	Some household oils
	Some rust-preventive oils
Scouring powder	Stainless steel cleaner
	Aluminum cleaner
Soap and water	Some jewelry cleaners
	Plant insecticides
	Plastic cleaners
	Some stain removers
Steel-wool scouring pads	Aluminum cleaner
	Some rust removers
	Stainless steel cleaner
Vinegar	Coffeepot cleaner
	Copper cleaner
	Some stain removers
Washing soda	Detergent boosters
	Drain cleaners
	Household detergents
	Water softeners

For details, check the individual product listings.

I hope that you will find all this as useful and, sometimes, as surprising as I have. My basic aim in writing this book was to make it possible for you, a lay person like me, to understand what goes into a whole class of products that we all use almost every day, usually without thinking twice about them.

An Alphabetical Listing of Household Products

Note

The product formulas and ingredients listed here are drawn from labels on products which were being sold in the summer of 1979, from personal correspondence, and from standard sources such as *The Clinical Toxicology of Commercial Products* and other reference material included in the list of sources which begins on page 221.

The fact that some of the products or ingredients listed here are described as allergenic, irritating, or poisonous to some people or in some specific situations does not necessarily mean that they will be allergenic, irritating, or poisonous to everyone or in all situations.

Air Freshener

What's in it: All air fresheners rely on fragrance for their "freshening" effect. The solid ones, like AIRWICK (Airwick), GLADE (S. C. Johnson & Son), RENUZIT (Drackett), and WIZARD (Boyle-Midway), are perfumed with essential oils or aromatic chemicals or both. There are also emulsifiers and stabilizers, such as carrageenan, to create a solid block, and usually a dye to make the air freshener look attractive. There may also be a preservative (formaldehyde) in the mix, although both essential oils and aromatic chemicals have some preservative properties.

Liquids—like AIRWICK—usually come in a bottle with a wick. The formulas are similar to those for solid air fresheners, except that the liquids also contain water and a smaller proportion of emulsifiers and stabilizers.

Aerosol air fresheners, such as AIR SWEET (Uncle Sam), GLADE, WIZARD, and RENUZIT sprays, are very simple products, containing perfume, water, and a propellant.

How it works: If you believe the advertising, air fresheners are something like dive-bombers, zooming in to attack and destroy nasty odors. The facts, of course, are a lot less hyperbolic. Air fresheners are simply perfumes that temporarily mask unpleasant smells. If you don't eventually open the window or door and let some air in, rooms in which you use air fresheners will begin to smell kind of heavy, like public rest rooms in which the smell of the deodorant is cloying and probably a lot more irritating than anything natural might have been.

What it can do to you: Any product containing formaldehyde or perfumes in very high concentrations would be poisonous if swallowed. It could cause nausea, vomiting, and gastric upset and the probable lethal dose for a small child (22 pounds/10 kilograms) might be less than a teaspoonful. Some air fresheners such as, AIRWICK liquids and solids, for example, do not contain formaldehyde and dilute their perfumes sufficiently to be able to put the word "nontoxic" on the label. However, because you are unlikely to find a complete list of ingredients on the package, it always makes sense to call the poison control center if a child in your home swallows any air freshener.

It's hard to swallow the deodorizer from a spray can, but aerosols present other problems. For one thing, many of the perfumes may cause allergic reactions, and an aerosol, which sprays perfume into the air around you, is more likely than other forms of air fresheners to set off such a reaction. In addition, the aerosol containers may explode if overheated or accidentally punctured. To further heat up the situation, the propellants and the aromatic chemicals in the aerosol cans are highly flammable.

What's better, safer, or cheaper: Aerosol sprays work best for quick attacks on nasty kitchen and bathroom smells, but they are terribly expensive when compared to solid or liquid products, and absurdly so when compared to old-fashioned remedies.

Your best ally when it comes to avoiding household smells is cleanliness. A clean closet, for example, or one that is aired out periodically, is less likely to smell bad. If your closet smells because it's damp, spraying or hanging up an air freshener inside is like sticking Band-Aids on a broken leg. You've got to locate and remove the source of the dampness, even if it means replastering a wall. In the end, the effort is worth it; no air freshener will keep your clothes from moldering in a damp closet. If you want to add perfume to your closets and drawers, try sachets made of herbs and spices sewn up in light linen or cotton bags.

In the kitchen, clean and clean again. Be sure the space under the sink is dry. Wash out the garbage can once a week (or as needed) with plain detergent or a chlorine bleach solution. Keep a box of baking soda open in the refrigerator to absorb the odors. Every once in a while, do a quick check to make sure nothing's rotting away on a back shelf. You just haven't lived until you've smelled an apple way, way, *way* past its prime. Seal smelly foods, like blue cheese, in plastic bags.

Cleanliness works in the bathroom, too. Be sure towels have adequate room to dry out, so they don't get to smelling musty. Keep the toilet bowl clean, and for emergency odor obliteration, keep a simple box of safety matches on a shelf near the toilet. When needed, strike a couple and let them burn for a moment. It really works.

Vacuum drapes and upholstery to get rid of any mustiness. Open the windows every day, even in the winter. When it comes to entertaining, you'll have to face the fact that unless you are willing to post No Smoking signs (we nonsmokers live in hope) and lose a few friends and relatives in the process, there's no way at all to avoid the horror of an atmosphere heavy with cigarette, cigar, or pipe smoke. Even open windows while the party's on won't help. Afterward, your furniture—not to mention your clothes, your hair, and *you*—will smell smoky. Maybe that's one time when a quick burst of air freshener, plus those open windows, is required.

Aluminum Cleaner

Safety Rating: HARMFUL IF SWALLOWED. CALL POISON CONTROL CENTER IMMEDIATELY FOR APPROPRIATE ANTIDOTE PROCEDURE.

What's in it: An aluminum cleaner in powder form like CAMEO (Purex) has an abrasive (silica), an acid (sulfamic acid is common), either non-ionic surfactants or detergents, and a fragrance. Liquid or cream polishes contain all these ingredients, plus a solvent (usually water).

How it works: Like all metal cleaners, aluminum cleaners dissolve or rub away dirt and grit. Since aluminum doesn't tarnish, no tarnish-preventives need be included.

What it can do to you: The powder can irritate your skin and your eyes, and if you inhale it, it will make you cough. If swallowed, the probable lethal dose for a small child (22 pounds/10 kilograms) may be as little as one fifth of an ounce.

What's better, safer, or cheaper: You really don't need a special cleaner to make your aluminum pots and pans shine. Any all-purpose metal cleaner or any cleaner meant for copper will work perfectly.

Actually, you don't even need one of those. Aluminum responds well to steel wool or to steel-wool scouring pads. You can give either brushed or smooth (mirror-finish) aluminum a radiant shine by rubbing it with steel wool. Be sure to rub in one direction only; never use a circular scrubbing motion, which can mar the finish. If you run out

17

of steel wool, try very fine sandpaper—in a small area first, though, to be certain that it isn't too abrasive.

One great kitchen remedy for stained or discolored aluminum is to boil water and vinegar (about three tablespoonsful vinegar to a pint of water) in the stained pot. Or, rubbing the stain with a cut lemon may remove the discoloration. You can avoid stains in the first place by not cooking alkaline foods in aluminum pans. When you bake a cheesecake by putting one pan inside another and filling the larger pan with water, you can avoid discoloring the aluminum by adding a teaspoonful of cream of tartar to the water.

Lime scale in the bottom of an aluminum teakettle can be removed by boiling water and vinegar in the kettle or leaving water and vinegar in it overnight. If the teakettle has an opening large enough to allow you to reach inside, finish the cleaning by shining with steel wool. Be sure to rinse the pot thoroughly before using.

Ammonia.

See **Household Ammonia.**

Antistatic Spray

> **Safety Rating: MAY BE HARMFUL IF SWALLOWED. CALL POISON CONTROL CENTER IMMEDIATELY FOR APPROPRIATE ANTIDOTE PROCEDURE.**

What's in it: Usually, antistatic sprays like STATIC GUARD (Armour-Dial) contain a conductor (ammonium chloride), plus a fragrance, non-ionic surfactants, and a propellant.

How it works: When you spray the antistatic preparation on your clothes or carpet, you coat the fabric with a conductor (ammonium chloride) that dissipates static electricity, keeping it from building up on the fabric. That means that your clothes won't cling to you, and your carpets won't snap back at you when you step on them.

18

What it can do to you: The spray can be irritating to your skin, either straight from the can or after it's dried on your clothes. It's also an eye irritant, and if you inhale the fine mist, it may irritate your respiratory tract. The biggest problems, though, are those it shares with any product housed in an aerosol can. The cans may explode if overheated or accidentally punctured, and the propellant gases may be flammable.

What's better, safer, or cheaper: If you can dunk your clothes in water, you may want to use a fabric softener (see in the alphabetical products listing) rather than an antistatic spray, since the softener may be much cheaper per application. If you stick to sprays, save pennies by not overspraying. Not only is that more economical, but it actually makes the spray work better, since too much spray may make your clothes or carpets feel slimy.

Bleach (Liquid)

> **Safety Rating: MAY BE HARMFUL IF SWALLOWED. CALL POISON CONTROL CENTER IMMEDIATELY FOR APPROPRIATE ANTIDOTE PROCEDURE.**

What's in it: Liquid chlorine bleaches get their whitening power from any one of a number of chlorine-source ingredients such as sodium hypochlorite. The chlorine-source ingredient accounts for up to 10 percent of the product. In addition, there will be up to 8 percent sodium chloride (table salt) plus a minute amount of a caustic such as sodium hydroxide or sodium carbonate (up to 0.5 percent), which helps remove stains. The rest of the bleach, as much as 90 percent, is plain water.

Bleach labels usually list the combination as "sodium hypochlorite 5.25 percent; inert ingredients 94.75 percent." The inert ingredients include the salt and the sodium hydroxide or sodium carbonate as well as the water. Since the caustic cleansers are hardly "inert" by anyone's definition (although there isn't enough of them in bleaches to do any harm), this ingredients list serves as a good example of what a household-product label means by the term "inert ingredients": ingredients that aren't crucial to the effect you want to get from the product.

How it works: Liquid chlorine bleaches like A & P (A & P), CLOROX (Clorox), PUREX (Purex), and TEXIZE (Texize) work like a charm on a wide range of stains, not to mention general dinginess. But they may damage or discolor some natural fabrics, including silk, wool, leather, and most synthetics (which will turn yellow). Naturally, you should never use a chlorine bleach on any garment if the label says not to, and it goes without saying that chlorine bleaches should never be used on material that isn't colorfast. If you aren't sure, dip a small edge of the fabric into a solution of bleach and water. If the fabric bleeds, even a little bit, forget the bleach.

If the wash is cotton and colorfast, however, chlorine bleach can be a boon. It's a terrific sanitizer if you live in an apartment house and use community washing machines, or if you are among those of us who are saving energy by using cool water for the wash. Just be sure that you never leave anything to soak in a chlorine bleach solution in a nonenameled metal container. Metal increases the action and power of the bleach tremendously, maybe even enough to damage fabrics that would otherwise have sailed through the bleach bath unscathed.

Liquid chlorine bleaches also work well as household cleaning aids. Mixed in a ratio of four tablespoonsful to a quart of warm water, the bleach can be applied to stubborn stains on porcelain tile, basins, tubs, or toilet bowls. Leave the solution on for about five minutes and then rinse off. Repeat a couple of times if necessary. In addition to bleaching out stains, the chlorine bleach will sanitize surfaces on which it's used, which is why it works so well on the inside of the garbage pail or in the toilet bowl. It also prevents the buildup of mold on the grout between the tiles on the floor and wall of the bathroom and can discourage the growth of mildew.

What it can do to you: Because they are alkaline, liquid chlorine bleaches used to be classified as corrosive poisons that could cause serious burns of mouth, throat, and stomach if swallowed. Modern animal experiments, however, have shown that this rarely happens. For one thing, the bleaches are not highly concentrated. For another, they are strongly emetic, which means that they cause prompt vomiting. In one series of experiments with laboratory dogs, the animals vomited within a minute or two after swallowing the bleach. Another survey showed that 23 of 26 children admitted to the University of

Oklahoma Health Sciences Center after swallowing bleach had vomited just as quickly as the laboratory dogs. As a result, although the liquids can cause a burning sensation, they rarely cause lasting damage. And according to one major poison control center, even when large quantities of bleach are used in suicide attempts, the most serious effect is apt to be vomiting.

But the bleaches are irritating. If you get some in your eye, you should flush the eye for as long as fifteen minutes with copious amounts of cool water. Then go to see your ophthalmologist, because the bleach can leave injuries you may not notice right away.

If you mistakenly happen to mix your chlorine bleach with straight ammonia or a household product containing significant amounts of ammonia, you'll know immediately that you've done something wrong. Mixing chlorine and ammonia can liberate chloramines, whose choking, burning fumes will almost certainly drive you right out of the bathroom or kitchen or basement or garage you've been cleaning. In unventilated spaces and in sufficient concentrations, chloramines can be deadly. In a wide-open, unventilated room, the worst effect will probably be a burning, irritated sore throat and a cough that can last as long as three or four days. Either way, it's a bad trip, the moral of which is: Don't mix cleaners.

What's better, safer, or cheaper: Years ago, housewives used to make their own version of a chlorine bleach, a solution called Javelle water. The raw ingredients in this solution were potentially caustic until diluted, and the final product wasn't as effective as the prepared chlorine bleaches on sale at every modern supermarket. In other words, this is one of those instances when modern chemistry and technology produced a better, safer, cheaper, more uniform product.

Bleach (Powder)

What's in it: Many people assume that all powder bleaches are "all-fabric" products, gentler than the liquid chlorine bleaches. The fact is that there are two kinds of powder bleaches, those with chlorine bleach and those with a peroxy or oxidizing bleach base.

The chlorine-based powders contain a source of chlorine, usually sodium hypochlorite (up to 20 percent), plus phosphates (up to 20 percent), brighteners (0.5 percent), bluing (0.5 percent), and an anticaking ingredient, such as sodium sulfate, which may account for as much as 90 percent of the powder.

Peroxy bleaches, the true "all-fabric" kind, contain sodium perborate (5–40 percent by volume), an alkali such as sodium carbonate (up to 70 percent), and minuscule amounts of anticaking agents, colors, fragrance, brighteners, or fluorescent dyes.

Chlorine bleach powders:

ACTION (Colgate-Palmolive)
AMWAY (Amway Corp.)
PUREX (Purex)

Peroxy bleach powders:

A & P ALL FABRIC BLEACH (A & P)
BIZ (Procter & Gamble; also contains enzymes)
CLOROX 2 (Clorox)
MIRACLE WHITE (Drackett)
PUREX GENTLE FABRIC BLEACH (Purex)
SNOWY BLEACH (Gold Seal)

How it works: As far as your clothes are concerned, there's no difference at all between liquid and powder chlorine bleaches. Both are excellent for fabrics other than silk, wool, leather, and most synthetics.

Peroxy bleaches are another story. They are gentler to fabrics, which means that they don't do as good a job of removing stains or making clothes and linens look white and bright. They can be used on just about any fabric, although it never hurts to be just a bit skeptical. To be certain, try dipping a small corner of the fabric you're washing in a little bit of the bleach plus water. Let it dry. If it doesn't run or fade, fine. If it does, don't use the bleach, no matter how safe the label says it is.

What it can do to you: The bleach in chlorine bleach powders is more concentrated than the bleach in liquid products. It is more irritating than the liquid if you spill it on your skin, inhale it as dust, get it in your eyes, or swallow it. However, just like the liquid bleaches (and most detergents), the chlorine bleach powders are emetic. Anyone who swallows them will regurgitate them fairly quickly. If there were time, it might make sense to give water or milk to anyone who swallows a chlorine bleach powder, in order to dilute the concentration of the active ingredients. But vomiting usually happens so fast that there simply isn't time—or, in most cases, need.

Peroxy bleach powders containing sodium perborate are another kettle of fish entirely. If swallowed, they may cause borate poisoning, the symptoms of which are vision problems, central nervous system disturbances, and gastritis. The probable lethal dose for a small child (22 pounds/10 kilograms) may range from about one eighth of a teaspoonful to one eighth of an ounce.

Occasionally, clothes or linens washed with chlorine bleaches, liquid or powder, are irritating to people with sensitive skins.

What's better, safer, or cheaper: A homemade peroxy bleach, which works like a charm for small spots on wool or synthetic fabrics, particularly those peculiar yellow or tan spots that seem to spring up on white wool sweaters or silky white synthetic blouses, is the old standby hair bleach: hydrogen peroxide and ammonia. To make this bleach, combine three parts bleaching peroxide to one part ammonia. Don't lean too close to the solution, because the fumes are irritating. Apply the bleach to stains and let it sit for an hour or two. Rinse off and reapply if necessary. If you happen to be one of those people who frosts or streaks her hair, there's an even simpler solution. The white bleaching paste you make by mixing the two components in a bleaching kit like Clairol's FROST AND TIP also contains bleaching peroxide and ammonia and is thick enough that it won't run or drip off a stain.

You just pick up a bit with a cotton swab and dab it on the stained spot. Then let it dry, brush off, and, if necessary, reapply. This one saved a white ski sweater which I picked up for a measly five bucks on Cape Cod, where the store owner practically gave it away because it had a funny brownish stain on the front, and a synthetic blouse which had gotten spotted as it aged. The Clairol paste erased both the sweater's stain and the blouse's age spots, without doing the slightest damage to the fabric underneath.

For the record, the probable lethal dose of this bleach for a small child is somewhere between one and four ounces. You'll never even have that much mixed up at one time. *Never* store a mixture of peroxide and ammonia—it can heat and then explode any sealed container such as a glass jar. Mix up just enough for one application and toss any leftovers in the trash can.

Bleach Substitute

> **Safety Rating: MAY BE HARMFUL IF SWALLOWED. CALL POISON CONTROL CENTER IMMEDIATELY FOR APPROPRIATE ANTIDOTE PROCEDURE.**

What's in it: Bleach substitutes are mildly alkaline detergent- or surfactant-based powders fortified with fluorescent brighteners and sometimes with enzymes. They do not contain either chlorine or peroxy bleaches. Laundry bluing (see in the alphabetical products listing) is often considered a bleach substitute.

Bleach substitutes with fluorescent brighteners:

BLU-WHITE (Purex)
BORATEEM (U.S. Borax & Chemical Corp.)
BORATEEM PLUS (U.S. Borax & Chemical Corp.)
LAFRANCE WHITENER/BRIGHTENER (Purex)

Bleach substitute with enzymes:

AXION (Colgate-Palmolive)

How it works: Bleach substitutes with fluorescent brighteners contain dyes that make white or neutral-colored clothes and fabrics look "whiter." They also brighten colored fabrics. Enzymes in bleach substitutes dissolve protein stains, such as food or blood.

Bleach substitutes can also be used as laundry detergent boosters (see in the alphabetical products listing), in which case you add about half a cup of the bleach substitute right along with the detergent. Of course, it doesn't make any sense to add the bleach substitute to detergents or soap powders that already have fluorescent brighteners or enzymes, so read the label on the detergent package first.

What it can do to you: Like all detergent products, bleach substitutes can cause vomiting, diarrhea, and gastric upset if swallowed. The probable lethal dose for a small child (22 pounds/10 kilograms) may be as low as one fifth of an ounce, depending upon the particular ingredients in a particular product and how concentrated they are. (Neither enzymes nor fluorescent brighteners make the product any more or less toxic.) If swallowed in quantity, the powders may block airways and cause suffocation. Bleach substitutes may also irritate and burn the eyes. If inhaled, the powders may be irritating to the respiratory tract.

What's better, safer, or cheaper: None of the bleach substitutes does a better job than ordinary bleaches; in fact, they really don't work any better than most detergents alone, since most laundry detergents contain either brighteners or enzymes or both. Verdict: an unnecessary expense. See Bleach (Liquid and Powder) in the alphabetical products listing for alternatives.

Brass Cleaner.

See **Copper Cleaner; Metal Cleaner (All-Purpose).**

Brown Glue.

See **Mucilage.**

Carpet Shampoo.

See **Rug and Carpet Shampoo (Liquid, Aerosol; Powder).**

Cat-Box Litter

What's in it: Cat-box litters are absorbent materials, such as processed clay (aluminum magnesium silicate) or alfalfa. Sometimes a deodorant is added.

Clay-based litters:

A & P PURRSCENT (A & P)

HARTZ CAT LITTER (Hartz Mountain)

KITTY PAN CAT LITTER, KITTY BOX CAT LITTER (Waverly Mineral Products)

KLEEN KITTY (Superior Cat Products)

Alfalfa litter:

LITTER GREEN (McFadden Co.)

How it works: The clay or alfalfa absorbs animal liquid wastes, and, presumably, the deodorant wipes out lingering odors. In practice, cleaning the box regularly is the only way to avoid having your house or apartment smell as if the cat owns the place. Adding a half cup of baking soda to the litter may be an effective way to increase its deodorizing powers.

Do not dump clay-based cat litters in the toilet. They swell so efficiently that they're likely to cause an annoying and expensive blockage of the pipes. Alfalfa litters won't swell, but they may block the pipes anyway.

What it can do to you: Clean litter is practically nontoxic. Because clay is so absorbent, however, if you swallow enough it may swell to form an obstruction in your intestines. Alfalfa litters won't do that, and they are so strictly nontoxic that—it says right on the bag—they can be used as feed for small herbivores like hamsters, gerbils, and rabbits.

Actually, the real problems with cat litter come after it's been used by the cat. Cat wastes contaminate the litter with all the bacteria that normally live in the cat's body, plus those that grow when urine and feces are exposed to the air. A cat's feces may also contain the cysts of toxoplasmosis, a parasite that can infect the central nervous system of the host who swallows them. In many parts of the world, as much as 94 percent of the population may be infected with toxoplasmosis, without showing any symptoms of the disease. However, if a pregnant woman is infected with toxoplasmosis parasites from cat feces, she may pass the infection along to her developing fetus. If this occurs early in pregnancy, the fetus may be spontaneously aborted. If it happens later in pregnancy, the woman may miscarry, or the child may be stillborn, or it may be born live but infected with the disease. Infected babies may be born blind or mentally retarded—or they may not show any symptoms at all, since toxoplasmosis parasites can remain dormant for months or even years after the baby is born. All in all, it's not a pretty picture to hang around the nursery, and the simplest way to avoid it is for pregnant women to avoid all exposure to feline wastes. (Dogs are less of a sanitary problem because they are commonly walked outdoors and their wastes do not remain around the house.)

What's better, safer, or cheaper: Shredded newspaper is cheaper than packaged cat litter, but it really isn't as absorbent, and it may not do the job at all if your cats are full-grown.

As far as I'm concerned, the most intriguing alternative to the cat litter box is a plastic device that is supposed to be able to train your cat to use the toilet. The device is a plastic circle that fits over the toilet bowl. It's weaker in the center, and it buckles if the cat steps there, so that he has to perch on the rim to do his business. That's providing you can get him up there in the first place. This gadget obviously requires a greater initial investment than a sack of cat litter, but if it works it sure is a more sanitary way to dispose of animal wastes. I can't really give you a balanced evaluation, because I don't know anyone who's used it, but if I had a cat I'd try it.

Cigarette-Lighter Fuel

> **Safety Rating: EXTREMELY HARMFUL IF SWALLOWED OR IF CONCENTRATED VAPORS ARE INHALED. CALL POISON CONTROL CENTER IMMEDIATELY FOR APPROPRIATE ANTIDOTE PROCEDURE.**

What's in it: All lighter fuels are petroleum distillates packaged either as liquids or as compressed gases. The commonest fuels are the naphthas (fluids) and butane (gas).

How it works: The fuels are, naturally, highly flammable. They ignite when struck by a spark from a lighter's flint or when exposed to the heat of an electric coil or wire.

What it can do to you: Petroleum distillate fumes are very toxic. If you inhale them, they can make you feel weak or nauseated, give you a headache, make you confused, drowsy, or, in extreme cases, cause coma and death. If swallowed, the fuels may cause nausea, vomiting, headache, weakness, and drowsiness, but they are unlikely to be fatal unless you aspirate some of the fluid into the lungs, which may cause a particularly lethal form of chemical pneumonia. That may happen if vomiting occurs, and therefore the probable lethal dose for a small child (22 pounds/10 kilograms) may start as low as one fifth of a teaspoonful.

What's better, safer, or cheaper: Simple matches. Or simply not smoking.

Closet Deodorizer

> **Safety Rating: MAY BE HARMFUL IF SWALLOWED OR IF CONCENTRATED VAPORS ARE INHALED. CALL POISON CONTROL CENTER IMMEDIATELY FOR APPROPRIATE ANTIDOTE PROCEDURE.**

What's in it: The deodorizers, which are usually sold as blocks attached to some kind of hanger, are made of *p*-dichlorobenzene, the insecticide found in moth blocks, chunks, or nuggets. There is usually some fragrance in the block, too.

How it works: The perfume in the deodorizer freshens your closet temporarily. The *p*-dichlorobenzene gives the space a kind of medicinal or sharp smell usually associated with disinfectants. It kills moths, too.

What it can do to you: The vapors from the blocks are irritating. They can make your eyes tear, scratch your throat, and, if you inhale them in a closed-in space for more than a few minutes, they may make you dizzy. If swallowed, the chemical is poisonous. Theoretically, the probable lethal dose for an adult may be an ounce or more (one seventh of an ounce for a small child), but people have survived doses as high as two thirds of an ounce without a single symptom, and there has never been a serious case of *p*-dichlorobenzene poisoning reported, probably because the smell is so bad.

What's better, safer, or cheaper: Keep your clothes clean and your closet aired and swept. That's the cheapest way to avoid odors. If you need additional perfuming fresheners, see the cheap alternatives under Air Freshener in this alphabetical products listing.

If your problem is the kind of dampness that leads to the musty, dusty odor of mildew, try leaving the light bulb in the closet burning for a couple of hours at a time. Even a small bulb will generate enough heat to make a real difference in the atmosphere around your clothes. Be careful, though, to see that the bulb *never* comes closer than twelve inches to any of the plastic bags that the cleaner sends back with your clothes, the heavier ones sold to keep clothes dust-free while they hang in the closet, or any other material or fabrics in the closet, including suitcases and boxes stored on high shelves. The heat from the bulb is enough to set these materials on fire. To be really safe, the bulb should be at least twelve inches from any of these cover-ups.

Coffeepot Cleaner

> **Safety Rating: MAY BE HARMFUL IF SWAL-
> LOWED. CALL POISON CONTROL CENTER
> IMMEDIATELY FOR APPROPRIATE ANTI-
> DOTE PROCEDURE.**

What's in it: DIP-IT (Economics Laboratory), MIRRO (Mirro), STAIN
AID (Lewis Research Labs.), and SUNBEAM COFFEE MAKER CLEANER
(Sunbeam Appliance Co.) are all mild alkaline cleaners based on detergent ingredients such as sodium metasilicate or sodium tripolyphosphate, plus a bleach (sodium perborate or chlorine bleach), an anticaking agent, and sometimes a surfactant.

How it works: Every time you use one of the electric percolators
for which these cleaners are made, the coffee leaves some nearly invisible oils on the inside of the pot and on the surface of the basket.
When you rinse out the pot, it may look clean but still have some of
the coffee oils left inside. These cleaners "cut" the oils and make it
possible to wash them easily out of the pot. You add a teaspoonful
or two of the cleaner to a potful of water and simply let the whole
thing sit there for as long as an hour. Then rinse out the coffeepot
with plain water and fill it up again, this time with water plus a teaspoonful or two of vinegar. Rinse again, and dry thoroughly. The result:
a percolator with insides absolutely free of oils.

What it can do to you: Like all detergents, coffeepot cleaners can
irritate your skin and eyes. If you inhale them, they can irritate your
nose and throat, too. If you swallow them, they may burn the inside
of your mouth, throat, and stomach, and they can definitely cause
nausea, vomiting, and general gastric upset. The probable lethal dose
for a small child (22 pounds/10 kilograms) is anywhere from slightly
less than a teaspoonful on up, but, as is the case with other detergents,
these cleaners are usually vomited up so quickly that they may not
have any lasting effects at all.

Cleaners with sodium perborate are more toxic than those with
a chlorine bleach or no bleach at all.

Coffeepot cleaners containing sodium perborate:

    DIP-IT
    STAIN AID

What's better, safer, or cheaper: You can use vinegar and water, or any dishwashing liquid or detergent, instead of this special cleaner. Or you can scour your pot thoroughly with a steel-wool pad. Either way, your best bet is to clean the pot completely every time you use it, so as to avoid a buildup of coffee oils.

Of course, you could also change from an aluminum electric percolator to a glass pot. The advantage here is that while the coffee oils may be hard to see inside an aluminum percolator, they're difficult to miss on the side of a glass pot. And glass is easy to clean. Just dunk the pot in soap or detergent suds. No special cleaner is needed, although, as with all glass or crystal, a bit of ammonia in the wash water will make it shine extra brightly.

Cold-Water Soap

> **Safety Rating: MAY BE HARMFUL IF SWALLOWED. CALL POISON CONTROL CENTER IMMEDIATELY FOR APPROPRIATE ANTIDOTE PROCEDURE.**

What's in it: "Cold-water soap" is a catchy but inaccurate name for products like WOOLKARE (Traum, David), WOOLITE (Boyle-Midway), and WOOL WASH (Reefer-Galler), all of which are really synthetic detergent/surfactant cleaners that contain no soap. The most prominent ingredient is a detergent, often alkyl sodium sulfate or alkyl aryl sulfonate, which dissolves easily in cold water. In addition, the powder cleaners usually contain an anticaking ingredient (sodium sulfate or sodium silicate), plus preservatives and such optional goodies as color brighteners and fragrances. The liquids also contain water.

How it works: Like all detergent/surfactant cleaners, these products are great at lifting dirt off a variety of fabrics. They got their big push as wool washes because they allow you to dunk a previously unwashable wool sweater in a sinkful of cold water and take it out clean and unshrunk. They work just as well on a number of other fabrics, including synthetics and synthetic knits, and they can be used in the washing machine as well as in the sink. However, a few words of caution are in order: There are lots of wools, including some fine wool knits, which should never be washed, not even in cold water. Garments with linings or with a particular line to them should almost always be dry-cleaned. For maximum safety, do yourself a favor and check with your neighborhood dry cleaner. Once dunked, a garment that should not have been washed usually cannot be made perfect again.

What it can do to you: Like all detergent products, these may be irritating to your skin or eyes. If swallowed, they may cause all the common symptoms of gastric upset associated with laundry detergents (nausea, vomiting, diarrhea). And, they may be caustic. In 1974, the *Journal of the American Medical Association* reported a case of throat ulcers in a teenager who had swallowed a cold-water soap that someone had slipped into the family sugar bowl as a practical joke.

The potentially lethal dose of cold-water soaps for a small child (22 pounds/10 kilograms) may be approximately one fifth of an ounce or more, depending on the concentration both of the detergent in the cleaner and of the cleaner itself. People with especially sensitive skin may be uncomfortable wearing clothes that have been washed in these detergents, and some people may be sensitive to the various fragrances, a common complaint where detergents are concerned.

What's better, safer, or cheaper: Because most modern laundry detergents work as well in cold water as in warm, you may be tempted to substitute one of the less expensive, all-purpose products for that expensive "wool wash." Resist the temptation. Most regular laundry products do work in cold water, but they have to be ruled out for hand washing because they often contain sodium carbonate, a water softener that may be corrosive in high concentrations and is certainly too strong to use when you're washing things by hand. Some detergents containing sodium carbonate: ALL, ARM & HAMMER, BOLD, CHEER, DASH, GAIN, OXYDOL, PUREX, RINSO, and TIDE. But neither COLD POWER XE nor TOTAL COLOR AJAX have sodium carbonate in the mix, and both have label directions that say they can be used for hand washing. Test them on something small first, to see if they work as well as the special cold-water soaps.

When you're choosing among the cold-water soaps, your most economical bet is almost always a powder. The one exception might come if you're buying the cleaner for traveling. In that case, you will probably opt for the expensive single-unit packets, which you can just toss into your suitcase. Of course, you could parcel out the bulk powders into individual bags, but the possibilities for spills boggle the mind. Who wants to have to sweep detergent powder out of the suitcase or off the clothes?

Contact Cement

What's in it: Contact cements are based on an elastomer, a synthetic, rubberlike ingredient, such as neoprene elastomer. The cements also contain a solvent. Nonflammable cements, such as ELMER'S NONFLAMMABLE SOLVENT CONTACT CEMENT (Borden Inc.), use 1,1,1-trichloroethane. The solvent in cements with a "flammable" warning on the label is usually toluol plus either acetone or isopropanol. Both kinds of contact cement may also contain inert resins and fillers for plasticity, body, and water resistance.

How it works: Elastomers harden and bond when the solvents evaporate.

What it can do to you: Elastomers are harmless. If you were to swallow some, they would simply congeal into rubbery blobs when mixed with saliva. But the addition of solvents makes all these cements potentially poisonous when swallowed, and the vapors of some solvents (notably toluol) are narcotic. The probable lethal dose of the cement for a small child (22 pounds/10 kilograms) may be less than an ounce. All the cements can be irritating to your skin and eyes.

What's better, safer, and cheaper: Sorry, as with most adhesives, there's really no simple, homemade alternative.

Copper Cleaner

What's in it: Powder cleaners like CAMEO COPPER CLEANER (Purex) or COPPER GLO (American Cyanamid) are mostly silica (an abrasive), plus sulfamic, citric, or tartaric acid (5–10 percent) to remove tarnish. They may also contain sodium chloride (table salt) to increase the action of the acid, as well as surfactants or detergents and fragrance. Paste cleaners like TWINKLE COPPER CLEANER (Drackett) contain the same ingredients, with water added to make the paste. Liquids, like GORHAM COPPER & BRASS POLISH (Gorham) and HAGERTY COPPER, BRASS AND METAL POLISH (Hagerty & Sons), contain a small amount of acid (such as phosphoric acid) in water.

How it works: Copper cleaners are less abrasive than all-purpose metal cleaners like NOXON. They can be used for aluminum, brass, and stainless steel, as well as for copper, but they are still too abrasive for silver flatware or jewelry made of gold or silver.

What it can do to you: If swallowed, copper cleaners are moderately toxic. The probable lethal dose for a small child (22 pounds/10 kilo-grams) is somewhere between one and five ounces. If you swallow small amounts of the cleaner, it may cause nausea, vomiting, and diar-rhea. *Note:* The green powder or "rust" that forms on copper when it comes in contact with vegetable juices is poisonous, just like all copper compounds. That's why copper pots and pans are always lined with chromium or tin and why you should absolutely never use a copper pan or teakettle on which the tin lining has worn thin.

What's better, safer, or cheaper: You can clean your copper utensils simply by rubbing them with an acid food such as vinegar, vinegar and salt, lemon juice and salt, or yogurt. Rinse the acid off as soon as you've cleaned the pot, and dry the copper to avoid water-spotting. For that greenish, powdery "rust," try soapsuds with a little ammonia.

For a more sophisticated homemade polishing paste, mix a table-spoon of salt with a tablespoon of all-purpose flour and add a tablespoon of vinegar to make a workable paste. When you're finished polishing, rinse it off and dry the copper thoroughly.

All-purpose metal cleaners are more caustic (they may contain oxalic acid) and probably more abrasive than copper cleaners, but not so abrasive that you can't use one all-purpose cleaner as an economical alternative to three or four different kinds of metal cleaners, for everything but silver. See Metal Cleaner (All-Purpose) in the alphabetical products listing.

Dishwasher Detergent
(for Automatic Dishwashers)

> **Safety Rating: IF SWALLOWED, THESE DE-TERGENTS MAY PRESENT A MEDICAL EMERGENCY REQUIRING *IMMEDIATE* MEDICAL ATTENTION.**

What's in it: CALGONITE (Beecham), CASCADE (Procter & Gamble), ELECTRASOL (Economics Laboratory), FINISH (Economics Laboratory), and others like them are powders made of strong alkalis and phosphates, such as washing soda or sodium carbonate, and sodium tripolyphosphate (10–40 percent each); anticaking agents, like sodium polysilicate (10–20 percent); surfactants (1–6 percent); bleaches, like sodium hypochlorite (1 percent or less); perfumes; and colorings.

How it works: When you wash dishes by hand, you want a mild solution that will get the food off your plates without burning your skin. The real cleaning power comes not from the detergent but from you, as you scrub away with cloth, brush, or sponge. The detergents for automatic dishwashers are much stronger, because they have to dissolve the food on the plate so that the mechanical action of the water spray can wash it away. Dishwasher detergents also have to contain some phosphates to prevent your dishes from spotting. The phosphates soften the wash water, keeping in solution the minerals that make it hard, so that they don't stick to the plates. Surfactants help to reduce spotting, too, by lessening the surface tension of the water so that it doesn't bead and cling to your china. Coloring agents and perfumes don't do a thing to help the detergent clean your dishes, but they may have some psychological effect; most of us seem to associate a cool blue color with a strong ability to clean.

What it can do to you: Detergents for dishwashers are so strongly alkaline that when swallowed in concentrated form they may cause injuries similar to those caused by lye. They may burn the inside of the mouth, throat, and stomach, and, in really severe cases, they have been known to burn right through the stomach walls. For a small child (22 pounds/10 kilograms), the probable lethal dose may be as low as one fifth or one seventh of a teaspoonful.

Needless to say, the detergents may be irritating to your skin and eyes, and, if inhaled, they can irritate the respiratory tract. The perfumes in them contribute to this effect; if you are sensitive to perfume, you may be interested to know that (as of 1979) ELECTRASOL appears to be the only one of these products without perfume in it.

What's better, safer, or cheaper: There really is no adequate substitute for commercial dishwasher detergents. You could try plain washing soda, of course, but it may not prevent those ugly water spots.

You should never, absolutely never, use ordinary dishwashing liquid as a substitute. It doesn't have enough cleaning power, and its suds can be devastating to your delicate electric dishwasher. They'll form a foamy cushion that can keep the water spray from cleaning off your plates, and they can clog the drain, causing the water in the dishwasher to spill over onto the floor.

Dishwasher Rinse Aid (for Automatic Dishwashers)

> **Safety Rating: MAY BE HARMFUL IF SWALLOWED. CALL POISON CONTROL CENTER IMMEDIATELY FOR APPROPRIATE ANTIDOTE PROCEDURE.**

What's in it: JET-DRY (Economics Laboratory), the only rinse aid I found on the shelves of my six local supermarkets, comes in both a liquid and a solid. The liquid is simply a surfactant in water solution; the solid contains surfactants and a small amount of phosphates.

How it works: All the detergents meant for use in automatic dishwashers contain surfactants and phosphates (see Dishwasher Detergent in the alphabetical products listing), but adding JET-DRY to the mix does seem to increase your chances of getting a really sparkling load of dishes out of the dishwasher. The extra surfactants boost the dishwasher detergent's ability to eliminate water-spotting. They make the water "wetter," helping it to slide off the dishes so that they dry more quickly, too. (The liquid JET-DRY is meant for dishwashers that have a special container for dispensing rinse aid; the solid goes in all other machines.)

What it can do to you: Like all detergent or surfactant products, the rinse aids can play all kinds of havoc with your gastric tract if swallowed. Even small doses can cause nausea, vomiting, and diarrhea. The probable lethal dose for a small child may be as small as a teaspoonful or less. Of course, these products may also be irritating to your skin and eyes.

What's better, safer, or cheaper: This is another product category for which there really isn't an adequate substitute. Whether or not you need to spend the extra pennies rinse aids cost really depends on how fanatic you are about sparkling dishes and glassware. Most dishwasher detergents do a competent job of eliminating spots. If that's good enough for you, put your extra pennies in a piggy bank. If not, use the rinse aid.

Dishwashing Liquid

> **Safety Rating: MAY BE HARMFUL IF SWAL-LOWED. CALL POISON CONTROL CENTER IMMEDIATELY FOR APPROPRIATE ANTI-DOTE PROCEDURE.**

What's in it: Dishwashing liquids may be as much as 70 percent water, plus about 10 percent surfactants and detergents such as alkyl aryl sulfonate. Sodium chloride (table salt) or potassium chloride is added to make the liquid thick and viscous, and ethyl alcohol, a solvent, keeps it flowing freely. Optional ingredients include opacifiers to make the liquid solid white; dyes that make it pink, yellow, blue, or green; and fragrance to give it that characteristic flowery, "fresh," or lemon scent.

How it works: The detergent and surfactants dissolve and loosen grease and food particles so that you, who do most of the work, can simply wipe them away with a dishcloth or brush. Foaming agents in the liquid produce suds, but no matter what the advertising tells you, the amount of suds you get from your dishwashing liquid has nothing at all to do with how well it cleans. In fact, a product like IVORY LIQUID (Procter & Gamble), which sudses up a storm, may actually make your job harder, because overabundant suds can clog the drain. If that happens, it will seem like forever as you stand there waiting for the dirty water to run out of the sink. Speed things along by shaking salt on the suds. The crystals will break up the bubbles in a hurry.

What it can do to you: Dishwashing liquids are the mildest of the household detergent products. Because they are diluted with water, they are generally less toxic than powders. But liquids are easier to swallow than powders, and the fact that some of these are perfumed with strawberry, lemon, or lime fragrances can make them inordinately attractive to an exploring child. The probable lethal dose for a small child (22 pounds/10 kilograms) may be anywhere from two ounces on up. However, if they are swallowed, the detergents usually cause vomiting so quickly that they rarely have any serious, lasting effect.

Allergies and irritations are a different story. The colors and the perfumes are the primary allergens. You can avoid the first, but as far as I can tell there's no dishwashing liquid made without some perfume or other. It's really a question of shopping around until you find one you can live with.

Naturally, the liquids can be irritating if you splash them in your eyes. They can be rough on your skin, too. Don't fall for the suggestion that a detergent with "protein" in it is kinder to your hands. Simple logic will tell you that you can't keep the protein on your skin while you're washing dishes; the water and detergent take it right off again. Hand creams or lotions, with or without protein, can help only if you slather them on after you get your hands out of the dishwater.

Wearing gloves is a much better bet, particularly if your skin is very sensitive. The smallest size you can get your hands into comfortably will give the best mobility and sense of touch. Never buy gloves that don't have a protective lining. Without the lining, you won't be able to tolerate really hot rinse water, and consequently your dishes won't get as clean.

What's better, safer, or cheaper: If you don't like spending money on dishwashing liquids, that well-known food writer M. F. K. Fisher has your number. She has written that she never uses a dishwashing product at all, since she finds that hot water and a really stiff brush get everything clean as a whistle anyway.

If you're simply psychologically unable to face a sinkful of dirty dishes without a pretty, nice-smelling bubbly liquid, then probably any one will do. Despite all the consumer-magazine ratings of dishwashing products, I've come to the conclusion that every last one of them does a fine job in my sink if I use enough (but not too much). Exactly how much is that? Try this simple test suggested by *Consumer Reports:* Put about a teaspoonful of dishwashing liquid in your dishpan. Scrub the dishes. If there are any suds left when you finish the panful of dishes, use a little less next time. Using this test, *Consumer Reports* found that the most "effective" liquids were AJAX (Colgate-Palmolive), DAWN (Procter & Gamble), DERMASSAGE (Colgate-Palmolive), LUX (Lever Brothers), and PALMOLIVE (Colgate-Palmolive). They're entitled to stand by their results. Personally, I think that all liquids, plus elbow grease, do about the same job.

If you like, you can exercise some consumer clout with your dish-washing-liquid pennies or dollars by picking the product with the most informative label: IVORY and JOY (both Procter & Gamble) give you label copy that lists ingredients and tells you what all of them do. Other than that, however, your most meaningful choice in dishwashing products seems to come down to color and perfume. Do you like white? Choose DOVE (Lever Brothers) or IVORY LIQUID. Prefer blue? Pick DAWN, which, inexplicably, hasn't got the same, informative label copy found on other Procter & Gamble products.

AJAX DISHWASHING LIQUID looks like thick yellow shampoo, and PALMOLIVE looks like Procter & Gamble's green PRELL shampoo. Appearances can be deceiving, though, and none of these dishwashing liquids, not even "gentle, white" IVORY LIQUID, should ever be used as a cheap substitute for real shampoo. The detergents are more concentrated, and there may be colors or bleaches or surfactants or other ingredients in the liquid that don't belong on your head or all over your body in a bubble bath. Stick to cosmetics for cosmetic purposes. It's (relatively) safer.

Disinfectant Cleaner

Safety Rating: MAY BE HARMFUL IF SWAL-
LOWED. CALL POISON CONTROL CENTER
IMMEDIATELY FOR APPROPRIATE ANTI-
DOTE PROCEDURE.

What's in it: Like general-purpose household cleaners, the disinfectant products begin with soaps or detergents, plus surfactants, water, and sometimes a dye to make the cleaner look pretty. The disinfectants also contain specific ingredients that destroy bacteria and thus eliminate odors. These ingredients vary from product to product. Here are some examples of liquid disinfectants:

Product	*Disinfectant Ingredients*
BREATH O PINE (Brondow)	Pine oil (40%)
CN (West Chemical)	Iodophors (12.3%)
LYSOL (Lehn & Fink)	
Regular	Phenol compounds (5.5%)
Fresh scent	Phenol compounds (3.2%)
Pine scent	Phenol compounds (4.5%), pine oil (5%)
PINE SOL (American Cyanamid)	Pine oil (30%)

An aerosol disinfectant cleaner contains everything that's in the liquids, plus a propellant.

How it works: The disinfectant ingredients in disinfectant products do kill microorganisms that cause mildew, mold, and those unpleasant odors around the garbage pail or toilet. In fact, the effectiveness of these products is a matter of record, since they are registered with the Environmental Protection Agency, which certifies that they do what they're supposed to do: kill germs.

It's important to remember, though, that the fact that a cleaner kills some germs and slows the rate at which others grow doesn't mean that it will sterilize your home, or even small areas in the bathroom or kitchen. Germs and bacteria are all around us, and about all you can count on a simple household disinfectant to do is to knock down the population for a little while.

What it can do to you: You might expect an effective disinfectant to be a lot more toxic than an ordinary household cleaner, and that would be true if there were more of the germ-killing ingredient in any of these disinfectants. As it is, there is usually so little of the active ingredient that, if swallowed, these cleaners may cause much the same side effects as the general-purpose liquid household cleaners. If swallowed, the disinfectants can make you sick to your stomach. Nausea, vomiting, and diarrhea would be expected symptoms. The cleaners can also irritate mucous membranes, and products containing pine oil or alcohol might cause the kind of momentary excitement followed by depression which we associate with ordinary inebriation.

Like most detergent or soap-based products, disinfectant cleaners may irritate your skin and eyes. Sensitive people may be allergic to specific dyes, detergents, or perfumes.

What's better, safer, or cheaper: There's really no need to use one of these expensive, special cleaners every time you tidy up. Simple thorough cleaning with an ordinary household detergent will keep down the bacteria population. Even just a regular swipe with a plain cloth dipped in water will eliminate a lot of bacteria. Keeping things dry is even better, since mildew, mold, and bacteria will not flourish for long without dampness.

The standard homemade disinfectant/deodorizer is a plain chlorine bleach. Mix one quarter cup with a quart of warm water and scrub away. If you want to add real cleaning power, mix one half cup of powder detergent. Be certain not to use a cleaner containing ammonia, since combining ammonia and chlorine bleach can liberate lethal chloramines.

Disinfectant Spray

> **Safety Rating: MAY BE HARMFUL IF SWALLOWED. CALL POISON CONTROL CENTER IMMEDIATELY FOR APPROPRIATE ANTIDOTE PROCEDURE.**

What's in it: This is a straight disinfectant, not a cleaner. An aerosol like DOW SPRAY DISINFECTANT (Dow Chemical) or LYSOL BRAND DISIN-

FECTANT SPRAY (Lehn & Fink) contains a tiny amount of an all-purpose germ-killer such as *o*-phenylphenol, plus alcohol (66–70 percent) and a propellant. No detergents, no soap, no surfactants.

How it works: According to the Environmental Protection Agency, the fine mist dispensed by the aerosol may get rid of some of the flu bugs, staph and strep organisms, cold viruses, viruses that cause herpes simplex, and mildew and mold organisms hanging around your house. Not that the aerosols sterilize the surfaces you spray them on; they'll just cut down the population of microorganisms for a while. There will always be a small population left to breed its way back up again.

The sprays are unique in that they can penetrate the surface of your mattress or curtains. They also work well on bathroom floors, toilet bowls, garbage cans, and all the other places nasty odors accumulate. One surface on which disinfectant sprays should never be used is wood furniture. The alcohol in the spray may dissolve or streak the finish.

What it can do to you: The disinfectant spray may irritate your skin and eyes, and if you breathe it in you'll feel it in your throat. It should never be used around food, because it can contaminate the things you eat, causing gastric upset if swallowed. The probable lethal dose for a small child (22 pounds/10 kilograms) may be one fifth of an ounce, but it is almost impossible to get that much out of an aerosol can.

The aerosols also present all the mechanical problems linked to other aerosols: The cans can explode if overheated or punctured, and the propellant gases may be flammable. The sprays should never be used around sparks or open flames.

What's better, safer, or cheaper: The special advantage of the aerosol sprays is that they evaporate quickly. They are perfect for mattresses or curtains, things that you don't want to dip into or swab down with a chlorine bleach and water solution, the normal cheapie disinfectant.

In other cases, though, this homemade solution may be just the ticket. It's fine for counter tops, garbage pails, toilet bowls, and even the telephone receiver. Closets, beds, and curtains may benefit from frequent airing; mold and mildew won't grow in clean, dry environments. As for the bathroom floor and the bottom of the shower, those surfaces are less likely to support the organisms which cause athlete's foot if you keep them clean and dry between uses.

Dog and Cat Repellent

> **Safety Rating: HARMFUL IF SWALLOWED. CALL POISON CONTROL CENTER IMMEDIATELY FOR APPROPRIATE ANTIDOTE PROCEDURE.**

What's in it: Products meant to keep your darling pet off the sofa so his not-so-darling claws or nails won't tear holes in the upholstery (not to mention the hair all over the place) usually contain one or more ingredients that smell bad or are irritating if touched or inhaled. Some of the common ones are allyl isothiocyanate (imitation oil of mustard), oleoresin capsicum (oil of an African chili), oil of lemongrass, oil of citronella, oxalic acid, formic acid, and methyl nonyl ketone. The repellents are mixed with a solvent-vehicle, and aerosol products include a propellant.

How it works: Hopefully, the smell of the repellent, or the irritation caused by it, will repel your pet. Needless to say, it doesn't always do the job.

What it can do to you: If it smells bad to Fido, it may smell bad to you, although a dog's sense of smell is so much more acute than ours that he may be put off by scents we don't even notice. More important, many if not all the ingredients in an animal repellent may be lethal if swallowed in quantity. Allyl isothiocyanate and oil of lemongrass are violent intestinal irritants. Oil of citronella, oxalic acid, formic acid—all may cause vomiting, shock, and death if swallowed in sufficient quantity. It is unlikely, of course, that you'd be able to swallow enough of a product that comes in an aerosol can.

Oleoresin capsicum is a skin irritant and an allergen; methyl nonyl ketone is similar to acetone, which is similar to alcohol. If you drink enough of any of them, they can be intoxicating or even fatal. Again, it's unlikely that such a thing could happen with aerosol products.

What's better, safer, or cheaper: Keeping pets off your furniture can be a problem, but not so much of a problem that you have to resort to some of the inhumane recommendations I have come across in various training manuals. Things like spraying pepper on the furniture (how do you keep from inhaling it yourself?); sprinkling ammonia around (won't it ruin the finish?); and scattering tacks on the pillows so that when Rover takes a running leap at the sofa he ends up with sharp tacks heaven knows where. Just about the only humane, intelligent, no-chemical repellent I came across was a pile of empty tin cans (with the sharp tops removed, of course). You balance these lightweight noisemakers on the arm of the sofa so that when your pet hits the sofa the cans hit the floor. The noise may discourage the pet's nestling into the pillows. Good luck.

Drain Cleaner (Crystal)

Safety Rating: IF SWALLOWED, DRAIN CLEANER CRYSTALS PRESENT A MEDICAL EMERGENCY REQUIRING *IMMEDIATE* MEDICAL ATTENTION.

What's in it: The single most important active ingredient in crystal drain cleaners is lye, usually listed on the label as sodium hydroxide. Sometimes, that's all there is in the product, for example, INDCO LYE (Independence Chemical Co.) and RED DEVIL LYE (Rasco). Multi-ingredient drain cleaners, like DRĀNO CONCENTRATED CRYSTAL DRAIN OPENER (Drackett), contain lye, plus sodium nitrate (a corrosion inhibitor) to protect the pipes, sodium chloride, and aluminum particles, which increase the heating action of the lye.

How it works: In its dry state, lye is not caustic. It becomes active when mixed with water. That's why the directions on most crystal drain cleaners tell you to pour a specific amount of lye into the drain and then follow it up with about a cupful of cool water. That makes the crystals dissolve. In doing so, they give off a considerable amount of heat. It has been suggested that a lye/aluminum particle mixture, for example, can produce temperatures as high as 220 degrees Fahrenheit inside your drainpipe. Usually, even that much heat is not enough to damage sound metal pipes. But it certainly might expand and crack porcelain surfaces, which is why you should never use crystal drain cleaners to unclog a stopped-up toilet. The last thing you need around the house is a cracked toilet bowl dripping lye and water all over the bathroom floor.

Plain lye, however, probably will not get hotter than about 160 degrees Fahrenheit when you mix it with water. Since that is usually not hot enough to crack porcelain, the manufacturers' plain lye products often suggest that you can use the lye to unclog your stopped-up toilet. Actually, I'm not sure it's all that hot an idea. Even if it doesn't actually reach boiling point, lye can spit back at you when you add it to an open container of water. The fact that there's no aluminum mixed with it has no effect at all on the lye's ability to burn your skin. And it may leave "hot spots" that mar the finish of the bowl. Less corrosive means of opening the toilet—a plunger or a mechanical snake—are almost certainly a better idea.

Note: never use caustic drain cleaner in the dishwasher or the garbage disposal. The lye will eat right through plastic or rubber parts, and it can damage aluminum, too.

What can go wrong: Caustic drain cleaners are the single most dangerous product in general home use. They can burn everything they touch, and, if swallowed, they can eat their way through mouth, esophagus, and stomach. Most frightening of all, there is absolutely no effective antidote.

Poison control experts suggest that it may help to give someone who has swallowed a caustic drain cleaner two glasses of milk and to do it immediately. The milk will dilute the cleaner and give it something other than body tissue to work on.

But the milk will not repair the damage the cleaner has done. Nor will anything else except, possibly, corrective surgery. In some cases, following the first-aid directions on a product label can be disastrous. For example, when a child in Missouri swallowed drain cleaner, his mother faithfully carried out the directions on the package and gave him vinegar to drink. The vinegar combined with the lye to produce a heat reaction severe enough to explode his stomach.

Scary? You bet.

The truth is that avoiding drain cleaners entirely is the only way to make sure children don't get into them. In one interesting marketing experiment, the Drackett Products Company, which makes DRĀNO, introduced small one-shot packages of DRĀNO II in 1973. The idea was to offer a package that wouldn't stand around open but would be used up in one application. What happened next may give some clue as to exactly how safety-conscious American consumers really are. When sales of the one-shot packages began, DRĀNO II had about 10 percent of the drain-cleaner market. One year later, that had slipped all the way down to 1 percent. Safety, it seems, comes second to the savings in the large economy size.

If you absolutely must have drain cleaners around the house, it helps to put them in a locked cabinet or on a shelf high enough to be beyond the reach of a small child. If you do that, don't ever underestimate the ability of that same small child to climb up toward something he or she really wants.

Healthwise, just about the only good thing you can say about crystal drain cleaners is that they will probably be less caustic than liquid ones if you happen to spill some on your skin. The dry crystals can be brushed off before they burn. Liquid products are already active and will burn the minute they hit the skin. All bets are off, of course, if you get the crystals in your eye, where they can be activated by the natural moistness of the tissues and should be flushed out immediately with copious amounts of cool water. Continue flushing for at least fifteen minutes.

What's better, safer, or cheaper: Start with a "plumber's helper," or plunger. If that doesn't work, calling the plumber may not be the cheapest way to deal with a stopped-up drain, but it's certainly safer and it's probably the best way. On really plugged drains, no dry or liquid drain cleaner works as well as a mechanical snake.

As for chemical substitutes, the handiest may be sodium carbonate, which is also known as sal soda or washing soda and is sold at the supermarket under a variety of brand names including ARM & HAMMER WASHING SODA. Sodium carbonate is alkaline and will do a competent job of removing minor obstructions in the drain. It's probably a more economical buy than any drain cleaner, because it has other uses. It's also a water softener and a laundry-detergent booster. Be warned, though—it's not harmless. Concentrated solutions can be very irritating to the skin and, if swallowed, will irritate and burn mouth, throat, and stomach.

Of course, the best, the safest, and the cheapest method for keeping drainpipes open is to treat them well in the first place. No, I don't mean you should pour old coffee grounds into the sink. That won't work. Neither will salt, which is simply too mild an alkali to eat through food or grease or hair. The trick is to start with a spanking clean drain and then keep it that way by (1) using a drain strainer, such as HAPPY HOME's, which goes for about 60 cents at the five-and-ten; (2) running hot tap water for a good five minutes after you finish washing the dishes or your hair; and (3) pouring a whole teakettleful of boiling water down the drain once or twice a week. If the drain is temporarily stopped up, try a plunger. You may never have to spend a cent, or risk a child's safety, on commercial drain cleaners again.

Drain Cleaner (Liquid)

> **Safety Rating: ALL LIQUID DRAIN CLEANERS MAY BE EXTREMELY HARMFUL IF SWALLOWED. PRODUCTS CONTAINING A CORROSIVE POISON (LYE, HYDROCHLORIC ACID) CAN PRESENT A MEDICAL EMERGENCY REQUIRING *IMMEDIATE* MEDICAL ATTENTION.**

What's in it: There are two basic kinds of liquid drain cleaners: caustic cleaners and cleaners based on solvents that dissolve grease. The caustics contain hydrochloric acid or lye (sodium or potassium hydroxide) in a water solution. The degreasing drain cleaners usually contain up to 100 percent 1,1,1-trichloroethane (a chlorinated hydrocarbon often used as a dry-cleaning fluid) plus a petroleum distillate solvent. The degreasing cleaners may also contain corrosion inhibitors and surfactants (wetting agents) to help the solvent work.

Caustic liquid drain cleaners:

GLAMORENE DRAIN POWER (Glamorene)
LIQUID DRĀNO (Drackett)
LIQUID-PLUMR (Clorox)
MR. PLUMBER DRAIN OPENER (Gromwell)
PLUNGE (Drackett)
SAFEGUARD (Safeguard)

Degreasing liquid drain cleaners:

AMWAY DRAIN MATE (Amway Corp.)
KITCHEN DRĀNO (Drackett)

How it works: Caustic liquid drain cleaners work exactly the same way caustic dry ones do, by literally eating away whatever is stopping up the pipe. Degreasing cleaners, however, dissolve only fatty substances. Naturally, they work best (sometimes even better than the corrosive liquids) on foods and fats.

Both the corrosive and the degreasing liquid cleaners can be poured directly into standing water; you don't have to bail out the sink to use them. Both kinds are best kept out of toilets, dishwashers, and garbage disposals. Caustic cleaners eat away at plastic, aluminum, or rubber parts, and degreasing cleaners can damage appliances too.

What it can do to you: If anything, caustic liquid drain cleaners are even more dangerous than caustic dry cleaners. For one thing, the liquids don't need the addition of water to make them corrosive to the dry skin. The liquid is already activated in the bottle. If you spill some on your skin, it will begin to burn right away. With a dry drain cleaner, however, you might be able to brush the crystals off before it causes any serious damage. It goes without saying that the caustic liquids can cause severe damage if swallowed.

Packaging also plays a part in making the liquid products more dangerous. The plastic bottles in which they are sold are usually flexible. If you squeeze too hard when you pick up the product, you can actually squeeze some of the liquid out of the bottle, splashing it on your hands or your face.

The "child-proof" caps on the corrosive liquids represent a real safety advance. According to the Glass Packaging Institute in Washington, D.C., there has been a 56 percent drop in the incidence of childhood injuries caused by swallowing lye-based products like these since the introduction of child-proof safety caps. That's a serious step forward, one which should give you pause the next time you are tempted to mutter unprintable things about a child-proof container that is resisting your best (adult) efforts to open it.

As for liquid drain cleaners based on degreasing solvents (petroleum distillates), they are poisonous but not corrosive. It is a marginal difference, to be sure, but it might make the difference between life and death. There are some antidote procedures that can lessen the effects of swallowing chlorinated hydrocarbons or petroleum distillates, but there are, as noted under Drain Cleaner (Crystal) in the alphabetical products listing, no practical antidotes for the corrosive action of lye-based products.

Note: Federal law requires that all products containing 10 percent or more lye have child-proof caps, and that all the caustic liquid drain cleaners have them. There is, however, no law requiring child-proof caps on products containing petroleum distillates, even though they are severely poisonous.

What's better, safer, or cheaper: See Drain Cleaner (Crystal) in the alphabetical products listing.

Drain Cleaner (Pressure-Type)

> **Safety Rating: THESE PRODUCTS ARE RARELY TOXIC BECAUSE IT IS VIRTUALLY IMPOSSIBLE TO SWALLOW OR INHALE THEIR CONTENTS.**

What's in it: The only ingredient in a pressure-type drain cleaner such as DRĀNO AEROSOL PLUNGER (Drackett) or DRAIN POWER (Airwick) is a propellant gas.

How it works: Pressure-type drain cleaners get their power from the whooooosh of propellant gas that escapes when you push the container into the drain opening. To be sure that all the whooooosh goes down the drain where it belongs, it's best to be certain that all overflow vents in the sink are covered or closed. Like liquid drain cleaners, the pressure-type products can be used right through standing water. They work best on drains that are only partially blocked; a really stopped-up drain almost always needs professional help, or at least the help of someone who can operate an electric snake.

What it can do to you: The side effects of aerosol drain cleaners are all pretty much mechanical ones. The cans should never be incinerated, for example; they will explode if heated past 120 degrees Fahrenheit. Don't puncture them; they will explode, scattering metal pieces like shrapnel. Don't use them after you've used a liquid or a crystal drain cleaner; the pressure from the aerosol can make the chemical cleaner splash back up at you. Don't lean down toward the aerosol when you use it; it can kick back, thumping you on the nose or chin or forehead if you haven't got a solid grip on it.

As for side effects to the drain itself, the pressure cleaners are supposed to be safe for pipes in sound condition, but I'd think twice or maybe even three times before using one on drainpipes that have been in place for more than twenty years.

What's better, safer, or cheaper: As with both liquid and crystal drain cleaners, the best, safest, and cheapest solution is to keep the drain free of debris in the first place. Nothing else is as safe or cheap as that.

Dust-Control Spray

Safety Rating: MAY BE HARMFUL IF SWALLOWED. PRODUCTS CONTAINING A PETROLEUM DISTILLATE MAY BE EXTREMELY HARMFUL. CALL POISON CONTROL CENTER IMMEDIATELY FOR APPROPRIATE ANTIDOTE PROCEDURE.

What's in it: Aerosol dusting sprays like DUST-SEAL (L. S. Green) and ENDUST (Drackett) are mostly mineral oil (up to 96 percent) plus either an alcohol or a petroleum distillate solvent, a surfactant, a fragrance, and a propellant.

How it works: The oil in the spray actually dampens and anchors dust, so that it's much easier to pick up with cloth or broom. Be sure to spray the dusting aid on your dustcloth or mop, not directly on furniture or floors. If sprayed on finished surfaces, the spray can remove or dissolve wax, leaving ugly streaks.

What it can do to you: Like all aerosols, these dusting sprays are flammable and should never be used around an open flame, nor should the cans be incinerated or accidentally punctured. Always check the direction of the nozzle before you push the spray button; a squirt in the eye will create a burning sensation. The solvents can make the products dangerous if swallowed. The probable lethal dose for a small child (22 pounds / 10 kilograms) may be as little as one fifth of a teaspoonful, but swallowing the contents of aerosol cans is kind of unlikely.

What's better, safer, or cheaper: Why pay aerosol prices for mineral oil when you can get the same thing dirt cheap at any drugstore? The answer is that the additional ingredients in the dust sprays and

50

the aerosol container make it possible to produce a fine mist that you simply cannot duplicate at home. Homemade sprays (mineral oil in a clean, empty pump-spray bottle originally used for window cleaner, for example) sound economical, but are just too heavy and greasy. If you must use a dust spray, you'll have to spring for the commercial product.

Dye.

See **Fabric Dye.**

Epoxy Resin Glue

Safety Rating: MAY BE HARMFUL IF SWALLOWED. CALL POISON CONTROL CENTER IMMEDIATELY FOR APPROPRIATE ANTIDOTE PROCEDURE.

What's in it: Epoxy resin glues are essentially two-ingredient products containing an epoxy resin plus an amine curing agent, the hardener. Some epoxy glues also contain fillers, but that's not the rule.

How it works: The resin and the hardener are packaged in separate containers to prevent their combining before you're ready to use them. Mixing carefully measured amounts of the two ingredients together causes a reaction that hardens the glue so that it can bind two surfaces together. Epoxy glues work best on nonporous surfaces like plastic, glass, china, and porcelain, and they are fairly water-resistant when dry.

What it can do to you: The epoxy resin is nontoxic whether swallowed or spilled on the skin, but the amine curing agent is alkaline and can burn your skin or the inside of your mouth, throat, and stomach. Its fumes are acrid and irritating to your eyes. They can cause reddening and conjunctivitis; skin rashes; asthmatic attacks in sensitive individuals, if inhaled; or ordinary coughing spells among the rest of us. The mixture of resin and hardener is less toxic than the hardener alone, more toxic than the resin alone. Probable lethal doses depend on how much hardener is ingested, so your best bet is to check immediately with your local poison control center. After it's hardened, the mixture is harmless unless you're allergic to it.

What's better, safer, or cheaper: Because you have to measure out accurate amounts of the resin and the hardener, and mix and apply them before they'll work, epoxy glues have always been notably messy to mess around with. The new containers such as DEVCON'S 2-IN-1 DISPENSER (Devcon Corp.) can make things a lot easier. The dispenser looks something like a plastic hypodermic needle with two chambers, side by side. The resin is in one, the hardener in the other, and when you press down on the plunger, a precisely measured mixture of the two appears at the tip that is the opening for both tubes. Spread it on the surfaces you're gluing, and you're in business.

Fabric Dye

Safety Rating: MAY (RARELY) BE HARM-FUL IF SWALLOWED IN QUANTITY. CALL POISON CONTROL CENTER IMMEDIATELY FOR APPROPRIATE ANTIDOTE PROCE-DURE.

What's in it: The popular fabric dyes, RIT (Best Foods) and TINTEX (Knomark), are relatively simple products. The powders have a coloring agent plus a surfactant (2 percent to help dye penetrate fabric, and sodium chloride, or common table salt (up to 98 percent). The liquids contain all these ingredients plus water. The exact amount of coloring in the dye depends on the shade. There's less dye in a light blue, for example, than in a dark blue or purple.

How it works: These dyes go to work when their molecules are changed around by hot water so that they can easily penetrate fabrics like cotton, rayon, or linen that are made from celluloselike fibers. The dyes work on wool, too, but the hot water may shrink the fabric.

The easiest way to dye clothes is to dissolve the dye in hot water in the washing machine. Then add clean, wet clothes for coloring; if the clothes aren't clean and wet, the dye won't penetrate evenly. Next, run the whole load through an entire wash cycle, ending with cold rinse water to "set" the dye. Run through a second cycle, with a little detergent added, to get rid of any excess dye that has survived the first go-round and to clean the machine at the same time.

If you insist, you can dye your clothes by boiling them in dye and water on top of the stove, but it's a long, hard process to wash out the excess dye by holding the clothes under cold running water. It's messy, too, because the dye running off the clothes can stain your porous porcelain tub or sink.

What you absolutely can't do is dye your clothes in the bathroom sink. The water isn't really hot enough to activate the dye, and it won't penetrate the fabric. It will simply drip all over everything, staining whatever it touches. At the end of the whole messy process, you're likely to find yourself with clothes that keep on running—on you, on other clothes, sometimes even on the fabric of chairs and sofas you sit on.

First aid for stains: If you've just got a few dye stains on a sink or tub, try scrubbing immediately with a little laundry detergent. Stubborn stains should yield to some chlorine bleach.

What it can do to you: There's some possibility that a few of the coloring agents in fabric dyes may be absorbed through intact skin. Protect yourself; always wear gloves when you dye clothes. Some people may be sensitive to the coloring agents, which can mean allergic reactions or, rarely, skin irritations. The dyes are irritating if you get them in your eyes.

The dyes are dangerous only if swallowed undiluted and in quantity. The relatively large amount of sodium chloride may cause salt poisoning: vomiting, diarrhea, dehydration, twitching muscles, convulsions, and, in extreme cases, death. The probable lethal dose for a small child (22 pounds/10 kilograms) may be less than a teaspoonful of the powder. There is proportionally less salt in the liquids, so they are marginally less toxic.

What's better, safer, or cheaper: The plain powder dyes, which you have to dilute yourself, are less expensive, ounce for ounce, than the already-prepared liquid dyes. When used intelligently and kept away from small children, both can be safe.

I suppose that if you're into natural things, you can muck around the kitchen with fruits and vegetables, cooking up some dyes of your own (beets for red, blueberries for blue, and so forth). But the truth of it is that no "natural" dye will give you the range and flexibility of the commercial dyes, which is why the commercial ones were invented in the first place.

Fabric Softener

What's in it: Liquid fabric softeners are mostly water (up to 90 percent), plus surfactants (up to 10 percent), emulsifiers (up to 10 percent), and fragrance. Some liquid softeners include optical brighteners or bluing.

Fabric-softening sheets, which go directly into the drier with the wash, are nonwoven sheets of rayon fibers saturated with surfactants and perfume.

Liquid fabric softeners:

DOWNY (Procter & Gamble)
FINAL TOUCH (Lever Brothers)
HANDLE WITH CARE (Drackett)
RAIN BARREL (S. C. Johnson & Son)

Fabric-softening sheets:

BOUNCE (Procter & Gamble)
CLING FREE (Beecham)
TOSS 'N SOFT (Purex)

How it works: Fabric softeners are really moisturizers for your clothes. They saturate the fabric with surfactants. The surfactants make the cloth more porous, so that it absorbs and holds moisture. As a result, ordinarily porous clothes like cotton and linen become softer and more pliable. The moisture acts as a conductor, dissipating static electricity before it can build up on your synthetics. Suddenly, as if by magic, they no longer cling like a second skin or stick to other fabrics.

What it can do to you: The surfactants can irritate your skin. Some people find them irritating even after they have dried on the fabric. They can irritate your eyes, too, and if you're allergic to the perfumes in the softeners, you can be uncomfortable wearing clothes that have been dunked in a softening product and water. You might try switching brands; one perfume may be less troublesome than another.

If swallowed, fabric softeners can cause nausea, vomiting, and all the symptoms of gastric upset associated with surfactants or detergents. The probable lethal dose for a small child (22 pounds/10 kilograms) may be as little as one fifth of a teaspoonful. On the other hand, since these things make you vomit so quickly, it is possible that even much larger doses may not be lethal.

What's better, safer, or cheaper: Certainly, liquid softeners like FINAL TOUCH are more economical than softening sheets like CLING FREE. And a steady hand as you pour can save you money every time; you probably need a lot less softener in the rinse water than the label on the package says you do. You may also find that the softening effect bestowed by one trip through the rinse can last through more than one washing. Try running softened garments through a couple of washings before you soften them again. That will give you a more accurate reading on exactly how often you have to repeat the process. For example, I have found that nylon petticoats can stand up to three washings before they start clinging to me and my skirts again.

Don't double up on softener to make it more powerful. If you pour too much into the rinse water, your clothes will come out feeling clammy or gummy. And watch your pennies. It's a waste of money to buy a softener with bluing if there's already some bluing or optical brightener in your detergent.

As far as I know, there's no homemade substitute for a commercial softener. Once upon a time, people used to put vinegar in the final rinse water. That softened clothes simply because the acid (vinegar) removed the alkali (soap) from the fabric. There wasn't any dulling or irritating film left. Modern detergents, though, aren't soap and don't leave a scum, so there's no reason at all to use vinegar, which won't provide any antistatic relief.

Floor Polish (for Synthetic Floor Coverings)

What's in it: A & P SELF POLISHING ACRYLIC FLOOR FINISH (A & P), AERO WAX CLEAR DRYING FLOOR CARE FORMULA (Boyle-Midway), BEACON SELF POLISHING FLOOR WAX (Lehn & Fink), BUTCHER'S GREEN STRIPE FLOOR WAX (Butcher Polish), JOHNSON'S GLO-COAT (S. C. Johnson & Son), KLEAR (S. C. Johnson & Son), MOP & GLO (Lehn & Fink), STEP SAVER (S. C. Johnson & Son) and SUPER BRAVO (S. C. Johnson & Son) are all water-based emulsions of natural or synthetic wax, plastic film-formers like acrylic or styrene copolymers, solvents, emulsifiers, humectants like carbitol or the glycols, and fragrance. Finishes that clean as well as polish your floor usually contain anionic or nonionic detergents or ammonia, or some other solvent, to melt away the wax or polish already on the floor.

How it works: As the water and solvents evaporate, the waxes and plastic film-formers create a lovely, clear plastic coating on your linoleum or vinyl floor. The coating really is terrifically resistant to heel marks or water-spotting, which means that cleaning up the kitchen is a (relative) joy. I am always particularly enchanted with the way crumbs skitter across the shiny surface right into the dustpan.

Note: Water-based polishes should never be used on wood or cork surfaces. Those surfaces require special, petroleum-solvent-based wood polish (see Wood Polish in the alphabetical products listing).

What it can do to you: Some solvents in some of the polishes are flammable. Check the label to be sure about any particular product. The detergents or ammonia or solvents in some of the polishes may also make them irritating to your skin, and you certainly wouldn't want to splash them in your eyes.

Because they're water-based, however, the polishes are likely to be less toxic than you might expect if someone swallows them. Depending upon the specific ingredients in a specific product, the probable

56

lethal dose for a small child (22 pounds/10 kilograms) may be as low as one seventh of an ounce or as "high" as two ounces or more. Since the manufacturers may switch ingredients around now and then, your best bet is to check with your local poison control center if anyone in your family swallows any floor polish.

What's better, safer, or cheaper: You want to save money on floor polish? Easy. Use about half as much as the manufacturer suggests on the label and polish the floor half as often as they say is necessary. Believe me, it works, As for upkeep, the trick is to make sure that when you damp-mop between polishings, you *damp*-mop. Don't flood the floor with water, which can soften the finish, and don't use detergents, which can strip the finish away with terrifying efficiency. In short, boring as it may sound, if you are nice to your floor polish, it will be nice to you.

Floor Polish (for Wood Floors).

See **Wood Polish.**

Floor-Polish Remover

> **Safety Rating: MAY BE HARMFUL IF SWAL-LOWED. CALL POISON CONTROL CENTER IMMEDIATELY FOR APPROPRIATE ANTI-DOTE PROCEDURE.**

What's in it: These are detergent-based degreasing cleaners meant to dissolve wax or acrylic floor polishes. The cleaning power of the detergents and surfactants in the water solution may be boosted by ammonia, as in ELECTROLUX FLOOR CLEANER (Electrolux) and PARSONS' WAX & ACRYLIC REMOVER (Armour-Dial). Or, the cleaner may contain an alcohol solvent, such as the ethylene glycol ether in BISSELL WAX REMOVER (Bissell) or the butyl cellosolve in BUTCHER'S KITCHEN FLOOR CLEANER & WAX REMOVER (Butcher Polish).

How it works: The detergents, solvents, and surfactants loosen the layers of wax or acrylic polish on your floor so that you can simply mop it up and start all over again. Naturally, these removers, which are up to 65 percent water, should be used only on washable floors.

What it can do to you: All detergent degreasing cleaners are hard on your hands, because the same ingredients that dissolve fatty waxes or acrylic polishes on the floor will irritate and maybe even damage your skin. The removers may burn if you get them in your eyes, and products containing ammonia may give off irritating fumes. Keep the windows open while using them.

If swallowed, floor-polish removers, like all detergents, can cause nausea, vomiting, and diarrhea. The probable lethal dose for a small child (22 pounds/10 kilograms) may be anything from one fifth of an ounce on up; removers containing alcohol solvents like butyl cellosolve are at the more toxic end of the scale. Products containing ammonia don't have enough ammonia in them to cause the kind of tissue burns associated with swallowing straight household ammonia. An additional word of warning: floor-polish removers containing alcohol solvents may be flammable. Don't smoke while cleaning.

What's better, safer, or cheaper: This is another product that comes under the heading of "Why spend money on a special cleaner when an ordinary one will do?" You can use your regular heavy-duty general-purpose household cleaner in place of these removers and get your floor just as clean. To boost the detergent's wax-removing power, add one half to one cupful of household ammonia to a solution of SPIC AND SPAN or SOILAX and water.

Or you can simply cut out your need for a floor-polish remover entirely by holding back on the polish when you clean the floor. Don't wax every time you clean. Wax once every week or two, and put down just enough polish to give you a water-resistant protective layer. Damp-mop in between polishings, and make sure the mop is damp, not sopping wet. Never use an abrasive cleaner on the floor. If you really watch it, you'll find that you're never again faced with a waxy buildup so yellow that you can't see the pattern on the floor through the polish.

Furniture Polish (All-Purpose: Liquid, Aerosol, Pump Spray)

> **Safety Rating: ALL FURNITURE POLISHES MAY BE HARMFUL IF SWALLOWED. PRODUCTS CONTAINING PETROLEUM DISTILLATES MAY BE EXTREMELY HARMFUL. CALL POISON CONTROL CENTER IMMEDIATELY FOR APPROPRIATE ANTIDOTE PROCEDURES.**

What's in it: As you may have suspected, there's not a dime's worth of difference among the leading all-purpose furniture polishes. BEHOLD (Drackett), FAVOR (S. C. Johnson & Son), KLEAN 'N SHINE (S. C. Johnson & Son), OLD ENGLISH (Boyle-Midway), and PLEDGE (S. C. Johnson & Son) all contain water, a petroleum distillate solvent, wax, silicone fluid, emulsifiers, and, if sold as an aerosol, propellant. Fragrances are optional, but lemon is the clear favorite. A "nonwax" polish such as FINIS (Scott's Liquid Gold) has an acrylic resin instead, and the most popular all-purpose liquid, JUBILEE KITCHEN WAX (S. C. Johnson & Son), also has a minute amount of a preservative/"germ-killer," a phenol compound.

How it works: All these spray and liquid polishes work like a dream on a variety of surfaces, including wood, vinyl, ceramic or plastic tiles, marble, and Formica counters. They should never be used on leather or on wood that has been polished with a specialized paste or liquid wood polish, since the solvents in the all-purpose spray can damage leather and dissolve wood polish. The manufacturers of KLEAN 'N SHINE specifically warn you against using the product on bathtubs, but frankly I had never thought of using these polishes there anyway. Had you?

Either spray or liquid will give you the same nice shine, but one advantage of using a spray is that the mist actually anchors any dust that may be floating around on your furniture or counter tops. You pick up the grounded dust and spread a protective layer of wax or acrylic resin at the same time.

Manufacturers of "nonwax" polishes like FINIS insist that the polishes will help you avoid a waxy buildup on the furniture, but the truth is that there's rarely any buildup with any of these polishes.

Each time you put a new layer on, the solvents in the polish more or less dissolve and remove the last layer.

To keep the finish shiny, always use a clean dustcloth, either to apply the polish or simply to dust later on. A dirty or grimy cloth will scratch the silicone finish that seals the polished surface, keeping spills from sinking in. If you scratch that shield, it won't be able to protect your furniture.

What it can do to you: All these polishes are flammable; the aerosols are doubly so, because they also contain flammable propellant gases.

In addition, the petroleum distillate solvents that help to make furniture polishes combustible also make them very dangerous if swallowed. It isn't so much that the solvents are deadly poisons in your stomach. The real problem is that aspiration of the solvents (getting them into your lungs) can cause a fatal form of chemical pneumonia so dangerous that aspiration of as little as a drop or two of solvent may be fatal for a small child.

That is why perfuming these products with fragrances which smell like food is so dangerous. It's also why an aerosol container may be marginally less dangerous to have around than a pump spray. Even a child can obtain a large handful of polish by pressing down on a pump handle, but it's almost impossible to get a mouthful of spray out of an aerosol can.

If a child does manage to swallow one of these polishes, he may appear drowsy, even drunk. Call your poison control center immediately for the appropriate antidote.

In addition to the problems they pose if swallowed, these polishes can irritate your skin and eyes, and you may find the fine mist of an aerosol irritating to breathe. Lots of people are sensitive to all the lemon perfume in the air; somehow, the woodsy fragrances don't seem quite so annoying.

What's better, safer, or cheaper: A liquid like JUBILEE is cheaper, ounce for ounce, than a pump spray, which in turn is cheaper than an aerosol. For wood surfaces, liquid or paste wood polishes (see in the alphabetical products listing) are almost certainly a better buy than the sprays. And they'll give your furniture a really deep, rich glow, more long-lasting than what you get from the sprays. Naturally, there's a catch. Even the easiest-to-use pastes and liquids take more time to apply and buff than the simple spray-on, wipe-off, all-purpose polishes. As for real cheap-cheaps, a plain detergent-and-water solution gets vinyl and enameled surfaces clean; it also works just dandy on various kinds of tile. For homemade wood polishes (which are really more trouble than they're worth and probably more dangerous to mess around with than the prepared stuff), see Wood Polish in the alphabetical products listing.

General-Purpose Household Cleaner (Liquid, Pump Spray)

> **Safety Rating: ALL LIQUID GENERAL-PURPOSE HOUSEHOLD CLEANERS MAY BE HARMFUL IF SWALLOWED. PRODUCTS CONTAINING PETROLEUM DISTILLATES MAY BE EXTREMELY HARMFUL. CALL POISON CONTROL CENTER IMMEDIATELY FOR APPROPRIATE ANTIDOTE PROCEDURE.**

What's in it: The most prominent ingredient in any of these cleaners is water, up to 95 percent. JANITOR IN A DRUM (Texize), MR. CLEAN and TOP JOB (both Procter & Gambe), and all other liquid cleaners contain detergents, chelating agents such as sodium citrate to keep the liquid clear, coloring agents, and fragrances. There is about 1 percent ammonia in AJAX WITH AMMONIA (Colgate-Palmolive). FANTASTIK (Texize) and FORMULA 409 (Clorox) pump sprays get extra cleaning power from ethylene glycol ether solvent. The solvent in LESTOIL HEAVY DUTY CLEANER (Noxell) is a petroleum distillate.

How it works: It isn't the bald giant or even the white tornado that gets your walls and floors clean. It's the detergents and solvents that lift and loosen dirt so that you can wipe it away. A product like LESTOIL *is* more effective, because of its petroleum distillate solvent, but it may be more dangerous to have around the house.

True to their name, the all-purpose cleaners can take the place of a lot of the specialized cleaners in your cabinet. They'll do bathroom surfaces, remove built-up wax or acrylic polish on the kitchen floor (products with ammonia are particularly effective at this job), and clean the windows (be sure to wipe off immediately or you'll get a hard-to-remove film). They will even, believe it or not, clean your paint-brushes. LESTOIL does the fastest job at that particular messy task, but *all* these liquid cleaners will get even oil paints off the brush, if you let them soak overnight before the paint has dried.

One thing you can't do with these cleaners is wash your carpets or upholstery. Despite the fact that they do look like carpet shampoos, the formulations are different. The carpet shampoos will dry so that you can just brush or vacuum them off. All-purpose cleaners have to be rinsed off thoroughly.

What it can do to you: Whether liquid cleaners without petroleum solvents are more or less lethal than powder cleaners like SPIC AND SPAN is an interesting question. By rights, the liquids ought to be less dangerous, since they are already diluted when you buy them. However, it appears to be a fact of life that liquids are more likely to be swallowed more often and in greater quantities than powders. If that happens, the liquids can cause nausea, vomiting, and diarrhea, and the probable lethal dose for a small child (22 pounds/10 kilograms) may be somewhere between two and five ounces.

A liquid that contains petroleum distillate solvents is potentially more dangerous because, if swallowed, the solvents may be aspirated into the lungs, causing pulmonary edema (swelling) or a kind of chemical pneumonia that is often fatal. It may only take a few drops of the solvent in the lungs to provoke this reaction.

It goes without saying that these cleaners can be irritating to the skin and eyes. The more solvents they contain, the more irritating they may be. Products containing ammonia, even in minute amounts, may give off irritating vapors and should never be mixed with any kind of chlorine bleach.

If you have small children around the house, you may wish to consider using either AMWAY ZOOM (Amway Corp.), which has a child-resistant cap, or FANTASTIK, a spray with an "off" position for the nozzle.

What's better, safer, or cheaper: You can dilute these cleaners if you like, but you can also use them full strength, which is the way they work best as floor-polish removers or paintbrush cleaners. This means that ounce for ounce the all-purpose powder cleaners like SOILAX or SPIC AND SPAN are a better buy; they'll go further for your money. For a large cleaning job, sprays are not as good a buy as the liquids; they work best as spot cleaners.

You can cut costs in all cases, though, with exactly the same homemade substitute: one half cup ammonia plus one third cup washing soda in a gallon of medium warm water. But be warned—this alternative is cheaper but not necessarily safer than the commercial cleaner. It is irritating to the skin and eyes, gives off annoying fumes, and may be poisonous if swallowed in sufficient quantity. In addition, the washing soda may burn tissues if the solution is swallowed. See Household Ammonia and Water Softener in the alphabetical products listing.

General-Purpose Household Cleaner (Powder)

> **Safety Rating: HARMFUL IF SWALLOWED. CALL POISON CONTROL CENTER IMMEDIATELY FOR APPROPRIATE ANTIDOTE PROCEDURE.**

What's in it: OAKITE (Clorox), SOILAX (Economics Laboratory), and SPIC AND SPAN (Procter & Gamble) all contain strongly alkaline detergents and surfactants like sodium carbonate and sodium sesquicarbonate, plus an anticaking agent, usually sodium sulfate.

How it works: You won't get any suds when you mix the standard heaping tablespoonful of cleaner with a gallon of warm water. That's because sudsing agents are cosmetics that manufacturers stick into mild detergents, like dishwashing liquids, to convince you that you're getting your money's worth. Since household cleaners are so strong, there's no need for this kind of psychological funny business.

The cleaners work best when you've got a really big job to do, since it's hardly worth whipping up a bucketful of cleaner-plus-water for a few spots here and there. (That's the time when it makes sense to use a liquid general-purpose cleaner, full-strength, right out of the bottle.) In any case, the detergents and surfactants cut through greasy marks on painted surfaces as well as on plain woodwork. These cleaners are very useful if you're planning to paint the house yourself. Wash down the walls or furniture slated for refurbishing. That way you'll get a nice clean, nongreasy surface to which all kinds of paint will cling as smoothly as panty hose on a perfect pair of legs. When you finish painting, put the brushes straightaway into a double-strength detergent solution. It will take the paint off as efficiently as those flammable, seriously poisonous paint removers or solvents. The double-strength solution is also a super-efficient floor-polish remover, which means that you don't need another, special product for that job either.

You can also use these powders, full-strength, as scouring powders for spot cleaning on tubs and tile surfaces.

What it can do to you: These are very strongly alkaline powders. They can irritate your skin and eyes, both in the pristine powder state and when they are mixed with water. If swallowed, like all detergents, they can make you sick to your stomach, causing nausea, vomiting, and diarrhea. More important, they may cause burns of the lining of the mouth, throat, and stomach. The probable lethal dose for a small child (22 pounds/10 kilograms) depends wholly upon the concentration of the powder. If taken straight, as little as one fifth of an ounce of the powder can be lethal. Naturally, the more diluted the solution is, the less dangerous it will be.

What's better, safer, or cheaper: The powder cleaners really are the cheaper all-purpose products. If they are not cheap enough for you, use the same substitute suggested for the liquid all-purpose cleaners: one half cup ammonia plus one third cup washing soda in a gallon of warm water. Remember, this is cheaper, not necessarily safer. It is an irritating and potentially caustic solution, and the separate ingredients present problems of their own (see Household Ammonia and Water Softener in the alphabetical products listing).

Glass Cleaner

> **Safety Rating: MAY BE HARMFUL IF SWALLOWED. CALL POISON CONTROL CENTER IMMEDIATELY FOR APPROPRIATE ANTIDOTE PROCEDURE.**

What's in it: Liquid glass cleaners such as A & P (A & P), EASY-OFF (Boyle-Midway), or WINDEX (Drackett) may be as much as 80 to 90 percent water, plus alcohols (up to 10 percent), surfactants (up to 1 percent), a trace of coloring and/or fragrance, and, if ammonia is touted on the label, a trace of that, too. Aerosols like AMWAY SEE SPRAY (Amway Corp.), A & P, EASY-OFF, WINDEX, and WIND-O-SHINE (Dolger) simply add a propellant.

How it works: The surfactants in the glass cleaner make it easier to apply; they also loosen dirt and grime. The alcohols do an instant defrosting job on glass that may be cold in the winter. They also keep the liquid you're working with from freezing on the glass. Coloring agents make the product look good; perfumes make it smell good. Ammonia adds cleaning power, but there's hardly enough in the bottle to make a real difference. Actually, it's the water that does the yeoman's job.

Glass cleaners are usually used on windows, but they work well on mirrors, aluminum and chrome fixtures, and enamel-surface appliances, too. They should always be put on and wiped off with clean cloths. When one rag gets dirty, don't just wring it out. Use a new cloth or you'll just keep spreading the same old grime around.

What it can do to you: If you swallow them, liquid glass cleaners can cause upset stomach, nausea, and vomiting. If you swallow enough, the alcohols in the mix can cause headache, dizziness, and stupor—symptoms normally associated with alcohol intoxication. "Enough," however, may be quite a lot. The probable lethal dose for a small child (22 pounds/10 kilograms) is estimated at a pint or more.

Aerosol products bring all their customary problems, including the potential for explosions if the cans are punctured or incinerated, and the possibility that you'll spray the stuff in your eye if you don't notice which way the nozzle is facing.

If you get a glass cleaner in your eye, you'll feel a temporary burning sensation. Wash the liquid out with copious amounts of cool or lukewarm water for at least fifteen minutes, and check with an ophthalmologist to be certain there are no "hidden" injuries.

The dyes and perfumes in the cleaners can be irritating for people with allergic sensitivities, and aerosol packaging intensifies the problem by dispensing a fine mist into the air you breathe.

What's better, safer, or cheaper: Liquids in plain or pump-spray bottles are always cheaper and safer than aerosols. Do-it-yourself mixes won't do a better job than the commercial products, but they will be a lot cheaper. The rock-bottom, penny-pincher's delight is plain, lukewarm water. Or, you can add a half cup of white vinegar to a quart of cool water. Or, you can use alcohol (a quarter cup to a quart of water). This works best in very cold weather, when the alcohol will keep your windows defrosted for a while. If you prefer ammonia, mix one tablespoonful with a quart of water and polish the glass or mirror with the kind of tissue paper you use to wrap gifts in (white only, please, lest the colors run all over the window and frame).

Clean newspaper, long touted as a super glass cleaner, never gets my vote because (1) the ink makes me sneeze and (2) it always gets all over my hands, which means that I end up leaving fingerprints on the window frame, and then I have to clean that off, and . . . well, the whole thing is endless.

Glass Wax

> **Safety Rating: MAY BE HARMFUL IF SWAL-LOWED. PRODUCTS CONTAINING PETRO-LEUM DISTILLATES MAY BE EXTREMELY HARMFUL. CALL POISON CONTROL CEN-TER IMMEDIATELY FOR APPROPRIATE ANTIDOTE PROCEDURE.**

What's in it: The active ingredient in a product such as GLASS WAX (Gold Seal) or WINDOW-LITE (Patterson Labs.) is a fine abrasive that is usually combined with some ammonia, wax, soap, and water. Some products also contain a petroleum distillate solvent.

How it works: On windows with an ordinary dirt film, an ammonia-and-water cleanser like WINDEX is usually sufficiently strong. But if the dirt is really caked on, you will probably need the abrasive particles in a glass wax to get through the grime. Glass waxes go on as a cream or lotion and dry to a fine powder, which may give you some extra cleanup work if the powder falls onto the windowsill. Be sure not to apply the wax itself to a painted window frame, because the ammonia in the wax may soften some paint finishes, particularly latex paint.

What it can do to you: Ammonia gives glass wax a sharp, penetrating aroma. Its fumes may be irritating to your eyes and throat, and if you spill it on your skin or splash it in your eyes, it is irritating. Depending on how much petroleum distillate solvent there is in the mix, the wax will be slightly or moderately toxic if swallowed. The probable lethal dose for a small child (22 pounds/10 kilograms) may be one third of an ounce or more.

What's better, safer, or cheaper: Plain ammonia and water (see Glass Cleaner in the alphabetical products listing) is always cheaper and usually as effective as a commercial glass cleaner. To keep mirrors from fogging—something glass waxes are particularly good at—make a solution of soap chips in water and rub a thin film over the mirror's surface (you can even use your fingers). Let the film dry, then polish off with a clean, soft cloth. There should be just enough of an almost invisible skim remaining to keep moisture from clinging to the mirror and beading up into "fog."

Glue

> *See* **Contact Cement; Epoxy Resin Glue; Instant Glue; Model Cement; Mucilage; White Glue.**

Household Ammonia

> **Safety Rating: HARMFUL IF SWALLOWED. CALL POISON CONTROL CENTER IMMEDIATELY FOR APPROPRIATE ANTIDOTE PROCEDURE.**

What's in it: Plain household ammonia like PARSONS' (Armour-Dial) or any one of the private-label brands available at supermarkets is a solution of ammonia gas dissolved in water (3–10 percent ammonia), plus a surfactant such as ethoxylated ethyl alcohol. The liquid may also contain a coloring agent, a fragrance, and a clarifier to keep it from clouding.

"Sudsy" ammonias include all the ingredients listed above, plus a detergent like linear alkyl benzene sulfonate to make it look soapy. Lemon or pine ammonias include the appropriate fragrance and color.

How it works: Ammonia solutions are grease-cutters which, like surfactants, easily dissolve and loosen the normal film and dirt found on enamel, glass, tile, or Formica surfaces in the kitchen and bathroom. They should never be used on painted, varnished, or lacquered surfaces, though, since they can soften and mar the finish.

What it can do to you: Ammonia solutions are potentially caustic. The higher the concentration of ammonia, the more caustic the solution. Household ammonia can irritate your skin and eyes, and, if swallowed, it can burn the lining of the mouth, throat, and stomach. Its fumes are irritating to the lining of nose and throat and lungs and can make your eyes tear. In high concentrations, ammonia fumes can be a choking poison.

When mixed with products containing chlorine bleach, ammonia combines with the chlorine to form irritating and potentially poisonous gases called chloramines (compounds containing nitrogen and chlorine). Never mix household ammonia with any of the following products or with any other product containing a chlorine bleach:

> • Liquid chlorine bleaches such as A & P (A & P), CLOROX (Clorox), PUREX (Purex), TEXIZE (Texize).
> • Powder chlorine bleaches such as ACTION (Colgate-Palmolive), AMWAY DRY CHLORINE BLEACH (Amway Corp.), PUREX (Purex).
> • Scouring powders with chlorine bleach such as ACME (Acme Products), AJAX (Colgate-Palmolive), A & P (A & P), COMET (Procter & Gamble), OLD DUTCH CLEANSER (Purex), ROKEACH FOAMING CLEANSER (I. Rokeach & Sons), WHITE ROSE CLEANSER (White Rose).

Products marked "with ammonia" generally don't contain much ammonia. Often it's only a trace. They will not produce great quantities of chloramines if mixed with a cleaner containing a chlorine bleach, but it isn't worth trying it to find out what happens. Besides, adding or combining products is often a waste of time and money, since most cleaning products are complete in themselves. The only major exception is adding a chlorine bleach to a simple laundry detergent.

What's better, safer, or cheaper: Few liquid household cleaners are more effective than a plain ammonia solution, although many are a lot more expensive. When used with caution, ammonia is probably no more dangerous than any other major cleaner. Be certain, however, that it is kept out of the reach of children, just like drain cleaner, toilet cleaner, oven cleaner, and all the other poisons in the house.

As for cheaper, years ago people looking for a cheap substitute for prepared household ammonia often picked up a bottle of a stronger ammonia solution (10–29 percent ammonia) at the drugstore and then diluted it with water (one part ammonia solution to three parts plain water). The result was similar to the ammonia available at the modern supermarket. Today, it's cheaper and much simpler to buy the ordinary household ammonia, since few drugstores still stock the stronger preparation.

Actually, household ammonia is itself a low-cost substitute for a number of other household products. It is a mild bleach and can be used to remove certain stains. For example, it can be applied full-strength to spots on all fabrics except silk or wool, or silk and wool blends. Leave the ammonia on until the spot begins to fade. Then rinse with water. If the color starts to bleed or change, apply some vinegar to the spot. Then rinse with water. That will "fix" the color. Ammonia is particularly good on urine stains or stains left by perspiration. One old-time home remedy for perspiration stains was to hold the stained fabric over an open ammonia bottle, presumably to let the fumes go to work on the stain. I can't swear by that one, but if you're going to try it, try it before you dry-clean and "fix" the stains.

Ammonia solution plus water is an excellent substitute for glass cleaner (see the alphabetical products listing). Household ammonia mixed with hydrogen peroxide is a stronger bleach than household ammonia alone. See Bleach (Liquid) in the alphabetical products listing.

Household Oil

Safety Rating: MAY BE HARMFUL IF SWALLOWED. CALL POISON CONTROL CENTER IMMEDIATELY FOR APPROPRIATE ANTIDOTE PROCEDURE.

What's in it: A general, all-purpose lubricant like 3-IN-1 HOUSEHOLD OIL (Boyle-Midway) usually contains mineral oil. It may also contain corrosion inhibitors (detergents, ammonia derivatives/amines, or fatty

oils), silicones to add "slipperiness," and fragrances. Aerosols such as
3-IN-1 HOUSEHOLD SPRAY contain a propellant.

How it works: The oils lubricate, while the corrosion inhibitors prevent (or at least slow down) the oxidation of the metal and the accumulation of dirt and grime on moving parts.

What it can do to you: Anything with a detergent in it can cause nausea, vomiting, and diarrhea if you swallow it. Mineral oils are usually nontoxic, although they, too, can cause diarrhea, which is why some forms of mineral oils are used as laxatives. The probable lethal dose for a general household oil may be as little as one seventh of an ounce or may range as high as two to five ounces for a small child (22 pounds/ 10 kilograms), depending on what's in it.

What's better, safer, or cheaper: Plain mineral oil may work as an emergency treatment for a squeaking door or machine part, but it won't give your motors or machines the protection offered by corrosion-inhibitor-enriched commercial oils. Vegetable oils like corn oil, peanut oil, soybean oil, or safflower oil are definite no-no's. They will rot or turn rancid and smell absolutely awful after a while.

Houseplant Cleaner

Safety Rating: RARELY HARMFUL, EVEN IF SWALLOWED. CALL POISON CONTROL CENTER IMMEDIATELY FOR APPROPRIATE ANTIDOTE PROCEDURE.

What's in it: Houseplant "polishes" like the venerable PLANT SHINE (Schultz Co.) or STIM-U-PLANT LEAF POLISH (Stim-u-plant) are simply combinations of water, waxes, and resins, with an emulsifier added to keep everything from separating.

How it works: When the water evaporates, the waxes and resins remain as a shiny coating on the plant.

What it can do to you: Plant cleaners are practically nontoxic. If you put some in your mouth, it will simply coalesce into what feels like a piece of soft rubber or plastic.

What's better, safer, or cheaper: In this case, what's cheaper for you is also probably better and safer for your plants. A little water and maybe some mild soap, like IVORY, is all you need to keep your houseplants clean. (Be sure to wash off the soap.) The oils and waxes and resins in the commercial cleaners may look good, but they can block the plant's respiration. And they give your plants a kind of standardized gleam that you're not likely to find in real living, growing things. If a plastic glow's what you want, why not go whole hog and buy real plastic plants?

Houseplant Fertilizer

Safety Rating: MAY BE HARMFUL IF SWAL-LOWED. CALL POISON CONTROL CENTER IMMEDIATELY FOR APPROPRIATE ANTI-DOTE PROCEDURE.

What's in it: All the popular houseplant foods or fertilizers start with three basic plant nutrients: nitrogen, phosphorus, and potash (potassium). The relative amounts of these ingredients are shown in the three numbers that appear on the label of all packages of plant food, for example, 3-6-19 or 5-10-5 or 20-20-20. These numbers always refer to nitrogen, phosphorus, and potash, and they're always listed in that particular order so it's easy to see which there's more (or less) of. There may also be traces of other plant nutrients like calcium, copper, iron, manganese, sulfur, and zinc.

How it works: Each of the three basic nutrients performs a specific job in the plant. Nitrogen makes the leaves green and shiny, phosphorus makes roots and stems strong, potash helps buds set and grow. So, although a truly refined manipulation of plant fertilizer can take the dedication and expertise of a real green-thumb type, you can make a few generalizations about what kind of food will work on your plants. Leaves yellowing? Try a formula high in nitrogen. Stems kind of twiggy? Try a bit more phosphorus. Buds about ready to bud? Potash. Not too often, of course, since unneeded or unused food can collect as a whitish crust on the soil or on the rim and sides of the pot. In the worst circumstances, a heavy hand with the fertilizer can actually make the soil unlivable for your plants. For the best feeding, follow the directions on the package.

What it can do to you: If swallowed, houseplant foods may cause nausea, vomiting, or diarrhea, but they are not often lethal. The single serious problem (which is most likely to occur in very young children) is the possibility that the nitrogen sources in the food may be converted by intestinal bacteria into nitrites. If this happens, they may cause a condition known as methemoglobinemia, or the replacement of the hemoglobin in your red blood cells with methemoglobin. Hemoglobin carries oxygen to all the cells of the body. Without it, you would end up oxygen-starved. Your skin would become flushed and your lips turn bluish (cyanosis); you would be headachy or dizzy and may vomit or suffer convulsions and go into a coma. If the oxygen deprivation is severe enough, you may die. Nitrates will do this only if swallowed; they can't be absorbed through your skin, so spilling plant food on your hands isn't dangerous.

Actually, it isn't only the plant food that can be poisonous. Many houseplants are also potentially lethal. Here is a partial list of the plants, shrubs, and trees around your house which can be harmful if eaten:

- azalea (entire plant)
- caladium (entire plant)
- castor bean (entire plant)
- cherry (twigs/leaves)
- daffodil (bulbs)
- dieffenbachia (leaves/stalks)
- hyacinth (bulbs)
- iris (stems)
- lantana (seeds/pods/flowers)
- laurel (leaves)
- lily of the valley (leaves/flowers)
- mistletoe (berries)
- narcissus (bulbs)
- oak (leaves/acorns)
- poinsettia (leaves)
- potato plant (leaves/stem)
- rhododendron (leaves)
- wisteria (seeds/pods)
- yew (berries/leaves)

Remember, these plants are also toxic for household pets.

What's better, safer, or cheaper: Plants get their nourishment out of the food only when the food has dissolved in water. In theory, therefore, it seems logical to assume that powders like HYPONEX (Hyponex Co.), which dissolve quickly as you water the plant, will work better than tablets like PLANTABBS (Plantabbs). In all fairness, though, I have to say that I've used both—and found that my plants react the same way to whatever I feed them.

One thing you can't feed a houseplant is fertilizer meant for lawns or trees or things that grow outside the house. The outdoor fertilizers are just too complicated; they take too long to convert to a form that can be taken up by your pet philodendron. Stick to the food meant for plants that live indoors.

Houseplant Insecticide.

See **Insecticide (Houseplant).**

Insecticide (Household)

> **Safety Rating: MANY BUT NOT ALL HOUSEHOLD INSECTICIDES ARE HARMFUL IF SWALLOWED, INHALED, OR ABSORBED THROUGH THE SKIN. PRODUCTS CONTAINING PETROLEUM DISTILLATES MAY BE EXTREMELY HARMFUL. CALL POISON CONTROL CENTER IMMEDIATELY FOR APPROPRIATE ANTIDOTE PROCEDURE.**

What's in it: All household insecticides—whether foggers, aerosols, spray liquids, powders, cakes, or strips—contain a specific insect poison (see page 75, "What It Can Do to You," for a detailed list of these poisons) plus a vehicle—liquid, solid, or powder—in which the insecticide is dispensed. Often the insecticide will also contain a synergist, such as MGK 264 or piperonyl butoxide, which boosts the action of the lethal ingredient. Aerosols also contain a propellant.

73

How it works: Foggers, such as D-CON FOUR GONE (d-Con), sit in the middle of the room and fill the space with poisonous fumes. Once you've turned the fogger on, you have to get out of its way, which means staying out of the house for about two or three hours and then opening all the windows to ventilate the space for a half hour or more before you move back in. Foggers work on all kinds of insects—crawlers as well as flying bugs.

Aerosol mists like ORTHO HOUSEHOLD INSECT SPRAY (Chevron Chemical) and HOT SHOT FLY AND MOSQUITO INSECT KILLER (Conwood Corp.) or liquid spray mists (liquid meant to be used in spray guns) like BLACK FLAG INSECT SPRAY (Boyle-Midway) are also used to hit the bugs on the wing, as it were. The main difference between the spray-gun liquids and the aerosols is that the aerosols contain a propellant.

Surface-directed aerosol sprays, like JOHNSTON'S NO-ROACH (Johnston, Gaston), spritz out large drops rather than a fine mist. The drops leave a coating of insecticide on floors or behind cabinets, and the coating stays deadly for as long as a couple of weeks. Aerosol powders, like D-CON WARPATH (d-Con), work on the same principle; they're just powder, instead of a liquid.

Liquid pump sprays like REAL KILL LIQUID ANT AND ROACH KILLER (Cook Chemical) and squirt bottles like D-CON ANT PRUFE (d-Con) are used in much the same way. Both are similar to the aerosol surface sprays, but without the propellant, and both require you to press a button or squeeze a bottle to apply the insecticide. The squeeze bottles may give you a stronger, more-directed stream of bug killer and may be easier to use when you're pointing them into cracks in the walls or spaces between cabinets.

Powders like ANTROL ANT KILLERS (Boyle-Midway) also come without propellant, but they may be more dangerous than the liquids because they blow around easily and can be inhaled or swallowed from the air.

There are two basic kinds of roach traps. The first are *bait traps*. These are boxes that you open and set behind a cabinet, under the sink, or in the back of a closet. The roaches are supposed to be attracted by the bait in the trap. When they wander in, they consume the bait, which is poison, and should expire on the spot. When the trap is full, you simply throw it out. So long as it isn't tipped over or broken open, it is relatively safe. Non-bait traps, like the ROACH MOTEL (Black Flag), are completely safe for humans. There is no poison in the trap, only a very sticky floor that catches and holds the roaches, who eventually

74

die in the trap. Obviously, the sticky surface is covered as the trap fills, and the last roaches to crawl in will be free to crawl out again, so you have to check these things from time to time to see that there's still room inside for more bugs. That's one reason why, although the trap is safe, you may prefer to have your roaches wander through a surface poison and then return decently to their cracks in the walls to die.

Insecticide tapes, such as RAID ROACH TAPE (Johnson Wax), are impregnated with insecticide, which the roach or ant picks up on his feet as he wanders across or around the strip.

Fumigant cakes like ENOZ (Enoz) release *p*-dichlorobenzene fumes, which knock down a number of bugs, including moths (see Mothproofer in the alphabetical products listing).

What it can do to you: You have to figure that anything that can wipe out a roach can have some effect on you, too. How much of an effect depends on exactly what's in the mixture. The following is a list of the most common insecticides in household bug killers, along with their probable lethal effects:

• *Aliphatic thiocyanates* are chemicals that release cynanide when swallowed or inhaled. The most toxic of the aliphatic thiocyanates used in insecticides is *Lethane 384* (also known as *beta-butoxy-beta-thiocyanodiethyl ether* or *2-butoxy-2-thiocyanodiethyl ether*); the probable lethal dose for a small child (22 pounds/ 10 kilograms) may be as little as one seventh of a teaspoonful. Other aliphatic thiocyanates in insecticides are *Lethane 60* and *Thanite* (also known as *isobornyl thiocyanoacetate*). If swallowed, all these ingredients can cause headache, drowsiness, cyanosis, convulsions, and coma.

• *Arsenates* are compounds containing arsenic. They can cause vomiting, diarrhea, and kidney and liver failure if swallowed. The arsenates found in household insecticides are usually *lead arsenate* or *arsenic trioxide*. Arsenic trioxide is marginally more toxic than lead arsenate, but the difference is not terribly important, since as little as a taste or two of either can be fatal for an adult.

• d-trans-*Allethrin* is a synthetic form of cinerin I, the active ingredient in pyrethrins (see below), and its toxicity is similar.

• *Boric acid* (also known as sodium borate) is one of those things that sound as if they should be safe but aren't. It is actually a poison that can cause nausea, vomiting, diarrhea, gastric bleeding, and convulsions if swallowed. It is also poisonous if absorbed through irritated or broken skin, and there have been instances of fatal boric acid poisoning in infants who were dusted with the powder for diaper rash.

• *O,O-Diethyl O-(2-isopropyl-4-methyl-6-pyrimidyl) phosphorothionate* (more conveniently known as *Diazinon*) can cause nausea, vomiting, cramps, blurred vision, convulsion, and coma if swallowed. It can also be absorbed through contact with the skin. The probable lethal oral dose for a small child may be as low as one seventh of a teaspoonful.

• *O,O-Dimethyl O-2,2-dichlorovinyl phosphate* (also known as *DDVP, Dichlorvos,* or *Vapona*) is rarely toxic in healthy human beings because it is rapidly inactivated by enzymes found in mammalian livers. *Note:* It may be dangerous to people ill with liver diseases.

• *2-Hydroxyethyl-*N-*octyl sulfide* (also known as *MGK 874*) is less toxic than most roach killers. In fact, rats have tolerated diets that were 2 percent MGK 874 for as long as ninety days with no ill effects. Nevertheless, the probable lethal dose for a small child (22 pounds/10 kilograms) may be slightly less than an ounce.

• *2-Isopropoxyphenyl* N-*methylcarbamate* (also known as *Propoxur, Baygon,* or *Unden*) is a roach killer that, if swallowed, may cause nausea, cramps, sweating, blurred vision, loss of muscle control, and coma. The probable lethal dose for a small child (22 pounds/10 kilograms) may be as small as a taste.

• *Pyrethrins* come from dried and ground-up flowers of a chrysanthemum, *Chrysanthemum cinerariaefolium.* They are used in mists and foggers meant to knock down both flying and crawling insects. One main problem pyrethrins present to human beings is the possibility of severe allergic reaction, including allergic shock in persons sensitive to pollen. Insecticides containing pyrethrins may be lethal if swallowed because they always contain petroleum distillate solvents as vehicles.

• *Resmethrin* is a synthetic derivative of natural pyrethrins. It is generally less allergenic than the natural stuff.

• *Silica gel* is virtually nontoxic to human beings. It's a different story for roaches, though. Bugs who wander across it find that particles stick to their bodies, causing them to dry out and kind of crackle to death. Silica gel doesn't work in humid weather.

• *Sodium fluoride,* the same chemical used to fluoridate water, is toxic in insecticides because so much of it is used. The normal proportion of fluorides in the water supply, for example, is only about one part per million; in insecticides, it may exceed 180,000 parts per million. If swallowed in concentrations this high, sodium fluoride can burn the mucous membranes and may cause depression of the central nervous system, shock, and kidney failure. It can also burn skin on contact.

• *Tetraethyl dithiopyrophosphate* (also known as *Sulfotepp*) is one of the—if not *the*—most toxic of the common insecticides. As little as a taste can be lethal for an adult. If swallowed, it may cause vision problems, vomiting, cramps, headache, mental confusion, coma, and death. Sulfotepp, which is usually sold in combination with Diazinon, can also be absorbed through the skin.

• *1,1,1-Trichloro-2,2-bis (p-methoxyphenyl)*, which is also known as *Methoxychlor* or *Methoxy-DDT,* is similar to DDT but only about one tenth as toxic if swallowed by humans. It can cause vomiting, convulsions, and respiratory failure, and about one seventh of an ounce may be lethal for a small child (22 pounds/10 kilograms).

What's better, safer, or cheaper: Trying to decide which of the commercial insecticides will be the least lethal to the humans and pets in your home is a complicated matter of juggling not only the active insecticidal ingredients but also the solvents and the forms in which the products are sold.

For example, unless you are allergic to them the pyrethrins, including *d-trans*-allethrin and resmethrin, are clearly less toxic than most other bug killers. DDVP, Dichlorvos or Vapona are rarely harmful to people whose livers are healthy enough to inactivate them. But both groups of insecticides are sold as solutions containing a petroleum distillate, which is both poisonous and flammable. Both are also available as aerosols containing a flammable propellant. And just to show how contrary these things can be, avoiding aerosols by purchasing powders and liquids may be more dangerous if you've got small children, since powders and liquids are much easier to swallow than the contents of a sealed aerosol can.

Just about the only nontoxic commercial insecticide is silica gel. Boric acid, found in a couple of commercial roach killers, is often touted as a safe, cheap, and effective way to get rid of bugs without resorting to dangerous poisons. It is cheap and it's certainly effective, as you can see from the list above, but it's anything but safe for kids and pets. To be fair, though, if all your pets are in fish tanks and everyone in your house is an adult, you really can save money and decimate the roach population by sprinkling simple boric acid straight from the container you buy at the drugstore, behind the refrigerator, along the baseboards, and so on. It will stick to your roaches' feet as they wander through it, and it will kill them when they lick it off, back in the nest.

Other than that, the only really effective way to get rid of roaches and such without commercial insecticides is to do all the simple, boring things like keeping your foodstuffs in sealed containers, cleaning up all drips and spots immediately, plugging up holes in the walls or baseboards, and fixing all leaks around sinks and toilets. One more thing: Never live in an apartment above one in which there are lots of ill-tended cats. I did that once, and the roaches who made the trek up from the apartment to mine laughed like crazy at me and the patient exterminator who showed up once every two weeks until the lease was up.

Insecticide (Houseplant)

> **Safety Rating: MOST BUT NOT ALL HOUSEPLANT INSECTICIDES ARE HARMFUL IF SWALLOWED. PRODUCTS CONTAINING PETROLEUM DISTILLATES MAY BE EXTREMELY HARMFUL. CALL POISON CONTROL CENTER IMMEDIATELY FOR APPROPRIATE ANTIDOTE PROCEDURE.**

What's in it: Both liquid and spray houseplant insecticides contain one or more insecticides such as cube extracts, Diazinon, malathion, pyrethrins, or rotenone in a petroleum distillate solvent. The insecticides may also contain a synergist, such as piperonyl butoxide, to boost the effectiveness of the bug killer, and the sprays contain propellants.

How it works: Liquids may be diluted and painted on the plant, or the whole plant can be turned upside down and dipped in a container filled with a solution of the insecticide and water, diluted according to label directions. The sprays, naturally, are sprayed on and are much easier to work with indoors.

What it can do to you: Most of the insecticides used in these products are a lot less toxic than the ones used in household insecticides. Here are the most common insecticides in houseplant bug killers, with their probable lethal effects:

- *Cube extracts* or derivatives are extracted from dried Derris roots from Malaya. They are similar in effect to rotenone (see below) but less toxic. The probable lethal dose for a small child (22 pounds/10 kilograms) may be one ounce or more.
- *Diazinon,* also known as O,O-*Diethyl O-(2-isopropyl-4-methyl-6-pyrimidyl) phosphorothionate,* is probably the most toxic of the ingredients in houseplant insecticides. It can be absorbed through the skin to cause the same symptoms it causes if swallowed: nausea, vomiting, cramps, blurred vision, mental confusion, coma. The probable lethal oral dose for a small child (22 pounds/10 kilograms) may be as little as one fifth of a teaspoonful.
- *Malathion,* known chemically as S-*(1,2-dicarbethoxyethyl)*-O,O *dimethyl dithiophosphate,* is an organophosphate poison similar to parathion (which was the first organophosphate poison) but much less toxic. It is a weak contact-sensitizer, which may cause a mild skin rash in large numbers of people. If swallowed, it may cause nausea, headache, dizziness, blurred vision, loss of muscle coordination, and respiratory failure. The probable lethal dose for a small child (22 pounds/10 kilograms) may be less than one ounce.
- *Pyrethrins,* which are also used in general household insecticides, are derived from dried and ground-up flowers of a chrysanthemum, *Chrysanthemum cinerariaefolium.* They are practically nontoxic to humans, except that they may cause serious, life-threatening allergic reactions in persons sensitive to pollens.
- *Rotenone* is a poison drawn from dried and powdered *Derris* root (found in Malaya) or *Lonchocarpus* (cube) root (found in Central or South America). It is potent against fish and birds and was used for centuries as the poison on Indian arrowheads. The Indians used fresh roots, not dried ones, and their poison was more toxic than the rotenone found in modern insecticides. Rotenone is relatively safe in ordinary use. It decomposes quickly

in light and air and, if swallowed, causes immediate vomiting so that it is quickly disgorged. Finally, although the probable lethal dose for a small child (22 pounds / 10 kilograms) may be less than one teaspoonful, there is rarely anything even approaching this amount in a commercial preparation.

The toxicity of any given insecticidal ingredient may be increased by the other ingredients in the bottle or spray. Piperonyl butoxide, for example, will increase the effectiveness (and thus the toxicity) of rotenone. The petroleum distillate solvents used in all these products are poisonous and, if aspirated into the lungs, can cause a form of chemical pneumonia. Needless to say, most of the aerosol propellants are flammable.

What's better, safer, or cheaper: Although individual insecticidal ingredients may vary in toxicity, most insecticidal products are combinations of ingredients and usually end up being equally toxic all around.

To avoid toxicity altogether, simply avoid commercial insecticides. You can keep your plants bug-free without them.

First, be certain that any new plant you bring in is clean. Wash it off under running water, then set it in its own corner for a week or two to see if anything turns up. If it turns out to have lots of bugs, return it immediately to the store where you bought it. If there are only a few bugs, wash it off every other day, and see if that does the trick. When it's been insect-free for a week or ten days, you can add it to the rest of your garden.

To keep them bug-free, mist or wash your plants at least once a week with plain, warm water. When crawling things appear, take the offending plant and turn it upside down into a bath of warm water and mild soap, such as IVORY SOAP or IVORY FLAKES. (Before you turn the plant upside down, put a collar of paper around the stem and over the soil so that the whole thing doesn't tumble out into the sink or bucket.)

Finally, if a plant is seriously infested, don't be sentimental. It costs less money, time, and energy just to give it a decent burial, down the incinerator or into the garbage can, where it can't contaminate anything else. There's no sense in trying to save one plant only to end up with creepy-crawlies running rampant through the rest.

Instant Glue

What's in it: Instant bonding agents such as DURO-3 SUPER GLUE (Duro Woodhill Chemical Corp.), EASTMAN 910 (Eastman Chemical), and KRAZY GLUE (Krazy Glue) are made of cyanoacrylate monomer, a liquid plastic.

How it works: Cyanoacrylate cements bond through polymerization. The liquid monomer molecules in the glue combine with the molecules in the surface to which you apply the glue, forming long chains of molecules called polymers. In short, the glue and the surface become one, which is why the bond is so strong and durable. The original instant glues worked only on solid surfaces such as glass, china, and steel. The newer cyanoacrylate cements, such as KRAZY GLUE FOR WOOD AND LEATHER (Krazy Glue), also work on porous surfaces such as fabrics and paper. At this time there is no instant glue that works on Teflon or polyethylene.

What it can do to you: Cyanoacrylate glues aren't flammable or toxic. Moisture on a surface inactivates them, and if you get some in your mouth, the saliva will turn the adhesive into little balls of plastic.

What about skin? If the instant glues bond everything else, can they make your fingers, say, stick together forever? Or if you touch a piece of china with a glue-smeared finger, are you going to spend the rest of your life with that dish at the end of your hand?

Hardly likely.

Instant glues certainly will bond skin surfaces instantly, but the bond isn't permanent. You can loosen it by rolling the stuck surfaces against each other so that the glue pills up into little balls, or, if you've got two fingers stuck together, you can stick them into a shot glass full of acetone (nail-polish remover), which will soften the glue.

The big problem comes when you stick a gluey finger to an eyelid or, worse, bond your eyelids together. That requires a doctor's touch to separate the skin surfaces, not because the bond is permanent but because it's in such a delicate area. (A little bit of glue in the eye will simply turn into a tiny blob, floating around in there. It, too, should be removed by a doctor, if it doesn't simply wash out in normal tearing.)

All things considered, tales of having to remove cyanoacrylate skin bonds surgically are foolish. Even if you did nothing at all to remove the glue, it would eventually fall off as your skin grew new layers of cells, pushing the older, top layer—and the glue—right off your body.

What's better, safer, or cheaper: Nothing. Cyanoacrylate adhesives are simply *sui generis*—there is nothing quite like them.

Jewelry Cleaner

> **Safety Rating: MAY BE HARMFUL IF SWALLOWED. CALL POISON CONTROL CENTER IMMEDIATELY FOR APPROPRIATE ANTIDOTE PROCEDURE.**

What's in it: The cleaning power in products like HAGERTY JEWEL CLEANER (Hagerty & Sons) comes from detergents (for example, sodium alkyl sulfate) and ammonia compounds. The cleaners also contain water, alcohol, and sometimes dyes and fragrance.

How it works: Ammonia compounds and detergents soften and dissolve dirt and grime. They are most effective if you apply the polish with a toothbrush to get it into all the small corners and crevices on your bracelet, ring, pin, or necklace. Once you've cleaned the jewelry, be sure to rinse it well in clear water. Otherwise, there'll be a dulling film left on the surface. Buff with a piece of plain, very soft tissue paper (the kind that comes in gift packages) for the best shine. Jewelry cleaners are meant for gold, silver, platinum, copper, and all kinds of stones. They should not be used on pearls, wood, or plastic beads.

What it can do to you: If swallowed, jewelry cleaners are moderately toxic; they can cause all kinds of stomach upset. The probable lethal dose for a small child (22 pounds/10 kilograms) may be approximately two ounces or more. The cleaners may also irritate your skin and eyes, and vapors can be irritating to eyes and throat.

What's better, safer, or cheaper: All your jewelry (except wooden beads or beads strung on leather) will benefit from an occasional soap-and-water bath. For precious stones, add a tablespoonful of ammonia to a quart of soapy water and swish. You can boil diamonds in this mixture and then rinse them in alcohol to get the incredible sparkle that sets them apart from all other jewels.

Silver jewelry shines up nicely with any good silver polish, but you should never use abrasive polish—not even a mild one like silver polish—on gold or gold-plated pieces. The metal is very soft and can be easily scarred or worn away. Pearls should be rubbed often with a soft chamois cloth, which removes dust and gives them a glowing luster. Dust your wooden bangles and beads. Never clean plastic with anything but warm, soapy water. Dust costume jewelry; never wash it in soap and water, lest you dissolve the glue or cement holding the stones in place.

Kitchen Wax.

See Furniture Polish.

Laundry Bluing (Liquid)

> **Safety Rating: UNLIKELY TO BE HARMFUL, EVEN IF SWALLOWED. CALL POISON CONTROL CENTER IMMEDIATELY FOR APPROPRIATE ANTIDOTE PROCEDURE.**

What's in it: A liquid laundry bluing such as BLUETTE (Walco-Linck) is mostly water (90–99 percent), plus a little blue dye (1–2 percent).

How it works: Like the fluorescent brighteners in some laundry detergents or bleach substitutes (see the alphabetical products listing), laundry bluing makes white clothes look whiter by adding a dye rather than by bleaching out stains. This is most apparent when too much bluing is used, giving the clothes a decidedly blue cast. If that happens, you can eliminate some of the dye from cotton clothes by pouring boiling water over them or by rinsing them in the washer, using the hottest water setting.

What it can do to you: Bluing may turn your fingers slightly blue if you leave them in the solution too long, but it is rarely toxic. The probable lethal dose for a small child (22 pounds/10 kilograms) is two ounces or more.

What's better, safer, or cheaper: Laundry bluing is a rather old-fashioned product. It made sense back in the tub-and-washboard days, when the only way to wash your clothes was to dunk them in plain laundry soap or soapflakes and water. Today, most laundry detergents are already packed with whiteners, brighteners, or bleaches, and it's a waste of good money to add bluing on top of all that.

Laundry Bluing (Powder)

See Bleach Substitute.

Laundry Detergent (Granular, Powder)

> Safety Rating: ALL LAUNDRY DETER-GENTS MAY BE HARMFUL IF SWAL-LOWED. CALL POISON CONTROL CENTER IMMEDIATELY FOR APPROPRIATE ANTI-DOTE PROCEDURE. IF SWALLOWED, PRODUCTS CONTAINING SODIUM CAR-BONATE MAY PRESENT A MEDICAL EMERGENCY REQUIRING *IMMEDIATE* MEDICAL ATTENTION.

What's in it: All the popular laundry detergent powders are based on a combination of anionic and nonionic detergents and surfactants. In addition, they usually contain an anticaking ingredient (sodium sulfate, sodium silicate, or both), whiteners or fluorescent brighteners, and perfumes. Where they are permitted, phosphates are usually included to soften hard water and boost the detergent's cleaning power. Where phosphates are banned, sodium carbonate is often substituted as a water softener. Optional extras include bleach (sodium perborate) and an anticorrosion agent, which may be added to nonphosphate detergents to protect the washing machine from the corrosive action of sodium carbonate.

Detergents with phosphates:

In areas where phosphates are permitted, they are included in most popular brands. When they are, they will be indicated on the label.

Detergents with nonphosphate water softener (sodium carbonate) and bleach (sodium perborate):

ALL (Lever Brothers)
OXYDOL (Procter & Gamble)

Detergents with nonphosphate water softener (sodium carbonate) only:

ARM & HAMMER (Church & Dwight Co.)
BOLD (Procter & Gamble)
CHEER (Procter & Gamble)
DASH (Procter & Gamble)
GAIN (Procter & Gamble)
PUREX (Purex)
RINSO (Lever Brothers)
TIDE (Procter & Gamble)

Detergents without water softener or bleach:

COLD POWER XE (Colgate-Palmolive)
FAB (Colgate-Palmolive)
TOTAL COLOR AJAX (Colgate-Palmolive)

How it works: When they were introduced, synthetic detergents represented a real leap forward in laundry cleaning power because they did a bang-up job of getting grease and other stains off washable woolens and synthetics even in plain, cold water. (Hot water and soap or soap powder is still the best way to get cottons clean.)

Of course, there's nothing magical about a detergent's ability to do this. It's all chemistry. Detergents are surfactants, "surface active agents," compounds that lessen the surface tension of liquids. Add a surfactant to water and you make the water "wetter," more able to penetrate fabrics, combining with grease or dirt to form an emulsion that simply lifts or floats off of the clothes in your washing machine.

Softeners in the detergent product enhance this effect by preventing the minerals (calcium and magnesium) in hard water from settling on your clothes to produce a "detergent scum" (really mineral deposits). Phosphates keep the minerals in suspension, floating around in the water. Sodium carbonate precipitates the minerals out of the water; that is, it combines with calcium and magnesium to form an insoluble mixture that simply falls to the bottom of the tub.

Fluorescent dyes or color brighteners make your wash look whiter or brighter; bleaches, naturally, bleach.

What it can do to you: The most publicized side effect of laundry detergent is what it may do to fish, plants, rivers, and lakes. Phosphates, the original water softeners and boosters in synthetic detergents, are basic nutrients for algae and other marine plants. The sudden infusion of enormous amounts of this plant food into rivers, lakes, and streams can produce a phenomenon known as *eutrophication,* a truly stunning overgrowth of vegetation which, at its most potent, can choke off all the fish and animal life in the water, "aging" or, quite literally, killing a lake as it goes.

Watching this happen, municipality after municipality began in the 1970s to ban detergents containing phosphates. Today, all the well-known products come in a phosphate and nonphosphate version, and even those with phosphates contain a lot less than the original ones did.

Did that solve all our detergent problems? Of course not. In fact, it created some new ones.

First, the least serious: Detergents without phosphates simply don't clean as well as detergents with phosphates do. Sometimes the difference is minimal; sometimes it's more apparent. In any case, in 1978, the state of Michigan sued Colgate-Palmolive, Procter & Gamble, and Lever Brothers for not making it clear that there was a difference in cleaning power between the two kinds of products. Under the state's consumer protection law, Michigan wanted manufacturers to come up with different packages or label copy for different detergents.

Next in order of seriousness is the fact that nonphosphate detergents are harder on your washing machine, because the chemical used as a substitute water softener, sodium carbonate, is caustic and corrosive. Manufacturers usually get around this by adding an anticorrosion ingredient to protect the machine, but that doesn't do anything to protect *you.*

Simple detergents, or detergents with added phosphates, can cause nausea, vomiting, diarrhea, and bloating if you swallow them, but they are rarely lethal. Detergents with sodium carbonate may be lethal. Sodium carbonate, or washing soda, is fairly innocuous when dry; if you spill it on your hand, you can simply brush it off quickly. But it begins to burn as soon as it gets wet—in your eyes or in your mouth and throat. Its power depends on its concentration, so there's really no way to predict how much will be deadly. But there's no doubt that if you swallow sodium carbonate, it can burn the inside of your mouth, your esophagus, and your stomach. It may also cause scarring serious enough to cause strictures, or scar formations that can block the throat, a few days or even weeks after it is swallowed.

Detergents with sodium perborate, a bleach, can cause symptoms of borate poisoning if swallowed: gastritis, blurred vision, and even disturbances of the central nervous system. As little as one seventh of an ounce of sodium perborate may be lethal for a small child (22 pounds/10 kilograms).

What's better, safer, or cheaper: Soaps or soap powders are really the only logical alternatives to laundry detergents. They're safer to store around the house if you've got small children, but they aren't noticeably cheaper and they really don't clean synthetic fabrics as well. Certainly, they won't work in cold water.

Among the commercial detergents, your best buy is probably the simplest one, without added water softeners or bleach. Those you can buy in bulk and add if necessary. Doing that, you have a certain freedom to play around that you give up by choosing a premixed product. You can use the same basic detergent for everything, from clothes that don't need bleach at all, to those that require an all-purpose sodium perborate bleach such as CLOROX 2, MIRACLE WHITE, PUREX GENTLE FABRIC BLEACH, or SNOWY, or those that really need the power of a chlorine bleach such as ACTION, CLOROX, PUREX (liquid or powder), or TEXIZE.

As for water softeners, before you pay a penny for them, either in bulk or in your detergent, be sure you really need them. The simplest way to tell is this: Pour two cupfuls of warm water from your tap into a quart jar. Add about a teaspoonful of soap powder such as IVORY FLAKES and shake hard. If you get suds that last about four or five minutes, forget the water softeners. You don't need them. No suds, or suds that break up fast, mean water softener is required. *Note:* This test may not work with a detergent like COLD POWER ALL (Lever Brothers), since many detergents are made to work without suds, so as to avoid clogging your washing machine.

Laundry Detergent (Liquid)

> **Safety Rating: MAY BE HARMFUL IF SWAL-LOWED. CALL POISON CONTROL CENTER IMMEDIATELY FOR APPROPRIATE ANTI-DOTE PROCEDURE.**

What's in it: Liquid laundry detergent products such as DYNAMO (Colgate-Palmolive), ENDIRT (Sunshine Chemical Corp.), ERA (Procter & Gamble), HEAVY DUTY ALL (Lever Brothers), WISK (Lever Brothers), and YES (Texize) are water-based solutions containing detergents and surfactants plus a number of other chemicals to improve the product's appearance or performance. For example, most liquid detergents include alcohol, which keeps the liquid flowing freely. There may be a thickener (resin or carboxymethyl cellulose), fragrance, brighteners, a coloring agent to make the detergent look pretty, an opacifier to give the liquid a "solid," heavy look, and an emulsifier such as sodium stearate to keep all the ingredients from separating in the pretty plastic bottle. Some products (YES is one) also contain a fabric softener.

How it works: Liquid detergents clean exactly the way powdered ones do, by allowing the wash water to form an emulsion with the dirt on the laundry and float or lift spots off the clothes. Liquid detergents are quite useful as prewash spot removers. They can be poured right on dirty, greasy stains like that dreaded "ring around the collar." And there are two real advantages to using a liquid detergent rather than one of the specialized prewash spot and stain removers (see in alphabetical products listing) or presoaks. First, it costs less to use one product instead of buying two different ones. Second, it may be safer. Some of the prewash spot and stain removers, like SHOUT and SPRAY 'N WASH, contain solvents, which may be flammable as well as poisonous. None of the liquid laundry detergents contains these solvents.

What it can do to you: In general, liquid laundry detergents are less dangerous than granular or powder ones. For one thing, liquids don't contain sodium carbonate, so they aren't caustic, even if swallowed straight from the bottle. They can cause the gastric symptoms associated with detergents—nausea, vomiting, and diarrhea—but they won't leave the kind of tissue burns that may result from swallowing concentrated powder detergent. The probable lethal dose for a small child (22 pounds/10 kilograms) may be two ounces or more. (Be warned, of course, that liquids are easier to swallow than powders.)

Like all detergents, these may irritate hands and eyes, and some people may be particularly sensitive to specific perfumes or colors or detergents. If that happens, try switching around until you find one you can live with comfortably.

What's better, safer, or cheaper: The prices of detergents vary, but the differences are purely arbitrary, based on marketing strategy. They have nothing at all to do with whether a detergent is a liquid or a powder. It can be said that the liquid detergents are easier to store (they come in smaller packages, after all), and, since none of them contains a water softener (sodium carbonate) or a bleach, they give you the chance to mix and match on your own.

Laundry Detergent Booster

> **Safety Rating: MAY BE HARMFUL IF SWALLOWED. CALL POISON CONTROL CENTER IMMEDIATELY FOR APPROPRIATE ANTIDOTE PROCEDURE.**

What's in it: There is no standard formula for a laundry detergent booster. Products being sold under that designation may contain a simple mild alkali, like the 100 percent borax in 20 MULE TEAM BORAX (U.S. Borax & Chemical Corp.), or they may contain a mild detergent, plus dyes, fragrance, and water, as AMWAY SMASHING WHITE (Amway Corp.) does. Or, like MIRACLE WHITE DETERGENT BOOSTER (Drackett), they may rely on a nonionic surfactant for their booster power.

How it works: Theoretically, detergent boosters increase the cleaning power of laundry detergents by contributing an element that is missing from the basic detergent product. So, bleach, bleach substitutes, and water softeners (see all in the alphabetical products listing) may be considered "detergent boosters," even if that isn't the way they're described on the package or bottle.

What it can do to you: The toxicity of detergent boosters depends on what's in the box or bottle. A good rule of thumb is that the probable lethal dose of powdered detergent products is generally assumed to be less than one ounce for a small child (22 pounds/10 kilograms). Products containing mild alkalis plus additives can cause nausea and vomiting when swallowed; products containing borax may cause mild symptoms of borate poisoning. Borates are toxic when absorbed through mucous membranes or broken skin, or when inhaled or swallowed.

Like detergents, detergent boosters may also be irritating to the skin. They can burn if you get them in your eye. If swallowed, they can burn mouth, throat, and stomach linings.

What's better, safer, or cheaper: Detergent boosters are often an unnecessary expense, since many laundry detergents already contain bleaches, brighteners, or water-softening chemicals. Always read the label before adding extra ingredients. For alternatives to specific products, see Bleach, Bleach Substitute, and Water Softener in the alphabetical products listing.

Laundry Presoak.

See Bleach; Bleach Substitute; Laundry Detergent (Granular, Powder; Liquid).

Laundry Starch (Aerosol)

> **Safety Rating: NONTOXIC; UNLIKELY TO BE HARMFUL IF SWALLOWED. CALL POISON CONTROL CENTER FOR APPROPRIATE ANTIDOTE PROCEDURE.**

What's in it: Aerosol spray starches such as EASY-ON (Boyle-Midway), NIAGARA (Best Foods), RENUZIT (Drackett), and WHITE ROSE (White Rose) are generally three-ingredient products containing cornstarch, silicone (sometimes given a sexy alias like NIAGARA's "SL 32"), and propellant. To all intents and purposes, aerosol "sizing" products, such as MAGIC EXTRA CRISP SIZING (Armour-Dial), are pretty much the same as aerosol starches. Some products also contain a corrosion inhibitor to keep the starch from damaging your iron.

How it works: Ostensibly, spray starches and sizing are easier to work with than either powder or liquid starches. All you have to do is press the little button; the starch then coats the fabric you're ironing, and the extra ingredient, silicone, allows the iron to go zipping along without sticking. In practice, though, you are likely to get more "hot spots" with spray starches than with powder or liquid products. You may hit the button a little bit harder at one point, or you may simply miss one spot entirely. You can keep the nozzle on the spray can from clogging by removing the plastic piece on top after each use (simply lift it off), rinsing it thoroughly, and allowing it to dry before replacing it. That way, there won't be any starch left in the nozzle to form a plug that keeps it from spritzing the next time you want to use it.

What it can do to you: Like all other aerosol products, spray starches are accidents waiting to happen. The propellant gases inside are flammable. The cans can explode if they get too hot or if they are accidentally punctured. Turn the thing the wrong way, and you can spray starch in your eyes or mouth. No matter which way you turn it, you are releasing a fine mist of ingredients into the air you breathe. And, to add insult to injury, spray starches are simply uneconomical. You get less starch for your penny than in any other form of the finish.

What's better, safer, or cheaper: Both powder and liquid starches qualify on all counts. For other alternatives, see the alphabetical products listing for Laundry Starch (Powder, Liquid).

Laundry Starch (Powder, Liquid)

What's in it: An old-fashioned laundry starch powder is mostly cornstarch (up to 95 percent). It may also contain small amounts of resin and wax to give extra body and flexibility to the finish and to help your iron glide smoothly over starched surfaces. There may also be small amounts of preservative.

These simple starches do not dissolve in water; they form suspensions, which means that the starch particles are simply suspended in the liquid. Modern starches, sometimes called "soluble starches," contain starch powders that have been treated with an acid so that they will indeed dissolve in water. These are likely to give a smoother finish than the nonsoluble products.

Liquid starches such as LINIT (Best Foods) contain cornstarch (up to 10 percent) that has already been mixed with water (up to 90 percent). There may also be dispersants in the liquid, plus stabilizers, detergents, and surfactants. If the product looks blue, it contains bluing.

How it works: New clothes, particularly cottons and linens, have a characteristic stiff finish when you first bring them home from the store. Laundering or cleaning can dissolve this finish, and starching is one way to put it back. For best results with a powder starch, be sure that the starch and water solution is really hot when you put the clean clothes into it. The hotter the water is, the better the starch will penetrate the cloth, giving you a smooth, even finish without those overstarch, shiny "hot spots" you get when the starch hasn't been evenly distributed on the fabric.

Liquid starches are easier to use, of course, but since they contain much less actual starch, the finish you get won't be as stiff as it is with the powder/water solutions.

How you wring out your clothes has a lot to do with how starchy they look when you iron them. Wringing them almost dry removes most starch and makes the clothes less stiff later on; wringing them out only part way, and then letting them dry naturally, makes them stiffer when dry.

Of course, you don't have to iron starched clothes the minute they dry. You can store them and then take them out when you are ready to go to work. Just sprinkle with warm water (even when you are working with a steam iron) and iron away.

What it can do to you: Virtually nothing. Cornstarch, the basic ingredient in starch powders, is perfectly safe unless you're allergic to it—in which case it will make you sneeze, make your eyes tear, or make your skin itchy and rashy. If that happens, avoid all products with the word "starch" in the name. They've all got cornstarch in them.

Otherwise, starch powders are practically nontoxic. The only real problem with a powder starch is the same one you face with any loose powder. If a small child stuffs a handful in his mouth, there's always the possibility that he will inhale some into his lungs or that it will block his air passages.

What's better, safer, or cheaper: Ounce for ounce, starch powders are much cheaper than the liquids. But you have to mix up the powder/water solution yourself, while liquid starches come all ready to use. Only you can judge whether your time is valuable enough to make it worth the money to get the prepared stuff.

I am told you can whip up starch the way your grandmother did, if you think it's worth the trouble. Mix from one to three tablespoonsful of cornstarch with about one and a half tablespoonsful of cold water, then add the paste to a pint of boiling water and mix in one quarter teaspoonful of white wax. Boil the whole thing for about fifteen minutes, then strain it through a double layer of cheesecloth to get rid of any lumps. Dilute it with more water (the more water, the less starchy the finished clothes will be), and drop in whatever you want to starch.

For really delicate stuff, like organdy or batiste, dissolve a packet of KNOX gelatin in a pint of hot water. Then dilute that with at least one quart of water and add your clothes. Try a small corner of the fabric, and let it dry to see if you've got the dilution right. If there wasn't enough water in the solution, the finish will end up sticky and gummy. Try again until you get it right.

You can mix up another starch for delicate fabrics by dissolving a tablespoonful or two of plain granulated white sugar in about a pint of warm water. Dip your clothes in the liquid. When the sugar solution dries, it leaves a crisp layer on the fabric, just the way evaporating beer leaves a "wave-setting" coating on your hair.

Lighter Fuel.

See Cigarette-Lighter Fuel.

Matches

Safety Rating: MATCH HEADS MAY BE HARMFUL IF SWALLOWED IN QUANTITY. CALL POISON CONTROL CENTER IMMEDIATELY FOR APPROPRIATE ANTIDOTE PROCEDURE.

What's in it: The active ingredient in match heads is potassium chlorate (40–60 percent), a flammable, explosive powder. The potassium chlorate is usually combined with glue, which holds it on the wooden or paper match, sulfur, thickeners like flour or starch, and coloring agents.

How it works: When you strike the match, the friction-created heat or spark ignites the potassium chlorate.

What it can do to you: Potassium chlorate is potentially lethal, but there is so little on a match head that it takes a lot of matches to produce a serious reaction. The smallest recorded lethal dose of match heads for an adult is about ninety book matches or sixty kitchen (safety) matches, or about one gram of potassium chlorate. Smaller amounts can cause nausea, vomiting, and diarrhea.

What's better, safer, or cheaper: Unless you plan to rub two sticks together to make a flame, there really is no better or cheaper substitute for kitchen matches. In fact, kitchen matches can help you lower your gas bill and increase your kitchen safety at the same time. Stoves with pilot lights consume gas all the time. And the burners on an ordinary kitchen stove are just about level with the top of a child's head. Buy a stove without a pilot light, or have your local utility company show you how to adapt your old stove, and you can cut down on the gas you use and lower your bill. Your kitchen will be safer, too, if you can fix things so that the burners must be lit with a match and don't go on when someone simply turns the knobs at the front. It's harder to convert burners than ovens, but it's certainly worth investigating.

Of course, the worst problems with matches are likely to arise from a child's playing with them. There's little you can do to erase the natural human interest in fire, but you can always buy safety matches which, true to their name, are a lot safer than matches that can be lit by striking them on any abrasive surface. And you can make sure that the matches, like the drain cleaner, the oven cleaner, and all the other problem products in the house, are either locked up or stored so high that they are always safely out of a child's reach. Check them out periodically; a growing child's reach gets longer every day.

Metal Cleaner (All-Purpose)

> **Safety Rating: HARMFUL IF SWALLOWED. CALL POISON CONTROL CENTER IMMEDIATELY FOR APPROPRIATE ANTIDOTE PROCEDURE.**

What's in it: All-purpose metal cleaners, like NOXON (Boyle-Midway) and WONDER METAL POLISH (Uncle Sam), contain silica (an abrasive) plus an acid (usually oxalic acid), ammonia, alcohols, and water. Some may also contain a petroleum distillate solvent.

How it works: These cleaners are formulated for use on all kinds of metal except silver, silver plate, and jewelry, for which they are simply too abrasive. They are stronger than most of the cleaners meant specifically for copper and aluminum.

What it can do to you: Because all-purpose metal cleaners contain ammonia, their fumes may be irritating to your eyes and nose. The cleaners themselves are eye and skin irritants that should be flushed off with lots of lukewarm water if you happen to spill or splash them on yourself. If swallowed, the probable lethal dose for a small child

(22 pounds/10 kilograms) can be anywhere from one fifth of a teaspoonful on up.

What's better, safer, or cheaper: Among commercial products, the all-purpose metal cleaner is a more economical buy than three or four special polishes. You may find that the all-purpose product is too abrasive for some of your metal pots, pans, and containers. To be truthful, I never have.

As a substitute, soapsuds with ammonia added work well for cleaning most metal surfaces, including chrome fittings on sink or tub. For other homemade alternatives, see Aluminum Cleaner, Copper Cleaner, Jewelry Cleaner, Silver Polish, and Stainless Steel Cleaner in the alphabetical products listing.

Mildew Preventive

> **Safety Rating: HARMFUL IF SWALLOWED OR ABSORBED THROUGH THE SKIN. CALL POISON CONTROL CENTER IMMEDIATELY FOR APPROPRIATE ANTIDOTE PROCEDURE.**

What's in it: There are a number of different kinds of mildew preventives, each containing different ingredients. The solid blocks are made of 100 percent paraformaldehyde. Saturated paper disks or hangers have been impregnated with a fungicide, such as biphenyl. Sprays or liquids contain cationic surfactants which serve as germicides, solvents (1,1,1-trichloroethane or isopropyl alcohol), fragrance, and, in aerosols, propellants.

How it works: Mildew is a mold that grows in warm, damp places. The chemicals in the mildew preventives are fungicides or disinfectants that make surfaces inhospitable for the mold.

What it can do to you: How toxic a mildew preventive is depends on what's in it. Paraformaldehyde produces symptoms similar to those caused by formaldehyde. Its vapors are irritating, and, if swallowed, it may cause gastric pain, internal bleeding, coma, and death. The probable lethal dose for a small child (22 pounds/10 kilograms) may be less than a half teaspoonful.

Biphenyl, while not a skin irritant, can be absorbed on contact through intact skin and may produce the same symptoms you might experience if you swallowed it. That means liver and kidney damage, respiratory problems, muscle weakness, coma, and death. The probable lethal dose for a small child (22 pounds/10 kilograms) may be as small as one seventh of an ounce.

Solvents such as isopropyl alcohol or 1,1,1-trichloroethane may cause dizziness, headache, and vertigo if you swallow them or inhale their vapors, but they are rarely lethal except in large amounts. However, they are flammable and may be irritating on your skin.

What's better, safer, or cheaper: Since dampness is the prime requisite for happiness among molds, keeping your closets dry can do a lot to eliminate mildew problems. Air closets out frequently, and leave the light burning for a couple of hours at a time every day. Be sure, though, that the light bulb is at least a foot away from any plastic clothes bags or any other material, including suitcases and boxes, since the bulb may get hot enough to set these things afire.

Mildew-Stain Remover

Safety Rating: IF SWALLOWED, PRODUCTS CONTAINING SODIUM CARBONATE OR CONCENTRATED SODIUM HYPOCHLORITE MAY PRESENT A MEDICAL EMERGENCY REQUIRING *IMMEDIATE* MEDICAL ATTENTION.

What's in it: A typical mildew-stain remover is a water-based solution containing a chlorine bleach disinfectant (sodium hypochlorite, calcium hypochlorite), plus a strong alkali such as sodium carbonate. One example: X-14 MILDEW STAIN REMOVER (White Laboratories).

How it works: The chlorine bleach bleaches out the stain and at the same time disinfects the surface you're using it on. Hopefully, it will kill the mildew or mold and prevent its growing (and staining) again.

What it can do to you: Sodium hypochlorite, calcium hypochlorite, and sodium carbonate are all irritating to the skin. Sodium carbonate may be caustic enough to burn the mouth, throat, and stomach if swallowed. How serious the burns will be depends on how concentrated the solution you swallow is. If it is concentrated enough, it can literally burn its way right through the stomach.

What's better, safer, or cheaper: Your mildew stains are really living things, molds that flourish on fabrics stored in damp, warm places. That means that the first step toward getting rid of the stain is getting rid of the mold. Brush the fabric vigorously, shake it out (out in the yard, or out the window—to avoid scattering mold spores indoors), and give it a good airing. You may find that stains on washable fabrics will respond well to simple soap-and-water washing. If more stringent methods are required, try one of the ordinary chlorine or sodium perborate laundry bleaches. It's always more economical to use one product for everything, rather than buying a special product for each job. Keep in mind, of course, that bleaches present their own safety problems. The best bet: Keep mildew from forming in the first place. To find out how, see Mildew Preventive in the alphabetical products listing.

Model Cement

> **Safety Rating: HARMFUL IF SWALLOWED OR INHALED. CALL POISON CONTROL CENTER IMMEDIATELY FOR APPROPRIATE ANTIDOTE PROCEDURE.**

What's in it: Cements for wood models are based on filler materials such as cellulose acetate, cellulose acetate butyrate, or nitrocellulose, plus a solvent (acetone, methyl ethyl ketone, toluol). Cements for plastic models are based on a synthetic resin (polyamide resin, polystyrene resin) plus a solvent (toluol). Both kinds of cement usually contain allyl isothiocyanate (imitation oil of mustard) as an "anti-sniff" ingredient.

How it works: The adhesives in these cements are thermoplastic substances that harden when exposed to room temperatures. Since you store these cements at room temperature anyway, the solvents are added to keep them plastic and workable in the tube. When you squeeze the cement out, the solvents evaporate and the cement hardens.

What it can do to you: All model cements are flammable. They should never be used around an open flame or while you're smoking. If you get the cement on your skin, you're likely to find that it's irritating, and it can certainly irritate your eyes. If swallowed, the adhesives are potentially toxic. The probable lethal dose for a small child (22 pounds/10 kilograms) may be less than a teaspoonful.

These products have such an unpleasant acrid smell that it is rare indeed for anyone to swallow anywhere near a lethal dose. The problem these cements pose is really for people who don't think they're a problem at all. As thousands of kids with brown paper bags have discovered, concentrating and inhaling the toluol or methyl ethyl ketone fumes from model cements can produce a euphoric high. Unfortunately, it's a high that can tumble over rather quickly into the ultimate low. If you inhale enough of these narcotic fumes in concentrated form, they may depress the central nervous system severely enough to cause coma, brain damage, and/or death. That's one reason why so many manufacturers add allyl isothiocyanate to cements containing either solvent. (The other is that it's required by law in some states.) This ingredient, which is also known as imitation oil of mustard, is very irritating to the mucous membranes and tremendously off-putting to anyone who tries to sniff the glue.

What's better, safer, or cheaper: Like so many specialized commercial adhesives, model cements do exactly what they're supposed to. There are no better or safer alternatives. As for cheaper substitutes, the only answer is to shop around among brands. Protect your investment by always cleaning off the top of the tube before you replace the cap—tightly closed—so that the cement doesn't dry out before you get a chance to use it.

Mothproofer

What's in it: The active ingredient in most modern mothballs and moth flakes is naphthalene, a major constituent of coal tar. Moth blocks, nuggets, or chunks contain *p*-dichlorobenzene (also known as paradichlorobenzene or paramoth).

How it works: Both naphthalene and *p*-dichlorobenzene are poisonous to moths. They can knock the creatures off in the larval stage before they get to be full-grown, wool-chomping insects. (These mothproofers will also keep down the populations of other insects in the closets and closet walls, keeping them away from your clothes, too.) Blocks of *p*-dichlorobenzene are also sold as "closet deodorizers." In that form, they contain some perfume to prettify the air in your closet.

What it can do to you: If you really have to have a chemical mothproofer, choose a product made of *p*-dichlorobenzene. It's poisonous, but much less dangerous than naphthalene. The vapors from *p*-dichlorobenzene can irritate your eyes, your skin, and your throat, and if you breathe high concentrations of *p*-dichlorobenzene vapors for more than a few minutes, it may make you dizzy and might eventually cause liver damage. Some experts even think *p*-dichlorobenzene may be a carcinogen.

So how can it be less dangerous than naphthalene? For one thing, the probable adult lethal dose of *p*-dichlorobenzene is estimated to be as great as one ounce. People have been known to walk away from doses as high as two thirds of an ounce, and there has never been a single case of serious oral poisoning reported.

Naphthalene, however, may be fatal if you swallow as little as one sixth to one half ounce. It can cause blood disorders, notably the destruction of red blood cells, and its other side effects include gastritis, nausea, vomiting, dizziness, weakness, confusion, convulsions, and coma. These effects are possible whether you swallow the naphthalene or inhale its fumes, and there is some evidence that it can do its dirty work on infants simply by being absorbed through the intact skin. It is also highly flammable.

And what's worse, you don't have to touch, swallow, or inhale the mothproofers directly to run into problems. People with sensitive skin or noses and throats that respond to a wide range of allergens may turn itchy, rashy, or worse just by wearing clothes that have been hanging in a naphthalene- or p-dichlorobenzene-saturated closet.

What's better, safer, or cheaper: There is virtually no chemical mothproofer that is totally safe. There are some that are cheaper. The Department of Agriculture, for example, used to suggest a mothproofing solution made of one ounce of sodium fluosilicate, plus one ounce of detergent mixed into a gallon of warm water. The idea was to soak washable clothes and linens in this solution and then store them for the summer. In concentrations like this, sodium fluosilicate isn't terribly poisonous, but this procedure is hardly practical, since so few people store their linens and "summer" clothes these days.

Actually, the safest and cheapest way of preventing damage by moths is to keep clothes clean. Moths are particularly mad for soiled wool and cotton—the more soiled the better. If clothes are cleaned or washed regularly, and if closets are vacuumed often enough to sweep up any moth eggs or larvae that might be lying around on the floor or shelves, it is possible to keep moths at bay without any chemicals at all. (Vacuum rugs and furniture regularly, too, and keep shelves where clothes are stored dust-free.) Of course, no matter how you keep them, your synthetics—nylon, dynel, orlon, Acrilan, spandex— will never attract any moths at all. The voracious pests simply don't enjoy chewing through plastic any more than you do, although they will somehow always manage to worm their way into plastic protective bags or sacks if you don't keep the cotton, woolen, feather, or fur garments inside clean.

Mucilage

What's in it: Mucilages such as ROSS MUCILAGE (Ross Chemical Co.) are translucent, brownish glues based on natural, sticky substances such as dextrin (a starch) or gum arabic. The solvent is always water, and optional ingredients include waterproofers (plasticizers or resins such as formaldehyde or phenylphenol) and humectants (glycerin).

How it works: Mucilages dry to form temporary bonds between paper, wood, and fabrics. They are not permanent adhesives, though, for as they dry out with age and they begin to flake off, the bond dissolves.

What it can do to you: The plasticizers and waterproofers in mucilage can be poisonous. If swallowed, the probable lethal dose for a small child (22 pounds/10 kilograms) may be somewhere between just under a teaspoonful to just under an ounce or more.

What's better, safer, or cheaper: There's really nothing more versatile, although mucilages are interchangeable with white glues (see in alphabetical products listing) for most purposes.

Nonstick Cooking Spray

What's in it: COOKING EASE (Clorox), MAZOLA NO-STICK (Best Foods), and PAM (Boyle-Midway) are all mixtures of plain vegetable oils plus propellants.

How it works: These sprays, which were invented to turn plain aluminum, iron, or stainless steel pots into imitations of those lined with Teflon or Silverstone, put a thin, even layer of oil on the pan's surface. They do an adequate job of keeping foods from sticking, and they really do reduce the amount of fat you'd ordinarily use. However, they can cause problems. Read on.

What it can do to you: Like all aerosols, the nonstick sprays are dangerous around heat and should never be used when the pan is on the stove. The propellants are flammable, the can may explode, and, if you spray the fat into a hot pan, it's liable to sizzle back at you.

What's better, safer, or cheaper: Plain fats, the kind you always used before, are cheaper and safer (from the mechanical point of view) than the nonstick sprays. To use as little fat as possible, use oil rather than butter or margarine, and give the pan a fast swipe with a paper towel to spread the oil all over the surface and pick up any excess.

Nonstick Furniture Spray

> **Safety Rating: IF SWALLOWED, PRODUCTS CONTAINING PETROLEUM DISTILLATES MAY BE EXTREMELY HARMFUL. CALL POISON CONTROL CENTER IMMEDIATELY FOR APPROPRIATE ANTIDOTE PROCEDURE.**

What's in it: Nonstick sprays like KRYLON SILICONE SPRAY (Borden Inc.) get their slippery power from a silicone compound such as methyl polysiloxane. There's also a solvent, usually a petroleum distillate, and, naturally, a propellant.

How it works: The silicone compound is a lubricator that makes the surface you spray it on slick, so these sprays keep drawers from sticking and may make it easier to open and close doors. Because silicones also repel water, they may keep drawer and door edges from swelling in damp weather.

What it can do to you: These sprays are very flammable, because they contain both propellant gases and petroleum distillate solvents.

The solvent vapors can make you dizzy and drowsy if you inhale them in an unventilated room.

What's better, safer, or cheaper: Once you're certain that your doors, drawers, and windows really fit their frames and aren't sticking simply because they're too large to slide easily, you might save money and eliminate the possible side effects of the silicone sprays by sliding a bar of soap along the drawer runners, down the side of the doors, and along the window-frame edges. The soap won't waterproof the way silicone does (your wooden doors, drawers, and window frames will still swell slightly and be hard to open in wet weather), but it will make the edges slippery enough so that you can open and close the dresser without swearing at it.

Oven Cleaner
(Paste, Liquid, Pump Spray, Aerosol)

> **Safety Rating: IF SWALLOWED, OVEN CLEANERS CONTAINING SODIUM HYDROXIDE (LYE) PRESENT A MEDICAL EMERGENCY REQUIRING *IMMEDIATE* MEDICAL ATTENTION.**

What's in it: The basic working ingredient in all oven cleaners is lye, otherwise known as sodium hydroxide, potassium hydroxide, or caustic soda. The simplest cleaner, a paste like EASY-OFF (Boyle-Midway), may contain about 8 percent sodium hydroxide, plus thickeners. A liquid, such as AMWAY HEAVY DUTY OVEN CLEANER (Amway Corp.), may have as much as 10 percent sodium hydroxide, plus surfactants, emulsifiers, detergents, and as much water as is needed to make a lotion that will spread easily but won't roll off the oven door onto your hand. A pump-spray oven cleaner, like EASY-OFF, puts the liquid in a plastic bottle with a pump-spray top. Aerosol oven cleaners such as DOW LEMON SCENTED (Dow Chemical), EASY-OFF, GLAMORENE 3 MINUTE (Glamorene), JIFOAM (Clorox), and MR. MUSCLE (Drackett) add propellant to sodium hydroxide (from 2.5 to 5 percent), detergents, surfactants, emulsifiers, and sometimes water.

104

How it works: There's nothing simpler than the way the lye in an oven cleaner dissolves and liquefies baked-on food and grease. When it's done, you can simply wipe the debris away with a damp cloth. This is one time when it pays to use a disposable rag, like a paper towel. There's just no percentage in washing out lye-saturated rags; you might as well toss them out with the garbage.

The more lye there is in the cleaner, the faster it will do the job. That's why the pastes and liquids will beat the aerosols every time. The aerosol manufacturers have made a virtue of this time disadvantage, though, suggesting that you use their product overnight, to let the cleaner work while you sleep. In the morning, the grease comes off easily.

No matter what kind of oven cleaner you use, be sure to close the oven door once you've spread, poured, or sprayed it on, so that the cleaner won't dry out. Wipe up spills before you touch them by mistake, because all oven cleaners can burn your skin. Be sure not to apply the cleaner to any surface it can harm, such as electrical connections, rubber, or aluminum. Use lined rubber gloves to protect your hands, and spread newspaper on the floor to catch any overflow. Be absolutely certain that the nozzle on the aerosol is pointed the right way—away from you—before you push the button. According to the Consumer Product Safety Commission, dozens of people spray aerosols in their eyes every year, and an eyeful of oven cleaner is no picnic.

What it can do to you: All these cleaners contain caustic poisons that will burn mouth, throat, and stomach if swallowed. Aerosols can explode if they get too hot or if you puncture them accidentally. In addition, when you use aerosols as directed you cannot avoid spraying a fine mist of caustic ingredients into the air you breathe. It goes without saying that you should never lean into the oven while you're spraying, and never spray oven cleaner into a hot oven. If you do, it can bounce right back at you.

What's better, safer, or cheaper: I hate to sound like the wicked witch of the kitchen, but the fact is that you won't need a caustic oven cleaner at all if you get into the habit of cleaning as you go. Wipe up spills as they happen, or give the *cooling* oven a swipe with a damp cloth, and there won't be any crusted food and grease buildup to get rid of later.

If you do forget once in a while, you can try cleaning up a moderate amount of newly baked-on goop with some ordinary dishwashing liquid or general-purpose powder household cleaner. Pour some of the liquid on the solid spots, or make a paste of the powder detergent and water and smear some of that on. Let it sit for a while, then scrub with one of those plastic sponges, like TUFFY, made for nonstick pots and pans (wet the sponge before scrubbing). You won't scratch the enamel finish, and you may just get the dirt off. Repeat once or twice if necessary, before giving up in favor of a standard caustic cleaner.

If you do end up using the commercial cleaner to get rid of built-up gunk, remember:

• The cheapest oven cleaner, ounce for ounce, is a paste, but it's also the most corrosive—so dangerous that standard poison textbooks will not even list a probable lethal dose. It all depends on concentration. Even a taste may be enough to burn a hole through a toddler's throat or stomach.

• Aerosols, despite their inherent problems, may be a slightly less dangerous form of the cleaner if you have a small child in the house. They are sealed containers, difficult for a small child to operate. For adults, aerosols are expensive, but they *do* let you get the cleaner onto the oven surface with the least effort (you have to spread the paste around with a brush).

Paint (Latex)

Safety Rating: **MOST INTERIOR LATEX PAINTS ARE RARELY HARMFUL, EVEN IF SWALLOWED. SOME EXTERIOR LATEX PAINTS MAY BE HARMFUL IF SWALLOWED. CALL POISON CONTROL CENTER IMMEDIATELY FOR APPROPRIATE ANTIDOTE PROCEDURE.**

What's in it: The latex paints usually used at home contain nontoxic pigments, plus a latex emulsion (a rubberlike synthetic) such as polyvinyl acetate elastomer, acrylic elastomer, or styrene butadiene elastomer, a solvent, and possibly vegetable oils, all in a water base. "Mildew resistant" exterior latex paints may contain small amounts of mercury fungicides.

How it works: As the water and solvent evaporate, the latex hardens into a protective coating which, if you make it too thick or put it on over an unproperly prepared surface, can be peeled off, just like a face mask that has dried. If you're going to apply latex paints over a badly worn, oil-painted surface, roughen up the surface with sandpaper or apply a primer coat. Otherwise, the latex paint may not adhere evenly.

What it can do to you: Small amounts of indoor latex paints will simply turn to plastic blobs if you put them in your mouth. The probable lethal dose for a small child (22 pounds/10 kilograms) is more than two ounces. Exterior latex paints may, if they are labeled "mildew resistant," contain potentially toxic levels of mercury fungicides. Any amounts in excess of 0.2 percent mercury must be noted on the label, and appropriate warning copy must be included. Without excessive mercury, exterior latex paints are pretty much nontoxic, too.

What's better, safer, or cheaper: As far as I'm concerned, latex paints *are* the better way. Because they do not contain mineral spirits, they do not smell as vile as oil-based paints and they are much less toxic. In addition, if you are a person who paints with abandon, splashing and splattering everywhere, these products can make cleaning-up a relative breeze. The experts say that the best way to mop up splashes is to go after them immediately with a damp or wet cloth, followed by a dry one. That works best when the splatters fall on a floor that is sealed with an impermeable finish: linoleum, kitchen tiles with a "no-wax" finish, or urethaned wood floors. However, when you drop this paint on an un-plasticized floor (like plain stained wood), adding water can aggravate problems by spreading the paint into the tiny cracks in the wood. Once that happens, it's almost impossible to get rid of the stain; you always seem to be left with a whitish film. So what I do when I drop latex paint on plain wood floors is to let the splatters dry and then peel them up with something like a putty knife, always being as careful as possible not to peel the finish off the floor.

Of course, whether the paint is latex or oil-based, nobody's ever come up with a better cleaning method than prevention, which means throwing dropcloths over everything before you start to paint. These dropcloths don't have to be exorbitantly expensive. I keep old sheets around the house for just this purpose. It's not a good idea to use those wonderfully cheap plastic dropcloths on the floor because they don't absorb paint: it just sits there in puddles waiting for you to step in it and track it all over the place. However, they are excellent for tossing over large pieces of furniture.

Paint (Metallic).

See Paint (Oil-Base).

Paint (Oil-Base)

> **Safety Rating: IF SWALLOWED, PRODUCTS CONTAINING PETROLEUM DISTILLATES MAY BE EXTREMELY HARMFUL. CALL POISON CONTROL CENTER IMMEDIATELY FOR APPROPRIATE ANTIDOTE PROCEDURE.**

What's in it: The pigments in white or pastel oil-base paints are white titanium dioxide plus 5 percent tinting colors. In the darker shades, color pigments take the place of most and sometimes all of the basic titanium compound. The paints also contain fillers such as clay, talc, or calcium carbonate, a resin or an oil varnish, and a petroleum distillate solvent (mineral spirits). What makes a gloss paint shinier than a satin-finish paint is the higher proportion of oil varnish and solvent in the glossy liquid. Aluminum, bronze, copper, gold, and silver paints are simply oil-base paints with coloring agents such as aluminum powder, gold-bronze powder, or copper-bronze powder substituting for regular color pigments. Spray paints contain a propellant.

How it works: Like all surface coatings, this one works when the solvent evaporates and the oil or resin oxidizes, leaving a hard skin of solids on the painted surface.

What it can do to you: Virtually all the nasty effects of oil-base paints can be traced to the solvent. It is flammable and its vapors are irritating, and, if swallowed, the paint is poisonous. In addition, the solvent can cause a potentially lethal form of chemical pneumonia if aspirated into your lungs. The probable lethal dose of oil-base paint for a small

108

child (22 pounds/10 kilograms) is less than half an ounce. If aspirated into the lungs, even a few drops can be fatal.

Until a few years ago, there was another problem to deal with if you used oil-base paints around the house: lead, which was used as a pigment. Babies who nibbled on their cribs or their toys or chewed up the pieces of paint that had chipped off the walls or the windowsill sometimes developed lead poisoning. As a result, in 1978, the Consumer Product Safety Commission required that house paint or paint used on furniture or toys be lead-free.

While it is certainly a step in the right direction, compliance with this regulation doesn't totally eliminate the possibility of lead poisoning, since there's still an awful lot of lead paint around on the walls and ceilings of older houses. In 1979, the Internal Revenue Service announced that parents could deduct the cost of removing lead paint from areas of the house that were "readily accessible" to children, so long as they were ordered to do so by a doctor. The IRS has interpreted "readily accessible" to mean rooms like the living room and the bedroom, not the attic. And only the cost of *removing* the paint is deductible. Covering the naked walls with new paint isn't. While the intent of the ruling is nifty, the language and interpretation leave one wondering how the IRS bureaucrats keep their kids out of the cellar and what they put on their walls. All in all, it's certainly a lovely piece of governmental hairsplitting.

What's better, safer, or cheaper: The safer, though not necessarily cheaper, alternative to oil-base paint is latex, or water-base, paint. It's nonflammable, relatively nontoxic, and thoroughly washable.

Paintbrush Cleaner.

See **General-Purpose Household Cleaner (Liquid, Pump Spray); Paint and Coating Solvent and Thinner; Paint Stripper.**

Paint and Coating Solvent and Thinner

> **Safety Rating: HARMFUL IF SWALLOWED. CALL POISON CONTROL CENTER IMMEDIATELY FOR APPROPRIATE ANTIDOTE PROCEDURE.**

What's in it: There are a lot of fairly volatile liquids that can be used to thin out paints and other coatings. For example, an oil-based paint is usually thinned with turpentine, mineral spirits, or linseed oil. Turpentine may also be used to thin out varnishes and oil-based primers. Denatured alcohol is the solvent used with shellacs and shellac-based sealer-primers. Denatured alcohol plus ketones is often used as a solvent for lacquers.

How it works: If you could keep your paint and coating cans sealed airtight, you'd probably never need solvents and thinners at all. Unfortunately, you can't. Whenever you open one of these cans the solution thickens, because the liquids in the mix begin to evaporate, leaving a more concentrated clump of the solid pigments, fillers, plasticizers, and resins. Solvents return the coating to its original state by dissolving the solids and putting them back into solution. All solvents also work as paintbrush cleaners. Brushes come clean more easily if you dunk them in the solvent as soon as you finish painting. You *can* clean them after the paint or coating has dried, but it takes longer, and somehow the brushes never come out as smooth and straight.

Splatters and spots are a different story. If you attack them with a solvent-soaked rag the minute they fall on the floor, you're likely to spread them around instead of cleaning them up. Much better to wait until they're dried, then pry up the really thick ones with a razor blade or sharp knife and gently go after the tiny ones with solvent. Along with the spots, you may pick up some of the finish on the floor, so be careful. Better yet, be careful while painting, and use drop cloths to protect furniture and floors.

What it can do to you: Virtually all solvents and thinners are flammable, and their vapors are usually combustible, too. Check the warnings on the labels. All these products are irritating to your skin and mucous membranes, and all give off irritating fumes that can make you drowsy

110

or restless or even high if you inhale them in concentrated form in an unventilated room.

The following list gives you the probable lethal dose for some of the more common paint and coating solvents if swallowed by a small child (22 pounds/10 kilograms).

Solvent	Probable lethal dose
Acetone (ketones)	May be less than one ounce
Alcohol (denatured alcohol, SD alcohol)	May be one ounce or more
Ethylene dichloride	May be one half ounce or more
Linseed oil (boiled)	May be less than one ounce*
Methanol (wood alcohol)	May be less than one ounce
Petroleum distillates (mineral spirits)	May be less than one ounce*
Toluene	May be less than one teaspoonful
Turpentine	May be less than one ounce
Xylene	May be less than one teaspoonful

* Minute amounts may be fatal if aspirated into the lungs.

What's better, safer, or cheaper: The only truly safe paint solvent is tap water, which is what's used to thin latex paints. You can save pennies by buying solvents in the least fancy containers, but don't try to save money by buying in quantity. Since these things are both flammable and poisonous, you don't want to keep them around any longer than you need to. Buy quantities small enough to use up and discard the container as soon as it is empty.

Sometimes you won't have to buy anything new at all. If you need a solvent for your shellac, for example, you don't have to travel any farther than the medicine cabinet. The rubbing alcohol you use to soothe muscle aches or to disinfect minor cuts is a perfect solvent for shellac, lacquer, and some primer coats.

Paint Stripper

What's in it: Paint strippers are solvents. The basic solvent in flammable paint strippers is benzene. Methylene chloride is the major active ingredient in nonflammable strippers. Both kinds of products also contain extra solvents (acetone, methanol, toluene), plus such thickeners as paraffin wax or ethyl or methyl cellulose. Optional ingredients include petroleum distillates (mineral spirits), detergents (borax), or non-ionic surfactants.

How it works: The solvents simply dissolve paint or varnish finishes so that they can be scraped or wiped away.

What it can do to you: Flammable paint strippers that contain benzene should never be used around an open flame; the vapors as well as the liquids are combustible. Benzene vapors are also narcotic. If inhaled, they can cause mental confusion, convulsions, coma, and death, and may also destroy blood cells and bone marrow. If swallowed, benzene can cause central nervous system depression and coma. With all that, it hardly seems to matter that the other solvents in the mix— acetone, methanol, mineral spirits—are also toxic in their own right. The probable lethal dose of a flammable, benzene paint stripper may be as little as one fifth of a teaspoonful for a small child (22 pounds/ 10 kilograms).

Nonflammable, methylene chloride strippers may be especially dangerous for smokers and heart patients. Inhalation of methylene chloride vapors can increase the amount of carbon dioxide in the blood, causing the heart muscles to work harder to supply oxygenated blood to the body. The vapors may also be narcotic in high concentrations, and the windows should be open when you are using any kind of paint stripper. If swallowed, the probable lethal dose of a nonflammable, methylene chloride stripper for a small child (22 pounds/10 kilograms) may be one seventh of an ounce or more.

Finally, anything that can dissolve paint can do a job on your skin. Wear gloves when using a paint stripper; if some drips on your skin, flush it off immediately with copious amounts of cool water.

What's better, safer, or cheaper: Having tried both chemical strippers and mechanical strippers (sanding machines), I think that the chemicals are quicker and more efficient, so long as you give them the respect they're due. The one that works best as far as I'm concerned is ZIP STRIP (Star Bronze Co.), a nonflammable, methylene chloride product that is measurably faster than any other paint stripper I've tried.

Plastic Coating

> **Safety Rating: IF SWALLOWED, PRODUCTS CONTAINING PETROLEUM DISTILLATES MAY BE EXTREMELY HARMFUL. CALL POISON CONTROL CENTER IMMEDIATELY FOR APPROPRIATE ANTIDOTE PROCEDURE.**

What's in it: Liquid plastic coatings—which are generally better known as "polyurethane" or "urethane" coatings—contain a plastic ingredient (polyurethane), plus mineral compounds, which work as "driers," and a solvent, usually mineral spirits, a petroleum distillate.

How it works: As the solvents evaporate, the plastics harden into water- and chip-resistant gloss or satin coatings. In addition to waterproofing, the coatings penetrate the wood, helping to harden and seal it.

What it can do to you: Plastic coatings contain combustible solvents, whose vapors are also combustible. If inhaled, the vapors can make you become dizzy and disoriented. The liquids are irritating to the skin, and, if swallowed, they are poisonous. Because they contain petroleum distillate solvents, these coatings may cause a potentially lethal form of chemical pneumonia if aspirated into the lungs. The probable lethal oral dose for a small child (22 pounds/10 kilograms) may be one seventh of an ounce or more.

What's better, safer, or cheaper: This is another one of those twentieth-century miracles for which there really is no effective substitute.

In fact, the plastic coatings are the preferred alternative to the old-fashioned varnishes and shellacs, which take forever to dry and are harder to work with.

If I have to choose between the two kinds of coatings, though—the gloss or the satin—I'll pick the satin every time. The gloss shows every single imperfection—the bubbles you couldn't get rid of, the teensy specks of dust from the air that settled into the coating while it was drying. The satin is much more forgiving; small imperfections kind of fit in.

You get the best finish from either kind of coating by applying the liquid, letting it dry, sanding it down, and applying another coat. You can do that ad infinitum, or as long as your patience lasts. The glow and the protection increase with each additional coating and sanding.

Plastic Wood.

See **Wood Filler.**

Prewash Spot and Stain Removers

> **Safety Rating: ALL PREWASH SPOT AND STAIN REMOVERS MAY BE HARMFUL IF SWALLOWED. PRODUCTS CONTAINING PETROLEUM DISTILLATE SOLVENTS MAY BE EXTREMELY HARMFUL. CALL POISON CONTROL CENTER IMMEDIATELY FOR APPROPRIATE ANTIDOTE PROCEDURE.**

What's in it: There are two basic kinds of prewash spot removers, those with either a petroleum distillate solvent (mineral spirits, naphtha) or an alcohol-base solvent (glycol ether) and those without. Nonsolvent products rely on nonionic or anionic surfactants to lift out the grime, plus fragrance, colors, and water.

Solvent-based prewash spot removers:

AMWAY PREWASH (Amway Corp.). Mineral spirits, naphtha. Aerosol.
MAGIC PREWASH (Armour-Dial). Glycol ether. Pump spray.
SHOUT (S. C. Johnson & Son). Petroleum solvents. Aerosol.
SPRAY 'N WASH (Texize). Petroleum solvents. Aerosol.

Surfactant-based prewash spot removers:

GREASE RELIEF (Texize). Pump spray.
MIRACLE WHITE (Beatrice Foods). Pump spray.

How it works: These products aren't general cleaners. They're meant for small stubborn spots, and they work best on greasy stains like food or oil or "ring around the collar." Since they aren't bleaches, they won't do as good a job on fruit or ink or urine stains, all of which respond nicely to chlorine or peroxy bleaches. Apply the remover to the spot, let it sit a while, then wash, using your regular detergent. Any prewash spot remover that works well in hot water will work well in cold water, too.

What it can do to you: Products with petroleum distillate or alcohol solvents are by far the more dangerous. They are poisonous if swallowed; the probable lethal dose for a small child (22 pounds/10 kilograms) may be less than half a teaspoonful. Their vapors are dangerous and can cause headache, nausea, weakness, and lack of coordination if you use them in a room without enough fresh air. Worse yet, the liquids and their vapors are combustible and flammable. Clothes sprayed or spotted with them may become marginally more flammable than normal, too, until they are thoroughly dry after washing and until all the solvent vapors have evaporated.

Prewash spot removers without petroleum distillate or alcohol solvents aren't flammable, but they are still potentially poisonous. The probable lethal dose for a small child (22 pounds/10 kilograms) may be anything from just under a teaspoonful on up.

Of course, both kinds of cleaners can irritate eyes and skin, and some sensitive individuals may have problems wearing clothes that have been treated with these cleaners, even after they've been washed.

What's better, safer, or cheaper: If you prefer to do it yourself, you should know that pouring salt on a greasy food stain as soon as it happens can get rid of a lot of the grease. You have to have a certain devil-may-care attitude to do this, though. Some people feel silly sitting at the table with salt falling off their ties or blouses.

Once the spot has dried, your only real alternative may be the dry cleaner. It's not cheap, but it's safe, since you don't have to handle flammable or poisonous materials. The professionals who do are apt to be better at protecting themselves.

Putty

> **Safety Rating: NONTOXIC AND RARELY HARMFUL IF SWALLOWED. CALL POISON CONTROL CENTER IMMEDIATELY FOR APPROPRIATE ANTIDOTE PROCEDURE.**

What's in it: Plain putty, used to fill cracks in the wall, contains calcium sulfate (plaster of Paris), dextrin (a vegetable gum derived from starch), and silica. Wood putties, used to patch wood surfaces, substitute wood flour for the silica.

How it works: As the moisture from the gum evaporates, the putty hardens. Like spackling compounds or other plasters, putties are more easily leveled when sticky than when dry.

What it can do to you: These are fairly innocuous products that are nontoxic if swallowed, although they can harden into an obstructive mass in your stomach if you swallow enough. Skin irritations are possible but rare.

What's better, safer, or cheaper: Actually, plain putty is the simpler alternative to spackling compound. Wood putty, while it doesn't perform as well as a plasticized wood filler (see in alphabetical products listing), is much safer, because it doesn't contain poisonous solvents.

116

Rat Poison

What's in it: Yellow phosphorus and strychnine, once the most popular rat poisons, have now been banned from sale to consumers in many areas of the United States. The most common rat poisons used in homes today are anticoagulants (hydroxycoumarin compounds such as Warfarin, or indanedione compounds such as Valone) and red squill, a convulsant.

How it works: Rat poisons may be used as fumigants, baits and baited traps, or pastes meant to be injected like caulks into narrow spaces. The specific actions of individual rat poisons are detailed below.

What it can do to you: The following list describes the toxicity and action of several popular rodenticides, as well as two outmoded ones:

• *Hydroxycoumarin compounds,* including *Coumachlor* (also known as *3-[alpha-acetonyl-4-chlorobenzyl]-4-hydroxycoumarin)*; *Coumafuryl,* or *Fumarin; Warfarin* (also known as *3-[alpha-acetonylbenzyl]-4-hydroxycoumarin)*. These are all anticoagulants that cause death by internal hemorrhage. Hydroxycoumarin compounds are often mixed with *sulfaquinoxaline,* or N^1-*(2-quinoxalyl)* sulfanilamide, which inhibits the growth of the intestinal bacteria that produce vitamin K. Vitamin K increases the ability of the blood to clot, so inhibiting its production makes an anticoagulant more powerful. Hydroxycoumarin compounds are rarely toxic in single doses, either for rats or for people, unless the single dose is relatively large.

• *Indanedione compounds,* such as *Diphenadione* (also known as *2-diphenylacetyl-1,3-indanedione)* or *Valone* (also known as

2-isovaleryl-1,3-indanedione). These are similar to hydroxycoumarin compounds in their anticoagulant effect, but they are more toxic. Both may be toxic to humans in single doses.

• *Red squill* is a natural poison, drawn from the inner scales of the bulb of the *Scilla maritima*. Its action is similar to digitalis: It causes violent convulsions. Red squill is also a strong emetic, which means that it causes severe vomiting. As a result, if swallowed by a human being or a household animal such as a dog or cat, red squill will be quickly vomited up. For this reason, it is usually considered unlikely to cause death when ingested by people, dogs, or cats, although the probable lethal dose for a small child (22 pounds/10 kilograms) has been estimated at about one seventh of an ounce. Rats, however, lack the ability to vomit and therefore cannot eliminate the poison from their bodies before it kills them.

• *Strychnine*, which has now been banned as a rat poison in many parts of the country, is one of the most potent poisons known to man. As little as a taste may be lethal for an adult as well as a child. It causes violent convulsions, powerful enough to fracture bones. And what's worse, it isn't even very effective with rats, because they may simply ignore it.

• *Yellow phosphorus* is another violent poison that has been banned in rat poisons by some states and cities. It is caustic and can burn skin and mucous membranes when inhaled. If swallowed it can cause liver damage, kidney failure, central nervous system damage, and shock. It can be absorbed in toxic amounts through the skin and is even more toxic when combined with solvents like alcohol. Finally, the symptoms of phosphorus poisoning may not show up for as long as eight days to two weeks after it is swallowed. As little as a taste may be fatal for adults as well as children.

What's better, safer, or cheaper: Perhaps the single most depressing fact about rats and people is that they are inseparable. Where people go, rats follow. Just about the best we can hope for is to keep us at least a wall apart.

The safest ways to do that are nonchemical. Begin by sealing up holes in the walls and other rodent entrances to your home. You may also want to employ living rat-killers, like the rat terrier, whose worst feature is that he may bring you the rat he's killed, so you can admire it. Ordinary cats can deal quite nicely with mice, but you need a really super cat to make hash of city rats.

Mice and gophers will be repelled by the smell of ordinary naphthalene mothproofers (see in alphabetical products listing), but rats won't be.

If you must use poisons for a short time to get rid of a sudden or virulent infestation, be sure to vary the poisons. After a while, rats (whose generational span can be measured in days) may become immune to whatever you're using.

For maximum safety, consider using a cartridge such as RAT NIP (NIP-CO), which fits into a caulking gun so that you can squirt it through cracks and holes into narrow spaces behind the walls. The cartridge is sealed, and nobody, not even you, has to touch or inhale the rodenticide in order to use it. Out of reach, it is usually out of harm's way. In addition, like all NIP-CO rodenticides, this one relies on red squill, a relatively safe but effective rat killer.

Rug and Carpet Shampoo (Liquid, Aerosol)

Safety Rating: MAY BE HARMFUL IF SWALLOWED. CALL POISON CONTROL CENTER IMMEDIATELY FOR APPROPRIATE ANTIDOTE PROCEDURE.

What's in it: Both liquid and aerosol shampoos contain exactly the same set of ingredients: detergents, surfactants, dyes or fluorescent brighteners, and water. There's more water in the liquids than in the sprays; the aerosols all contain a propellant. Very foamy aerosols contain a plasticizer such as maleic anhydride-styrene copolymer to give you all that nearly solid fluff.

Upholstery cleaners like BISSELL UPHOLSTERY SHAMPOO (Bissell) or WOOLITE UPHOLSTERY CLEANER (Boyle-Midway) are pretty much the same as the rug and carpet shampoos. For all practical purposes, the products are interchangeable, which is why some companies simply advertise one product for both jobs—for example, CARBONA RUG AND UPHOLSTERY SHAMPOO (Carbona) or GLAMORENE SHAMPOO FOR RUGS & UPHOLSTERY (Glamorene).

How it works: These cleaners lift dirt and grime to the surface of the carpet, so that once the shampoo has dried you can simply pick up the ick with your vacuum cleaner.

The liquids, like GLORY (S. C. Johnson & Son) and TURBO (Electrolux), are meant to be diluted with water and poured into one of those automatic carpet cleaners with the two whirling brushes on the bottom. If you haven't got one of those, CARBONA'S SHAMPOOZER (Carbona) lets you do the job by hand. The shampoozer is a plastic squeeze bottle full of already-diluted shampoo. There's a stiff plastic brush on top, so that when you turn the bottle upside down the shampoo flows out through the brush. This means that you can scrub away at the carpet, inch by inch, on your hands and knees. Personally, I think I'd rather have dirty rugs.

As for the aerosols, they come in two versions, one that you simply spray on and then vacuum up when the spray dries, and another that you spray on, sponge in with a damp mop or cloth, and then vacuum up when it dries. If you chose the easier method, you may find you have to do the whole thing twice. The tedious sponge-in technique usually gives better penetration and cleaning power. There is, as we all know, no justice in this world.

Spray/vacuum aerosols:

CARBONA SPRAY FOAM (Carbona)
GLAMORENE SPRAY 'N VAC (Glamorene)
LESTOIL DEODORIZING RUG SHAMPOO (Noxell)

Spray/sponge/vacuum aerosols:

GLORY SPRAY FOAM (S. C. Johnson & Son)
WOOLITE SPRAY FOAM RUG CLEANER (Woolite)

What it can do to you: On the scale of detergent harshness, these solutions are midway between the mildest (dishwashing liquids) and the really tough heavy-duty ones (the disinfectant household cleaners). They may irritate your skin and eyes if you splash them around carelessly, and, if swallowed, they can cause nausea, vomiting, and diarrhea. The probable lethal dose for a small child (22 pounds/10 kilograms) can be as low as one fifth of an ounce.

The aerosol packaging carries its own potential for injury, because the containers can explode if you overheat or accidentally puncture them. When you use any aerosol, you should take a quick look to make sure that the nozzle is pointed away from you before you release a jet of detergent. Elementary, but essential.

What's better, safer, or cheaper: Begin with the basics: Regular vacuuming is the best way to keep your rugs and carpets looking good. Whenever you do the rugs, make it a habit to slip that stubby brush attachment onto the vacuum and go over the furniture, too. You won't believe how many crumbs you can pick up before they get ground into stains, and vacuuming keeps your furniture from developing that gray, dusty look.

How often you haul the vacuum cleaner out of the closet really depends on two things: where you live and whether or not you have a dog. Obviously, you'll have to vacuum more often in a place like New York City than in Tucson, Arizona, and having a dog like mine, who sheds all over everything all the time, makes all other calculations meaningless.

As for shampooing the rugs, carpets, and furniture, the best job is almost always done by a professional, who will be happy to cart your removable rugs off once every year or so and give them a thorough cleaning at his plant. Wall-to-wall carpeting has to be cleaned in your home, so whether you hand the job over to a professional depends on how well you think you can wield an electric shampooer filled with one of the liquid shampoos.

You can't substitute any other general household detergent for rug and carpet shampoo. The formulations aren't the same, and the general cleaners won't come up off the rug the way the shampoos for rugs do.

However, you can do emergency spot removal with cleaners other than the special shampoos. Plain, all-purpose detergent and water, for example, will wipe out most small, common stains. Before you use that or any of the variations listed below, be sure you know what *not* to do. The rug or upholstery you save may be your own.

• *Don't* wait for the stain to dry out before you attack it. The sooner, the better.

• *Don't*, however, attack like the marines going into the South Pacific. Blot gently, so as to avoid grinding the stain into the fabric.

• *Don't* apply any cleaning solution broadside without testing it first in a small, inconspicuous spot. Blot it on, wipe off the excess, then blow dry with your hairdryer. If the patch of rug has not shrunk, and the color hasn't run, go after the stain.

A few pertinent specifics on stain removal:

• *Alcoholic beverages.* Blot gently with a clean cloth. Then rinse off with a solution of detergent and water (prepared as directed

121

on the label). Finally, blot off the detergent with plain, cool water or a solution of water and vinegar.

• *Bloodstains.* Try a teaspoonful of either ammonia or salt in a cup of cold water. Apply, rinse off, and apply again until the spot is gone.

• *Cigarette burns.* If the burn has gone straight through the fabric, forget it. Only reweaving will heal the wound. If you've only singed and discolored a few threads, however, carefully trim off the burned ends and sponge lightly with a little detergent and water. Then rinse off. As a final touch, try sponging gently with a solution of all-purpose peroxy bleach (or plain peroxide) and water.

• *Food stains.* If the food is greasy, scrape off the excess, then sprinkle on some salt or cornstarch to soak up the oil. Blot gently and apply a bit of solvent-based prewash spot and stain remover. For fruit stains, use a solution of detergent and water or ammonia and water.

• *Urine.* Sponge fresh urine stains gently with ammonia and water. Older stains may respond better to vinegar and water.

Rug and Carpet Shampoo (Powder)

> **Safety Rating: HARMFUL IF SWALLOWED. CALL POISON CONTROL CENTER IMMEDIATELY FOR APPROPRIATE ANTIDOTE PROCEDURE.**

What's in it: Dry powder shampoos like BISSELL DRY RUG CLEANER (Bissell) and CARBONA DRY CLEAN RUG POWDER (Carbona) start with an absorbent ingredient such as diatomaceous earth or sawdust. They include some detergents and perhaps a small amount of a petroleum distillate solvent.

How it works: Dry rug and carpet shampoos work pretty much the same way a dry hair shampoo acts on your hair. The absorbents pick up dirt and grease, and you simply brush or vacuum them both out. Like the dry shampoos meant for your head, the dry shampoos for rugs are great in a pinch, but they don't really do as good a job as the liquid or spray types.

What it can do to you: The powders can be irritating to your skin and eyes, and if you breathe in a cloud of them, they can make you sneeze. Because they contain detergents, they can cause nausea, vomiting, and diarrhea if you swallow them. The petroleum solvents that help to remove spots make them more dangerous than simple detergents, though, and the probable lethal dose of dry shampoo for a small child may be as small as one seventh of a teaspoon. And don't forget that if a toddler stuffs a handful of the powder into his mouth, there's always the chance that it can block his airways, causing suffocation.

What's better, safer, or cheaper: On the theory that what works on my hair should work on my rug, I tried the common "natural" dry shampoo—cornstarch—on the carpet. The rug did look cleaner than usual when I vacuumed up the cornstarch, and if you vacuum really thoroughly, going over each part of the rug five or six times, you may be satisfied with the homemade stuff. But it's likely that the commercial cleaner, with its dirt-dissolving detergents and solvents, will still do a better job. Only you can decide how significant the difference is, and your answer may well be that the extra cleaning power isn't worth the extra cost and risk.

Rust Preventive

> **Safety Rating: ALL RUST PREVENTIVES MAY BE HARMFUL IF SWALLOWED. PRODUCTS CONTAINING PETROLEUM DISTILLATES MAY BE EXTREMELY HARMFUL. CALL POISON CONTROL CENTER IMMEDIATELY FOR APPROPRIATE ANTIDOTE PROCEDURE.**

What's in it: There are two basic kinds of rust preventives likely to be found around the home: surface coatings (paints and primers) and oils.

The coatings, such as those sold under the RUST-O-LEUM brand name, are similar to oil-based paints. They contain heat- and light-resistant inorganic pigments such as zinc chromate or zinc oxide, plus inert fillers (magnesium silicate or diatomaceous earth), resins (alkyd resin, polyamide resins), oils, and a petroleum distillate solvent.

The oils, which are used to prevent the formation of rust on small tools or moving parts inside machinery, are simple, ordinary household oils (see in alphabetical products listing) which may or may not be combined with a petroleum distillate solvent, plus silicones for "slipperiness" and resins for extra waterproofing.

How it works: The reddish powder we call rust is really ferric oxide, the end product of a chemical interaction between iron and oxygen. Moisture can cause rust to form more quickly, but it's the oxygen, not the water, that starts the ball rolling.

To keep ferric oxide from forming on metal surfaces, you just have to keep air, which contains oxygen, away from the metal with the iron in it. That's exactly what rust-preventing coatings and oils do.

What it can do to you: Anything that can go wrong when you use an oil-based paint can go wrong when you use a rust-preventive coating. First, the liquid is flammable. Its vapors are irritating to eyes and throat. The coatings are also irritating to your skin, and if you swallow them they may be lethal. The probable lethal dose for a small child (22 pounds/10 kilograms) may be as small as one seventh of an ounce. But the major danger with these coatings, as with any product containing a petroleum distillate solvent, is that even a drop or two may cause a potentially fatal form of chemical pneumonia if aspirated into the lungs.

You have to read each individual label to check the toxicity of rust-preventing oils. Obviously, those containing petroleum distillate solvents are potentially the most toxic.

What's better, safer, or cheaper: You don't have to buy a special kind of paint to rust-proof metal furniture; any good oil-based paint will do the job. Be absolutely certain, though, that before you paint you scrape off every last speck of rust. Even the tiniest smidgen left under the paint will continue to spread until, one morning, you'll wake up to find it's eaten a hole right through the metal.

Ordinary mineral oil is as good as any special product for keeping your small tools safe from rust. Wipe the tools down after each use, leaving a slight skim of oil on the surface. The emphasis there is on the *slight*, of course; you don't want to put so much on that a pool of oil forms at the bottom of the toolbox. And, never use a food oil, like peanut, soybean, or safflower oil. It may rot on the tools and smell horrendous.

Rust Remover

> **Safety Rating: IF SWALLOWED, THIS PRODUCT PRESENTS A MEDICAL EMERGENCY REQUIRING *IMMEDIATE* MEDICAL ATTENTION.**

What's in it: The chemicals that give rust removers their almost magical ability to wipe away ugly rust are corrosive mineral acids: phosphoric acid, which is found in BALKAMP NAVAL JELLY (Balkamp), RUSTICIDE (Rusticide), RUST JELLY (Sheffield Bronze Paint), and RUST NIP (NIP-CO); hydrochloric acid, which does the job in RUST-GO (Holcomb); or oxalic acid, found in ZUD (Boyle-Midway). Also in the mix: petroleum distillate solvents or water, plus surfactants.

How it works: The acids simply dislodge rust so that you can wipe it away.

What it can do to you: Mineral acids are extremely corrosive. They can burn your skin and eyes, and, if swallowed, they can literally burn holes in your mouth, throat, or stomach. Internal injuries that seem minor at the start sometimes develop strictures (that is, scar formations) that may block off throat or stomach passageways. Strictures may form days or even weeks after the original injury occurs.

There is no way to measure a probable lethal dose of these acids. The damage they do if swallowed, spilled, or splashed depends entirely upon how concentrated they are.

What's better, safer, or cheaper: You can get rust off safely and cheaply with fine sandpaper or steel wool (just watch out for splinters in your thumb). Unfortunately, this safe, cheap way is also the hard and tedious one, and most people eagerly relinquish the safety of the mechanical removers for the convenience of the chemical ones. If that's your choice, be sure to cover all bases by stashing the rust remover away in the same safe place you store the drain cleaner and the toilet bowl cleaner. When using rust removers, wear protective gloves. For "stitch in nine"-type protection, see Rust Preventive in the alphabetical products listing.

Scouring Pad

> **Safety Rating: THE CLEANER ON SOAP-SATURATED PADS MAY BE HARMFUL IF SWALLOWED. CALL POISON CONTROL CENTER IMMEDIATELY FOR APPROPRIATE ANTIDOTE PROCEDURE.**

What's in it: There are at least seven different kinds of scouring pads. Listed in descending order of abrasiveness, the most abrasive first, they are:

1. Abrasive pads, alone or bonded to synthetic sponges. The pads get their gritty quality from fine particles of silica or other non-metal abrasives. Example: RESCUE II (3M).

2. Plain steel-wool pads, like SUPREME (Purex).

3. Steel-wool pads with cleaner added. Examples: BRILLO (Purex) and S.O.S. (Miles Laboratories). The cleaner in the pad is a mixture of soap powder, surfactants, dye, rust inhibitors, anticaking agents, fragrance, and some water to bind them all together.

4. Abrasive cloths, like GOLDEN FLEECE (General Cable Corp.), with abrasive particles or fibers in the cloth.

5. Plain metal coils and balls, like CHORE BOY COPPER and CHORE BOY STAINLESS STEEL (General Cable Corp.)

None of these heavy-duty scouring pads should be used on glass, plastic, porcelain, or nonstick surfaces. For those, choose from:

6. Reinforced sponges, which are sponges covered with a plastic mesh or sponges with a mildly abrasive surface, like the one on SCOTCH-BRITE COOKWARE SCRUB'N SPONGE (3M).

7. Plain plastic mesh pads like TUFFY (Miles Laboratories).

How they work: Sometimes scouring pads work even more efficiently than you think they will, which is another way of saying that you have to be careful which one you pick for the job. Metal or steel-wool pads, which work best on rust stains, have a deservedly rough reputation, but some of the synthetic abrasive pads, like RESCUE II, can be even tougher. Perhaps the best way to protect your pots and pans, not to mention your counters, cabinets, and kitchen sink, is to do as the label on SCOTCH-BRITE SCRUB'N SPONGE (a synthetic sponge that is much too abrasive for Teflon pans) suggests: "Test first with light pressure to determine whether any surface may scratch."

That's not to say that scratching is always bad. Actually, a good hard scrubbing with a steel-wool pad can sometimes make brushed aluminum or stainless steel surfaces look shiny and terrific. And, while a light-duty pad may work well on nonstick surfaces and porcelain basins and sinks, you will almost certainly need the heavy hitters to get at baked-on food and dirt.

What it can do to you: If you are allergic to one perfume or another in one of the soap-filled pads, try switching brands. Soap or detergent-saturated pads may be harmful if swallowed, causing nausea, vomiting, and gastric upset, but the problems with scouring pads are more likely to be mechanical ones, like steel-wool splinters in your hand. If swallowed, any of the pads may block the throat and cause suffocation, just as any other foreign body might, and steel-wool pads could leave splinters.

What's better, safer, or cheaper: The truth of it is that if you clean things up as you use them, you will probably never have to spend a cent on scouring pads. Don't let crusted food dry on pot surfaces. Add water right away and let the pot soak. The food absorbs the moisture, swells, and floats away from the side of the pan. For really stubborn crusting, fill the pot with cool water, add about a cup of salt, and let the solution sit for a couple of hours or maybe even overnight. Then turn on the burner under the pot and let the saltwater heat until boiling. That should loosen even the worst burned-on food. Sometimes you'll be able just to pour it out or wipe it off. If not, then it's time for the scouring pad.

At that point, it's to your advantage to know that the least economical, least versatile, and even least sanitary of the scouring pads are the soap-filled steel-wool ones, like BRILLO or S.O.S. They rust as soon as you rinse out the soap (which contains the rust inhibitors), and they never do rinse clean once you've used them on anything covered with food. The same goes for plain steel wool.

Other pads won't rust, but some of them—the reinforced sponges, the abrasive pads bonded to sponges, and the abrasive cloths—are also hard to get clean.

The safest, cleanest, and most economical products are the plastic mesh pads like TUFFY. They are gentle enough to be used on Teflon or other nonstick surfaces, although continued use may eventually wear down the finish, and a plain sponge is even safer. You can make mesh pads more abrasive by adding some scouring powder, but don't waste time and money dousing them with liquid detergent. The liquid falls right through, and that's not economical at all. Maybe the best bet is to scrub with a plastic mesh pad and hot water, swish the dish or pot through soapy water, then give it a final rinse. Or any variation thereof.

Scouring Powder

> **Safety Rating: MAY BE HARMFUL IF SWALLOWED. CALL POISON CONTROL CENTER IMMEDIATELY FOR APPROPRIATE ANTIDOTE PROCEDURE.**

What's in it: The basic ingredient in any scouring powder is the abrasive (silica, volcanic ash, or feldspar), combined with a filler (clay) and a cleaner (soap or detergent). This mixture of dry ingredients makes up as much as 90 percent of the product. Modern scouring powders usually include a bleach (up to 0.5 percent of the product), plus a phosphate builder (up to 25 percent) to increase the cleaning action of the detergent.

Until we get full-disclosure ingredient labeling, you probably won't find all these ingredients listed on the label, but you will always know when there is a bleach inside the can. You may find it listed as "chlorine bleach" or as some consumer-oriented euphemism such as COMET's "Chlorinol-G" (actually sodium dichloro-*s*-triazinetrone sulfonate, sometimes known as trichloroisocyanuric acid).

Liquid scouring cleaners, such as SOFT SCRUB (Clorox), contain all the above-mentioned ingredients, plus water.

Scouring powders with chlorine bleach and phosphate builders:

AJAX (Colgate-Palmolive)
COMET WITH CHLORINOL-G (Procter & Gamble)

Scouring powders with chlorine bleach but no phosphate builders:

ACME (Acme Products)
A & P (A & P)
OLD DUTCH CLEANSER (Purex)
WHITE ROSE CLEANSER (White Rose)

Scouring powders without bleaches or phosphate builders:

BON AMI CLEANING POWDER (Faultless Starch Co.)
BON AMI POLISHING CLEANSER (Faultless Starch Co.)

How it works: Scouring powders work just the way their name implies they do, by scouring or abrading the surface on which they are used. Unfortunately, in doing that they can take off the top layer of the finish as well as the dirt. After a while, the scratches left by the scouring powder can create little pits and crevices into which dirt nestles as comfortably as the proverbial bug in the rug. When that happens, the only thing that can get the dirt out again is the scouring powder, which reaches down into the tiny scratches to rub the dirt, and makes more scratches, which require more scouring powder. In other words, by using the stuff in the first place, you make it necessary to use more later on. A manufacturer's dream!

But it can be a nightmare for you, because scratched surfaces not only wear out sooner (some experts estimate that scouring powders can shorten a tub's or basin's life by as much as ten or fifteen years), but they are hard to clean and unsanitary to boot. If your appliances and basins are already scratched, you may have to grin and bear it. But you can avoid more of the same by never using an abrasive scouring powder on new tubs or basins, plastic or Formica counters and cabinets, enamel appliances, or enameled or glass pots and pans.

And that holds no matter what the label says. AJAX, for example, has a label that tells you to use the cleanser with "caution" when you apply it to plastic surfaces. My experience, though, is that it will scratch no matter how cautious you are. As for BON AMI's claim that its cleanser, like the chick on the package, "hasn't scratched yet," well, there's some slight justification for saying that. Unlike most scouring powders, which are based on silica, or fine sand, BON AMI is based on feldspar. The particles are smaller and smoother than those of silica, so BON AMI cleansers are somewhat less abrasive, but they still should not be used on glass or plastic.

One special product deserves special mention. SOFT SCRUB is a creamy liquid in a plastic squeeze bottle. It looks something like hand cream and has a psychological advantage in that it just seems likely to be less abrasive than the scouring powders. In fact, when it was introduced a few years ago, it was touted as a totally nonabrasive scouring powder. Eventually, though, both consumers and consumer groups discovered that it left the same old scratches on the same old surfaces. As a result, in February 1979, the Federal Trade Commission announced that Clorox had agreed to add label copy warning that SOFT SCRUB might mar enamel or plastic surfaces. *Caveat emptor.*

What can go wrong: All scouring powders can cause bloating, nausea, vomiting, and diarrhea if swallowed, but simple scouring powders, without phosphate builders or bleaches, are rarely truly dangerous. Products containing sodium perborate (a nonchlorine bleach) can cause symptoms of borate poisoning if swallowed: eye damage, gastritis, and central nervous system disturbances. Powders with chlorine bleaches may in rare cases be corrosive if swallowed, but the amount of the damage depends not just on how much powder is taken in but also on the concentration of the bleach. The same rule applies to other potentially corrosive substances such as soda ash and sodium carbonate.

All scouring powders can be irritating to the skin and, if inhaled, to the respiratory tract. If combined with ammonia, scouring powders made with chlorine bleach can release chloramines, gases that are irritating to the eyes and respiratory tract, and can be lethal if inhaled in high concentrations.

What's better, safer, or cheaper: Is there a better or more economical way to clean the basins, tubs, tile, and counters?

Sure.

Plain old SPIC AND SPAN, SOILAX, or any other heavy-duty laundry detergent or detergent powder can be used to clean these surfaces without scratching. Mix them with water and apply with a plastic mesh sponge meant for cleaning Teflon pots and pans. That way you'll get cleaning power plus friction without abrasion. For really tough basin stains, you can use a plain liquid or powder bleach. Pour it on (if liquid) or make a paste (if powder). Leave it in place for a while, then remove. Once again, never mix your bleach with ammonia; the chemical reaction can be dangerous.

You can whip up your own scouring cleansers with whiting, an abrasive chalk powder often found in paint and/or hardware stores. Mix nine parts whiting with one part soap or detergent powder, and use as you would a scouring powder. The result may or may not be less abrasive than the cleanser you used to use, but it will probably be cheaper, and you can control what goes into it. The simpler the soap powder you use, the simpler and safer the product will be.

One final money-saving note: All scouring powders will cake in the can if they get wet, and once that happens, they won't be worth the cans they come in. You can save money by keeping your powder dry. The best way is to store them in dry, cool places, and that rules out the space under the sink or in the bathroom—which is too bad because that's exactly where you need the cleanser—close at hand. Compromise by putting your cleanser into a sealed glass jar or by sealing the container the powder comes in with one of those plastic caps made for soft drink cans. It's not foolproof, but it will help.

Shellac

Safety Rating: HARMFUL IF SWALLOWED. CALL POISON CONTROL CENTER IMMEDIATELY FOR APPROPRIATE ANTIDOTE PROCEDURE.

What's in it: Shellac (the ingredient) is a resinous substance excreted by an insect that lives on the kusum tree in India. Shellac (the wood finish) is a solution of this resin, a whitish powder, in methanol (wood alcohol). Occasionally a coloring agent (an arsenic compound) may be added to darken the shellac.

How it works: As the solvent evaporates, the resin hardens to a shiny finish.

What it can do to you: The shellac resin is fairly innocuous, but methanol is poisonous, whether swallowed or absorbed through the skin. It can cause weakness, muscle cramps, convulsions, blindness, and coma.

If the shellac contains arsenic compounds, they, too, are poisonous. The probable lethal dose of shellac for a small child can be as small as one fifth of a teaspoonful.

In addition, the shellac solution is flammable and can be irritating to your skin.

What's better, safer, or cheaper: For all practical purposes, shellac and varnish (see Varnish in alphabetical products listing) are interchangeable on wood surfaces. They are almost equally toxic. Polyurethane or polyhydric alcohol plastic coatings (see Plastic Coating in alphabetical products listing) dry faster and are easier to work with.

Silver Polish

Safety Rating: MAY BE HARMFUL IF SWALLOWED. CALL POISON CONTROL CENTER IMMEDIATELY FOR APPROPRIATE ANTIDOTE PROCEDURE. PRODUCTS CONTAINING AN ACID ARE MORE HARMFUL THAN THE ABRASIVE POLISHES.

What's in it: There are three basic types of silver cleaners: those that simply wipe off dirt and tarnish; those that both clean and polish; and those that clean, polish, and also add a shield against fast retarnishing.

The simple cleaners (either dip-in/wipe-off or wipe-on/wipe-off liquids) are generally mixtures of an acid (commonly sulfuric acid), thiourea (an ammonia derivative), a surfactant, fragrance, and enough water to make them workable.

Examples of simple cleaners:

AFTA SILVER DIP (Afta Corp.)
E-Z-EST SILVERDIP (E-Z-Est)
GODDARD'S SILVER DIP (S. C. Johnson & Son)
INSTANT-DIP (Lewal Industries)
QUIK-DIP (Boyle-Midway)
TARN-X (Jelmar Co.)

Polishing cleaners clean with ammonia compounds and polish with mild abrasives (diatomaceous earth). These cleaners also contain solvents and perfumes.

Examples of polishing cleaners:

GORHAM SILVER POLISH (Gorham)

HAGERTY SILVER FOAM (Hagerty & Sons)

INTERNATIONAL SILVER POLISH (International Silver)

SILVO (R. T. French)

WRIGHT'S SILVER CREAM (J. A. Wright & Co.)

Antitarnish cleaners contain all the ingredients found in polishing cleaners. They also contain an antitarnish ingredient, either an antioxidant like polyethylene glycol or a wax.

Examples of antitarnish cleaners:

AMWAY ANTI-TARNISH (Amway Corp.)

E-Z-EST TARNISH PREVENTIVE (E-Z-Est)

GODDARD'S LONG TERM SILVER FOAM and LONG TERM SILVER POLISH (S. C. Johnson & Son)

HAGERTY SILVERSMITHS' POLISH and SILVERSMITHS' WASH (Hagerty & Sons)

TARNI-SHIELD (3M)

TWINKLE (Drackett)

WRIGHT'S ANTI-TARNISH SILVER CREAM (J. A. Wright & Co.)

How it works: The good news about the dip cleaners is that they are particularly good on heavily tarnished, intricately patterned flatware, the kind you'd otherwise have to scrub with a toothbrush. The bad news is that the same chemicals that make these cleaners so effective also make them offensive. They smell terrible. Their fumes are acrid. They're hard on your hands, and they're absolute hell on the stainless steel used as blades on so many sterling silver or silver-plated knives. And they don't polish at all. Instead, they leave a dull film that you'll have to polish off afterward.

Polishing cleaners are a lot more congenial. The abrasive/ammonia mixture is less acrid than the acid dips, and the products do exactly what they're supposed to: clean and shine. Naturally, you'll want to buff your silver with a soft clean cloth to bring out the best glow.

Polishing cleaners with antitarnish ingredients really do what they're meant to do, although some work better than others. Which one works best is a matter of opinion. Goddard and Hagerty products score well in *Consumer Reports* and *Consumers' Research Magazine* ratings, but not necessarily in the same order in both places.

Don't forget to consider the type of finish on your silver when you choose a cleaner. All cleaners work well on bright-finish pieces, but certain cleaners may remove some of the finish on antiqued silver and may be too efficient for satin-finish pieces, making them too shiny. Test the polish on a small, inconspicuous area before applying it to the whole piece. You will probably find that the nonpolishing dips do the best job on satin-finish pieces, since they won't make them too shiny. But the acids may chew their way right through the antique finishes, leaving shiny spots.

What it can do to you: Although the acid-based dips are the worst offenders, all silver polishes can irritate your skin. You should always wear rubber gloves when using them and always be careful about splashing them near your face and eyes.

The fumes of the acid-based cleaners are very irritating if you inhale them, and they can cause severe headaches. That's why neither these nor any other silver cleaners (or metal cleaners in general) should be used in a room without proper ventilation. In addition, since the vapors of some polishes are flammable (even though it doesn't say so on the label), never use any polish near an open flame.

If swallowed, all silver polishes can cause gastric upset, ranging from mild to severe. Cleaners with acid in them can burn the lining of the mouth, throat, and stomach; in really high concentrations, these burns may go right through internal tissues. The precise toxicity of acid-based cleaners depends on the concentration of the acid and how much cleaner is swallowed; the probable lethal dose of nonacid cleaner for a small child (22 pounds/10 kilograms) may be as little as one fifth of a teaspoonful.

What's better, safer, or cheaper: There really is no correlation between price and type. Some brands, like Goddard or Hagerty, always seem to be more expensive than other brands, like Gorham or International. If you like to experiment, you can make your own silver polish from whiting, a fine abrasive stocked by hardware stores. Dust some on a cloth that has been dampened with a solution of water plus a teaspoonful of alcohol or ammonia. Test carefully to be certain that this polish isn't too abrasive for your silver. In the long run, Grandma's flatware or your mother-in-law's silver serving plate may deserve the commercial polish.

If you don't like chemicals at all, you can clean your silver electrolytically. Electrolytic cleaning relies on a chemical reaction among aluminum, salt, and baking soda to jar the tarnish loose from your silver. Take an aluminum pan (or put a sheet of aluminum foil in the bottom of an enameled pan), add an inch or two or three of water, pour in a teaspoonful of salt and one of baking soda, and bring to a boil. Then, carefully slip in your silverware and let it boil for two or three minutes (be sure there's enough water to cover the silver). Remove the silver, wash it in warm soapsuds, rinse, dry, and buff. The silver will be clean and shiny; the tarnish will be lying on the bottom of the pan. *Caution:* Never try this on flatware with hollow handles. The hot water can dissolve the glue that holds the handles in place.

To prevent tarnish in the first place, keep your silverware in special gray or blue felt bags. The cloth is impregnated with an antitarnish ingredient that keeps it from getting dull. Or, you can wrap the silverware in plastic wrap. Just be sure you don't use rubber bands to secure the plastic, since rubber corrodes silver, even through the plastic.

Silver-Polishing Cloth

> **Safety Rating: THE POLISHES ON THESE CLOTHS MAY BE HARMFUL IF SWALLOWED. CALL POISON CONTROL CENTER IMMEDIATELY FOR APPROPRIATE ANTIDOTE PROCEDURE.**

What's in it: Polishing cloths are nonwoven fabrics saturated with a wet or dry silver polish (see Silver Polish in alphabetical products listing). Dry-polish cloths include GODDARD'S LONG SHINE SILVER CLOTH (Goddard & Sons) and HAGERTY'S SILVERSMITHS' GLOVES (Hagerty & Sons). GORHAM SILVERSMITH ANTI-TARNISH POLISH SATURATED CLOTHS (Gorham) are wet-polish cloths in foil packets.

How it works: All the cloths loosen and remove tarnish. To polish, you have to buff with a second, clean cloth. If your silver is really tarnished or grimy, none of these polishers will do as good a job as regular silver polish, but they may work as well for light touch-ups.

What it can do to you: If you're sensitive to any of the ingredients in the polish, the cloth may be irritating to your skin. The vapors may be irritating if you breathe them in or if you get them in your eyes, and, if swallowed, the polish can cause gastric upset.

What's better, safer, or cheaper: The polishing cloths are handy, but they're a lot less economical than the regular polishes. For alternatives, see Silver Polish in the alphabetical products listing.

Sizing.

See **Laundry Starch (Aerosol).**

Soap (Cold-Water).

See **Cold-Water Soap.**

Soap Flakes/Powder

> **Safety Rating: RARELY HARMFUL, EVEN IF SWALLOWED. CALL POISON CONTROL CENTER IMMEDIATELY FOR APPROPRIATE ANTIDOTE PROCEDURE.**

What's in it: Basic soap products such as IVORY SNOW or IVORY FLAKES (both Procter & Gamble) are made of soap, plus fabric whiteners and fragrance. The particles may also contain glycerin to keep them from drying out.

How it works: Detergents dissolve in cold water, but soaps require hot or at least very warm water to melt them down so that they can begin to lift the dirt off your laundry. In places where the water is very hard, you'll have to add a softener to the wash water to avoid a very definite soap-scum buildup on your clothes and linens.

What it can do to you: The disadvantage of soap powders and flakes is that they don't contain many of the bleaches or softeners that are

136

standard in detergents, which means they may not clean as well. The advantage is that without all the extras, soap products are a lot less dangerous than detergents. In fact, they are practically nontoxic. If you swallow one, it may cause vomiting or minor gastric upset, perhaps some bloating, but serious side effects are so rare as to be virtually nonexistent.

Soap powders and flakes will sting if you get them in your eyes and, like other powders, they can be irritating if you inhale them. Some people may find one perfume or another annoying, and often people who end up itchy and scratching when they wear clothes washed in detergents may find some relief by switching to a plain soap powder. *Note:* These powders should never be used as bubble baths, since the whiteners and perfumes don't really belong all over your body.

What's better, safer, or cheaper: Just about the only way to get your soap powder cheaper is to save the slivers of used bath soap you'd ordinarily throw out. The saving there comes not because the bath soap is, ounce for ounce, cheaper than the laundry product but because you're making use of something you'd otherwise waste. Be warned, though, that the formula isn't exactly the same. The bath bar (both soap and detergent) may leave a bit more coating on your clothes than you like. If you use this kind of cleaner, be double-sure to rinse with hot water so as to get rid of the residue.

Spackling Compound

Safety Rating: MAY BE HARMFUL IF SWALLOWED. CALL POISON CONTROL CENTER IMMEDIATELY FOR APPROPRIATE ANTIDOTE PROCEDURE.

What's in it: Spackling compounds are essentially bouncy or stretchable plasters. Premixed spacklers like DAP VINYL PASTE SPACKLING COMPOUND (DAP), SPACKLE (Muralo), or UGL 222 SPACKLING PASTE (United Gilsonite) start with calcium carbonate or calcium sulfate (plaster of Paris), plus polyvinyl plastic for elasticity, an acetate resin emulsion for strength, and water. Mica and glue may also be included. Powder spackling products such as SAVOGRAN SPACKLING COMPOUND (Savogran) or UGL CERFEX SPACKLING COMPOUND (United Gilsonite) have everything but water, which you add when you're ready to use the product.

How it works: As the moisture evaporates, the spackling compound hardens, to fill in imperfections in your walls and provide a surface that is immediately ready for painting. If you've done a good job of repairing gouges, holes, or cracks—which means leveling the spackle patches with a paint scraper as you go—you'll have a nice smooth surface. You *can* sand down imperfections once the paste has dried, but it's hard and boring work; much better to level while the spackle is still damp.

What it can do to you: Once upon a time, there were likely to be asbestos fibers in your spackling compound, but in 1979, the Consumer Product Safety Commission banned the manufacture and sale of spacklers containing asbestos. When sanding old surfaces that may have been repaired with spackling compounds or other puttylike products containing asbestos, it is best to avoid breathing in the dust raised by the sanding. You might even want to wear a mask over your mouth and nose to cut down your possible exposure to floating asbestos fibers. Today's spackling powders may be irritating if you inhale them, but neither they nor the pastes are likely sources of asbestos fibers.

If swallowed, both powders and pastes are virtually nonpoisonous. They're not entirely harmless, however. Like all products containing lots of calcium carbonate or calcium sulfate, spackling compound can harden into an obstructive mass in your stomach if swallowed in sufficient quantity. And if you're sensitive to plastics, they may be irritating to your skin.

What's better, safer, or cheaper: Although each type of spackling compound has its partisans, there's really very little difference in performance between pastes and powders. Resistance to cracking or shrinking, for example, varies among individual products, not by product type.

When it comes to saving pennies, though, the powders may come out ahead, mainly because they can't dry out between uses. You mix them as required, adding powder to water until you get a smooth, thick, but not stiff, paste. It will be workable for about an hour after you mix it, so you've got to be prepared to get cracking right away.

If you prefer paste, you can cut down on waste by keeping the container tightly closed when it is not in use, so the compound doesn't dry out and become useless.

Spot Remover

> **Safety Rating: ALL SPOT REMOVERS MAY BE HARMFUL IF SWALLOWED. PRODUCTS CONTAINING PETROLEUM DISTILLATES MAY BE EXTREMELY HARMFUL. CALL POISON CONTROL CENTER IMMEDIATELY FOR APPROPRIATE ANTIDOTE PROCEDURE.**

What's in it: Whether liquid, paste, or aerosol, all spot removers contain essentially the same ingredients: chlorinated hydrocarbons (like perchloroethylene or tetrachloroethylene) or petroleum distillate solvents (commonly naphtha) or a combination of the two. CARBONA CLEANING FLUID (Carbona), for example, is a combination product, while ENERGINE SPOT REMOVER (d-Con) is 100 percent naphtha. An aerosol, like K2R AEROSOL SPOT LIFTER (Texize), is solvent plus propellant.

How it works: Commercial spot removers do their best work on grease stains, which the solvents dissolve and lift up to the surface of the material. They do too effective a job on some fabrics—like rubber, leather, suede, and plastics—dissolving the fabric along with the spot. And they are probably overkill for a lot of simple stains, like blood and liquor, which will come out if you rinse them right away with plain soap and water.

What it can do to you: The petroleum solvents used in these products are flammable. Their vapors are flammable, too, and clothes to which they are applied may burn more quickly afterward.

If your spot cleaner has the word "nonflammable" on the label, the solvent inside is usually a dry-cleaning fluid, perchloroethylene or tetrachloroethylene. These solvents won't burn, but their vapors can make you drowsy if inhaled in high concentrations. Always keep

139

a window open while you're working with a spot remover, and wear gloves. Solvents work by dissolving grease and fat, and they may be very irritating to your skin if you spill them by mistake.

All spot removers are potentially deadly. They are poisonous if swallowed, and the probable lethal dose for a small child (22 pounds/ 10 kilograms) is less than a teaspoonful. As with other products containing petroleum distillates, the possibility of chemical pneumonia exists if someone who has swallowed the spot remover is forced to vomit it up. While the remover is coming up from the stomach, it may be aspirated, or drawn into the lungs. The resulting pneumonia can be fatal.

What's better, safer, or cheaper: As you have no doubt surmised, simple, homemade cleaners are much safer. In some cases, they may even work better. For example, try the following:

> • *Bleaches.* Ordinary peroxide or chlorine bleach can be applied as needed to small, nongrease spots. Test on a small, hidden patch of fabric first to be certain that the surrounding colors/dyes won't run. The bleaches work best on white or cream-colored fabrics, of synthetic as well as "natural" fibers. However, follow label directions for best results. Never use any bleach on a fabric for which it is not intended.
>
> • *Cornstarch, cornmeal, or white talcum powder.* These adsorbent powders "soak up" grease spots if you apply them quickly enough. Shake right from the box, or make a thick paste (with water), smear on, let dry, and scrape or shake off. Reapply as necessary.
>
> • *Acetone or acetone-based nail-polish remover.* (Check the label to be certain that your nail-polish remover is acetone, not amyl acetate.) Softens and removes gums like chewing gum or the sticky stuff from adhesive tapes. Never use on plastics, synthetics, or varnished furniture; it will take the fabric or finish off along with the spot.
>
> • *Petroleum jelly or vaseline.* A first step in removing crusted spots or stains like paint, tar, or lipstick. Softens and loosens the stain so that you can lift it off.
>
> • *Salt.* Another adsorbent that works on grease stains. Particularly useful for pouring from the shaker onto a tie that's just fallen into the gravy.

- *Water.* With soap. Probably the simplest way to remove your basic blood, alcohol, and other nongrease stains if you use it immediately, before they "set." Splash water on the stain, or swish the fabric around in soapsuds. Naturally, you use this only on washable fabrics.
- *White vinegar.* Works on "acid" stains, like fruit juice and urine.

Obviously, these are all first aid treatments meant to get rid of an occasional spot in a hurry. Alas, they may also leave your clothes feeling and smelling funny and, sometimes, even with the best attention in the world, they won't really get rid of the spot. It is always worth your while to consider the services of a professional dry cleaner for really good clothes.

Whether you use a cleaner who gives individual attention to each garment or one of the less expensive coin-operated machine dry cleaners is up to you. When you are cleaning blankets, for example, there's really no point in spending a bundle; the coin-operated places will do just as well. But you might not trust them with your favorite beaded dress, or with chiffons. This is a choice you will have to make almost on a garment by garment basis.

Stainless Steel Cleaner

> **Safety Rating: MAY BE HARMFUL IF SWALLOWED. CALL POISON CONTROL CENTER FOR APPROPRIATE ANTIDOTE PROCEDURE.**

What's in it: Like all other metal polishes, stainless steel cleaners contain diluted sulfamic, citric, or tartaric acid; sodium chloride to increase the product's bulk; a surfactant to help lift dirt off, a corrosion inhibitor (borax), and some fine abrasive for polishing. An example: GODDARD'S STAINLESS STEEL CARE (S. C. Johnson & Son).

How it works: All metal cleaners dissolve or lift off dirt. Some also polish the surface of the metal through abrasion. Stainless steel requires less care than most metals. It doesn't stain or tarnish, and it won't rust either.

What it can do to you: These cleaners can irritate your skin and eyes, and they are slightly toxic if swallowed. The probable lethal dose for a small child (22 pounds/10 kilograms) is two ounces or more.

What's better, safer, or cheaper: You don't have to spend a lot of money to keep stainless steel looking great, but you do have to give it some time.

Wash it in warm, soapy water. Adding a tablespoonful of ammonia to the wash water helps shine up the metal. Always dry stainless steel as soon as you take it out of the sink, otherwise it will water-spot and get dull. Polish with a soft cloth. Never use any scratchy or abrasive cleaners, although you may want to try polishing with feldspar, the very fine abrasive found in BON AMI CLEANING POWDER and BON AMI POLISHING CLEANSER. Try this on a very small spot first. It probably won't make any marks on brushed stainless steel, but you should be very cautious on smooth- or mirror-finish pieces.

When it comes to storing, treat your stainless steel cutlery with tender loving care. Keep it in a drawer with individual slots for forks, knives, and so on. That way it won't bang against itself and get scratched. Naturally, you'll want to avoid letting it lie around in the sink, since it may bang up against dishes and utensils.

If you must use a commercial polish, it may make more sense economically to use an all-purpose metal polish like NOXON. Try this on a small part of one piece to be certain that it isn't too scratchy; although all-purpose polishes are supposed to work on stainless steel, they may contain a cleaner that is more abrasive or gritty than you want. The finish on the steel and your tolerance for tiny marks really have a lot to do with which kind of cleaner you think does the job best.

Steam-Iron Cleaner

> **Safety Rating: MAY BE HARMFUL IF SWALLOWED. CALL POISON CONTROL CENTER IMMEDIATELY FOR APPROPRIATE ANTIDOTE PROCEDURE.**

What's in it: Pour-in cleaners like SUNBEAM STEAM IRON CLEANER (Sunbeam Appliance Co.) contain alkalis, detergents, and such optionals as dyes and/or fragrances.

How it works: The alkaline cleaners soften and remove mineral deposits left when hard water is used to create steam.

What it can do to you: Like all alkaline cleaners, these can be irritating to your skin and can cause caustic burns if they splash in your eyes or if you swallow them. How serious the burns are depends on how much alkali is in the cleaner and how concentrated it is. In general, less than an ounce of the cleaners may be lethal if swallowed by a small (22 pounds/10 kilograms) child.

What's better, safer, or cheaper: The easiest way to save money on steam-iron cleaners is to eliminate the need to use them. Do that by using only distilled water in your iron. If you have to use tap water, be sure to press down on the steam button several times after you've turned the iron off, so as to expel as much water as possible from the iron. Never let the iron sit around with water in it once you've finished ironing.

Teflon Cleaner

Safety Rating: MAY BE HARMFUL IF SWALLOWED. CALL POISON CONTROL CENTER IMMEDIATELY FOR APPROPRIATE ANTIDOTE PROCEDURE.

What's in it: "Teflon" is DuPont's trade name for a kind of plastic used to coat pots and pans. Powders used to clean this sort of plastic-coated surface usually contain an alkali (sodium metasilicate), a bleach (sodium perborate), and detergents.

How it works: The alkali is gently abrasive, just enough to remove foods without scratching the plastic surface underneath. The bleach is most useful for removing stains from light-color plastic coatings.

What it can do to you: Sodium metasilicate is corrosive. If swallowed, it may burn the inside of your mouth, your esophagus, and your stomach lining. How strong it is depends on how concentrated it is. The probable lethal dose of Teflon cleaner for a small child (22 pounds/10 kilograms) may be as low as one fifth of an ounce.

The detergents themselves can cause nausea, vomiting, and diarrhea if swallowed. If vomiting occurs, the burns administered by the sodium metasilicate may be more severe.

Naturally, these powders may also be irritating to skin and eyes, and it's really a good idea to wear protective gloves when using them.

What's better, safer, or cheaper: Is anyone at all surprised to hear that you can get plastic-coated pots and pans clean without any detergent product at all? Of course not. Use one of those plastic-net pads or sponges meant for coated surfaces, and scrub away under very hot water. That does the job without any of the expensive liquids or powders.

Toilet Bowl Cleaner (In-Bowl)

> **Safety Rating: IF SWALLOWED, BOTH LIQUID AND GRANULAR IN-BOWL TOILET CLEANERS PRESENT A MEDICAL EMERGENCY REQUIRING *IMMEDIATE* MEDICAL ATTENTION.**

What's in it: Both liquid and granular toilet bowl cleaners are acid-based products. Granular cleaners may contain 70 to 100 percent sodium bisulfate, plus a small amount of detergents, surfactants, alkalis, and perfume. Liquid cleaners get their power from hydrochloric acid (8–30 percent), plus detergents, surfactants, fragrance, dyes, and water.

Granular cleaners:

AMWAY BOWL CLEANER (Amway Corp.). 74.4% (by weight) sodium bisulfate.*

---

* Percentages of active ingredients obtained from product labels or formulas listed in *Clinical Toxicology of Commercial Products* (Baltimore: Williams & Wilkins, 1977).

144

BOWLENE (Climalene). 83.5% sodium bisulfate.
SANI-FLUSH (Boyle-Midway). 75% sodium bisulfate.
VANISH (Drackett). 62% sodium bisulfate.

Liquid cleaners:

LYSOL BRAND DISINFECTANT TOILET BOWL CLEANER (Lehn & Fink). 8.50% hydrochloric acid.
SANI-FLUSH (Boyle-Midway). 7% hydrochloric acid.

How it works: The powerful acids in the in-bowl cleaners easily soften and dissolve the scum that collects on the sides and under the rim of the bowl.

For general cleaning, liquid products are probably more efficient than granular ones. You can direct the stream of cleaner up under the rim and let it run down the sides. Granular cleaners make an impressive show when you pour them into the toilet, but all the fizzing and bubbling tends to dilute the acidity of the cleaner and thus weaken its power. However, granular cleaners do work well on stains below the waterline. If you are the lazy type, you can pour them into the toilet before you go to sleep and let them work away during the night. (Don't do this if you've got small children around the house, since there's always the possibility that they will dip a finger into the bowl or even drink from it. Pets too.)

Never use either kind of in-bowl cleaner on any other kind of bathroom fixture. There's almost certainly a metal frame under the enamel porcelain finish on your tub or basin, and the acid cleaners can corrode the metal. They'll get to it through tiny, almost invisible cracks in the finish.

Don't try to increase the cleaning power of the toilet bowl cleaner either. Never mix it with any other kind of cleaner. You may be adding chemicals that will interact with the acids in the cleaner. For example, if mixed with chlorine bleach, both hydrochloric acid and sodium bisulfate will release potentially lethal chloramines, irritating gases that can be lethal if inhaled in high concentrations.

What it can do to you: Sodium bisulfate, the acid in granular toilet bowl cleaners, turns into sulfuric acid when you mix it with water. Sulfuric acid is a corrosive poison, just like hydrochloric acid, the active ingredient in liquid cleaners.

Both sulfuric acid and hydrochloric acid can burn your skin and your eyes on contact. Both can corrode the mucous membranes lining your mouth, throat, and stomach. If swallowed, they may produce very painful burns, often painful enough to keep someone from swallowing a second mouthful. If you swallow just a little, there may be nausea and vomiting. If you swallow a lot, there may be circulatory collapse, leading to death.

There's no fixed lethal dosage for liquid or granulated bowl cleaners, because the damage they do depends on how concentrated the products are. However, the concentrations in toilet bowl cleaners are definitely dangerous. As little as one seventh of a teaspoonful of either kind of cleaner can be lethal for a small child (22 pounds/10 kilograms) if he swallowed it right out of the bottle. Obviously, the concentration would be weaker if the cleaners are diluted in water, as in the toilet bowl.

What's better, safer, or cheaper: Practically everything. Plain chlorine bleach, for example, will sanitize and clean the toilet. Pour a half cup of bleach into the bowl and let it sit there while you clean the rest of the bathroom. Then scrub with a toilet brush and flush.

General household cleaners work well, too, although you may have to scrub harder than you would with one of the prepared cleaners if you let stains and dirt build up in the bowl. That's because they don't have the acids that make the toilet cleaners so effective. But it's a worthwhile trade-off because the general cleaners aren't corrosive either.

What *not* to use: scouring powders or liquids. These cleaners may scratch the surface of the porcelain bowl, creating tiny nicks and crevices for dirt and germs to hide in.

Toilet Bowl Cleaner (In-Tank Automatic)

> **Safety Rating: MAY BE HARMFUL IF SWALLOWED. CALL POISON CONTROL CENTER FOR APPROPRIATE ANTIDOTE PROCEDURE.**

What's in it: In-tank cleaners may come in liquid or solid form. Either way, the basic ingredients are a concentrated dye, a detergent, fragrance, and water. Some in-tank cleaners also include a germ-killing ingredient such as urea or a phenol compound.

Detergent cleaners:

BLU BOY (Northwest Sanitation Products). Solid.
TY-D-BOWL (Knomark). Liquid, solid.
VANISH (Drackett). Liquid.
WHITE ROSE (White Rose). Solid.

Detergent cleaners plus germ-killer:

SANI-FLUSH (Boyle-Midway). Liquid, solid. Phenol compound.
VANISH (Drackett). Solid. Urea.

How it works: Every time you flush the toilet, water runs through the in-tank cleaner, sending chemicals down into the toilet bowl. These chemicals show up rather dramatically in the form of blue dye. Technicolor effects aside, though, the cleaner doesn't really do an effective job of cleaning the bowl—unless you go in with a toilet brush and scrub down the surface. It follows, of course, that if it doesn't clean well it can't disinfect or deodorize effectively either, no matter what's in it. In sum, automatic, in-tank cleaners may be pretty, but they're not very hardworking.

What it can do to you: If swallowed, in-tank cleaners may be harmful. Those with disinfectants or germ-killers in them are potentially more harmful than plain detergent-plus-dye. Both kinds are less harmful if swallowed in diluted form, that is, directly from the toilet bowl rather than from the container.

The blue dye in the cleaner is concentrated and may be hard to wash off your hands. More important is the fact that a blue dye in the water can mask the appearance of blood in the stool, an important early warning sign of colon-rectum cancers.

What's better, safer, or cheaper: Liquid or crystal in-bowl cleaners work better than in-tank cleaners. Ordinary cleaners like chlorine bleach or household detergents are both cheaper and more effective. See Toilet Bowl Cleaner (In-Bowl) in the alphabetical products listing.

Toilet Bowl Deodorizer Block

> **Safety Rating: MAY BE HARMFUL IF SWAL-LOWED. CALL POISON CONTROL CENTER IMMEDIATELY FOR APPROPRIATE ANTI-DOTE PROCEDURE.**

What's in it: Toilet bowl deodorizer blocks may be 100 percent *p*-dichlorobenzene, or they may contain a trace of fragrance.

How it works: The deodorant blocks hang inside the rim of the bowl, releasing an aromatic solution every time you flush. They mask the odor of wastes in the water and on the porcelain surface of the bowl, but they don't clean the toilet bowl.

What it can do to you: *P*-dichlorobenzene, which is also used in moth blocks or chunks, is poisonous. Theoretically, the probable lethal dose for an adult may be one ounce or more; for a small child (22 pounds/ 10 kilograms), one seventh of an ounce or more. Nevertheless, cases of serious *p*-dichlorobenzene poisoning are rare; people have been known to walk away unharmed after swallowing as much as two thirds of an ounce.

One paradoxical side effect of these deodorizing products is that a lot of people can't stand the way they smell, finding the sometimes thick, often sweet odor downright unpleasant.

What's better, safer, or cheaper: Just keeping the toilet bowl clean with regular scrubbings can go a long way toward keeping it sanitary and clean-smelling. If you're looking for extra protection, clean with chlorine bleach, which is a germ-killer. Pour in a half cup of bleach, let it sit for a while, then scrub with a toilet brush and flush away.

Tub and Tile Cleaner

What's in it: Like most liquid cleaners, these tub and tile shiner-uppers are mostly water (sometimes as much as 90 percent). The general formulation also includes detergents, surfactants, grease-dissolving solvents such as ethylene glycol ethers or butyl cellosolve, fragrance, and coloring agents. Such disinfectants as alkyl ammonium chloride or phenol compounds are optional. So are propellants, which turn the liquids into foams.

Tub/tile cleaners with disinfectant:

CREW BATHROOM CLEANER (S. C. Johnson & Son). Aerosol. Phenol compound: *o*-phenylphenol.

DOW BATHROOM CLEANER (Dow Chemical). Aerosol. Phenol compound: *o*-phenylphenol.

FANTASTIK BATHROOM CLEANER (Texize). Aerosol. Phenol compound: *o*-benzyl-*p*-chlorophenol.

FORMULA 409 (Clorox). Nonaerosol. Phenol compound: *o*-phenylphenol.

LYSOL BRAND DISINFECTANT BASIN/TUB/TILE CLEANER (Lehn & Fink). Aerosol. Alkyl ammonium chloride.

Tub/tile cleaner without disinfectant:

PINE SOL FOAM BATHROOM CLEANER (American Cyanamid). Aerosol.

How it works: These light detergent foams and liquids are particularly good at dislodging and wiping away the gritty, often invisible layer of sticky grime that often builds up on tiled bathroom walls and floors. They also work well on enameled sinks and toilets, but a really scratched-up bathtub may require a harder working scouring powder. You can use tub and tile cleaners on the mirror or to wipe off the bathroom window, but they should never be sprayed or poured on painted surfaces, because the same solvents that do such a good job at dissolving grime may soften or "melt" paints, particularly water-based latex enamels.

These cleaners also wipe away the beginnings of the ugly black mold that sometimes grows on the grout between tiles, but if you're looking for a true-blue disinfectant, look elsewhere. Despite occasionally extravagant label claims, there is so little disinfectant in these cleaners, and the concentration is so weak, that they really won't keep you from catching colds or flu or other common infections. But while it won't "disinfect" the toilet bowl, a squirt of the often sweet-smelling detergent in the bowl once in a while can help mask odors.

What it can do to you: Like most detergents, these cleaners can cause upset stomachs—nausea, diarrhea, vomiting—if swallowed and should never be sprayed freely around food or surfaces on which food is prepared. They are moderately toxic; the probable lethal dose for a small child (22 pounds/10 kilograms) may start at less than an ounce, which, when you're talking about a light foam, may be a couple of teaspoonsful.

Tub and tile cleaners may also be irritating to your skin and eyes, and a lot of people find one perfume or another irritating or unpleasant. If that's your problem, try shopping around. There really is a wide variety of fragrances available, since each product has its own distinctive scent.

All the common prohibitions related to aerosol products apply to these: Don't overheat them; don't puncture the can; be sure the nozzle is pointing away from you before you push the button.

What's better, safer, or cheaper: Before I begin to list the alternatives to the common tub and tile cleaners on your supermarket shelf, I have a confession to make.

Most people have some little secret vice sneaking around in their lives. Some people drink red wine with fish. Some people steal pennies from their kids' piggy banks. Me, I am crazy about DOW BATHROOM CLEANER. I know all the arguments against aerosols, but those "scrubbing bubbles" (which don't really scrub hard; it's *me* that wields the sponge) are the stuff of shameful dreams, as far as I'm concerned. Cleaning the bathroom is at best a bore. Somehow the nice fresh smell of the foam, not to mention the fun of watching those white bubbles burble out of the can, almost makes it bearable. I don't tell you any of this to urge you on to buy the cleaner, just to let you know I understand if you really have an unbearable compulsion to use some equally expensive or unnecessary product.

If you're one of those people who simply don't get turned on

150

by a commercial tub and tile cleaner (and there must be millions of you), you can save a bundle by passing them by. Instead of the expensive aerosols, use a simple ammonia-and-water solution to scrub down the tiles, walls, and floors. A solution of a water softener like CALGON and water, or even plain washing soda and water, will also do yeoman's work on tubs and basins, as well as on tiles. For really scratched bathtubs, where the enamel's so pocked that the dirt collects in the crevices and won't come out for anything but scouring powder, use that. Or substitute that all-purpose house cleaner, baking soda. A paste of cream of tartar moistened with ordinary hydrogen peroxide can be used to scrub away stains.

The best inexpensive disinfectant is chlorine bleach in water, which can be used on both tile and enamel. It should *never* be used in combination with ammonia or any product containing ammonia. Together, the two chemicals produce chloramines, irritating gases that may be lethal if inhaled in high concentrations.

The nonaerosol tub and tile cleaners are more economical than the foams. The performance of *all* the tub and tile cleaners is pretty much the same.

Typewriter Cleaner

> **Safety Rating: MAY BE HARMFUL IF SWALLOWED, INHALED, OR ABSORBED THROUGH THE SKIN. CALL POISON CONTROL CENTER IMMEDIATELY FOR APPROPRIATE ANTIDOTE PROCEDURE.**

What's in it: Typewriter cleaners are single-ingredient products, and the single ingredient is usually 1,1,1-trichloroethane, a solvent.

How it works: The fast evaporating solvent dissolves or loosens dirt and grime and ink, so that it is easy to wipe away.

What it can do to you: Trichloroethane is nonflammable and only mildly irritating to your skin, but its fumes can irritate your eyes or mucous membranes. They may also produce vomiting, drowsiness, and coma if inhaled in sufficient concentrations or absorbed through the skin or swallowed. The probable lethal oral dose for a small child (22 pounds/10 kilograms) can be less than an ounce.

What's better, safer, or cheaper: You can keep your typewriter relatively clean by using a clean, lint-free cloth to wipe off the keys or typing element and the platen. General dusting of the machine helps, too. The safest way to get a typewriter cleaned thoroughly is to deliver it to the professionals once every year or eighteen months. The checkup can also prolong the useful life of the typewriter.

Upholstery Shampoo.
See **Rug and Carpet Shampoo (Liquid, Aerosol).**

Varnish

> **Safety Rating: IF SWALLOWED, PRODUCTS CONTAINING PETROLEUM DISTILLATES MAY BE EXTREMELY HARMFUL. CALL POISON CONTROL CENTER IMMEDIATELY FOR APPROPRIATE ANTIDOTE PROCEDURE.**

What's in it: Varnishes contain common oils (such as linseed oil), synthetic resins such as phenolic castor oil, plus minerals (which serve as drying agents), and a petroleum distillate solvent (mineral spirits).

How it works: As the solvent evaporates, the resins oxidize and harden to form a shiny protective coating. Once the varnish has dried, the coating may show milky stains. They are the result of moisture being absorbed by the varnish, and you may be able to get rid of them simply by polishing with oil. If that doesn't work, try a teaspoonful of vinegar in about two cups of water. If that fails, too, your only option may be to redo the coating.

152

What it can do to you: Like shellac solutions, varnishes are flammable. They are also extremely toxic if swallowed, and as little as one fifth of a teaspoonful may be the probable lethal dose for a small child (22 pounds/10 kilograms). In addition, the petroleum distillate solvent can cause a chemical pneumonia if aspirated into the lungs. Not surprisingly, the liquids are also irritating to your skin, and the vapors may irritate your eyes or, if you inhale them, your lungs.

What's better, safer, or cheaper: Polyurethane plastic coatings are a lot more convenient than either shellac or varnish since they dry so much faster. Varnish is the slowest drying of the three; if you varnish on a wet day, the stuff can take as long as forty-eight hours or more to dry thoroughly. The plastic coatings are marginally safer, too. All three are potentially lethal, but varnish is the most toxic.

Wallpaper Cleaner

> **Safety Rating: MAY BE HARMFUL IF SWAL-
> LOWED. CALL POISON CONTROL CENTER
> IMMEDIATELY FOR APPROPRIATE ANTI-
> DOTE PROCEDURE.**

What's in it: Wallpaper cleaners, which usually look like putty or a lump of uncooked bread dough, are made of an absorbent powder such as wheat flour or kaolin, plus a solvent (water, kerosine, naphtha, ethylene glycol ether). There may be ammonia, borax, or soap for extra cleaning powder, and dyes (for the cleaner, not the paper) are optional.

How it works: Depending on the nature of the stain, the putty or doughlike lump will either rub a stain off, the way an eraser rubs lead pencil off paper, or absorb it, like a blotter. The blotting action is most effective with grease stains that haven't dried yet. The solvents in the cleaner dissolve or liquefy stains so that they come off more easily.

What it can do to you: Without poisonous solvents, wallpaper cleaners would be absolutely innocuous; you could eat them with no ill effects at all. If they contain petroleum distillate or alcohol solvents, they may be lethal. As little as one seventh of an ounce of cleaner with petroleum solvent may be fatal if swallowed by a small child (22 pounds/10 kilograms). If aspirated into the lungs, the solvent can cause a form of chemical pneumonia that can prove fatal.

What's better, safer, or cheaper: One of the really wizard inventions of modern life is vinyl wallpaper, which is expensive but nearly stain-proof. Almost everything washes off easily with plain soap or detergent and water, which means that a commercial cleaner is a waste of money. *Note:* Be sparing with the water. If you flood it on, some water may seep in between the seams, loosening the paper.

For nonwashable papers, try one of these cheap, safe alternatives:

• A rubber eraser or art gum can be used to rub off pencil marks or other nongreasy, light stains.

• The inside of a loaf of bread (stale bread hangs together better than fresh) can be used as an absorbent for greasy stains. It also blots up ink nicely.

• Another nifty homemade absorbent is a powder like fuller's earth or chalk plus water. Pat the "paste" on, then brush it off as it soaks up the stain.

If these first-aid measures pick up the stain but don't remove it completely, you may be reduced to using a commercial spot remover or cleaning fluid. Pour a little on a lint-free dustcloth, and pat gently at the stain. Once the stain is off, a few applications of your homemade absorbent may be needed to get rid of the residue of the cleaning fluid.

Wallpaper Remover

> **Safety Rating: MAY BE HARMFUL IF SWALLOWED. CALL POISON CONTROL CENTER FOR APPROPRIATE ANTIDOTE PROCEDURE.**

What's in it: Paper strippers like EASY OFF WALLPAPER REMOVER (Klean-Stripp) are water-based solutions of surfactants plus humectants (glycolic acid, or hydroxyacetic acid).

How it works: The surfactants and humectants help to push the water into and behind the wallpaper, dissolving and loosening the glue that holds the paper to the wall. Sometimes this happens with almost magical speed. Sometimes it seems to take forever.

What it can do to you: Both the surfactants and the humectants may be irritating to your skin and eyes, and, if you swallow the remover, it may cause all kinds of gastric upset, including nausea, vomiting, and diarrhea.

What's better, safer, or cheaper: A solution of very hot water and ordinary household cleaner (like SPIC AND SPAN), which is loaded with surfactants, can be a handy alternative to the commercial strippers.

Some people prefer to use a special steaming iron that forces hot moisture into the wallpaper and helps dissolve the glue. Could you use your own steam iron to do the job? Sorry, no. It simply hasn't got either the water capacity or the power to produce the kind of steam bursts you need to get the job done, and it can get much too hot to handle used in this way.

Of course, you can avoid all this mess (and it *is* a messy job) by using the strippable, canvas-backed paper next time. This kind of paper simply peels off the wall when you're ready for a change. It's almost always more expensive, but it's worth it.

Water-repellent Fabric Spray

> **Safety Rating: HARMFUL IF SWALLOWED, INHALED, OR ABSORBED THROUGH THE SKIN. CALL POISON CONTROL CENTER IMMEDIATELY FOR APPROPRIATE ANTIDOTE PROCEDURE.** .

What's in it: All fabric water-repellent sprays contain either silicones or a synthetic resin, plus a solvent (usually trichloroethane) and a propellant. Silicone-based sprays include CAMP DRI (Kiwi Polish Co.) and G-96 (Jet-aer). SCOTCHGARD (3M) gets its water-repellent power from a synthetic resin.

How it works: The solvent makes it possible for the silicone or synthetic resin to penetrate the fibers of the fabric you are making water-repellent. When the solvent evaporates and the spray dries, you're left with a surprisingly effective layer of protection. The silicone or resins that remain in the fabric repel water, causing it to bead up and roll off. Of course, the water won't roll off your sofa or couch as easily as it might roll off the proverbial duck's back, but the sprays will help you cope with the ordinary spills and stains of daily life in an active household. Out in the rain, the water-repellents will give added water resistance to cotton, cotton/Dacron, or nylon raincoats. In a heavy downpour, you'd still do better with a rubber or plastic slicker, and it's always smart to have a serviceable umbrella handy. The water-repellents do wear off, so it's a good idea to check from time to time to see if you need another spritzing.

Of course, it's also a good idea to test the fabric before you spray a whole garment or piece of furniture, just to be sure the spray won't damage the color, the pattern, or the fabric itself. Spray a small corner and move onto the whole thing only if the test area looks and feels good once the spray has dried. For maximum protection, be sure the fabric is as clean as possible before you spray. Brush, vacuum, or rinse, if necessary, to get rid of dust or detergents, which might keep the spray from penetrating and coating evenly.

What it can do to you: One major problem with these sprays is that they are flammable in the can as well as when you first spray them on a fabric. Whether they increase the flammability of fabrics on which they are sprayed is an open question. According to tests conducted by *Consumers' Research Magazine* in 1977, the flammability of cotton and cotton/Dacron fabrics actually seemed to be reduced after spraying. But nylon's different. It burned even brighter when coated with silicone spray (SCOTCHGARD resin-based spray didn't have that effect), and, as the magazine cautions, that's important to keep in mind next time you start to waterproof your nylon camping tent. Treating it with a water-repellent may be hazardous to your health. *Note:* All the sprays were more flammable before the solvent had evaporated, and so were the fabrics they were sprayed on.

There's another thing you should know about water-repellent sprays: The trichloroethane solvent can make you feel dizzy and rather out of focus if you inhale highly concentrated vapors or if you absorb it through your skin. If you take in enough of it through your skin or your lungs, it may also damage your liver or your kidneys. The solution: Keep the windows open while you spray, and wear gloves until the spray dries and the solvent has evaporated.

Other than that, aerosol water-repellents should be handled like any aerosols. Don't use them around an open flame, lest they go *boom!*—right in your hand. Don't incinerate or overheat or puncture the cans. Aim the nozzle in the right direction—away from you, of course. You'd be surprised how many people forget that one.

What's better, safer, or cheaper: Unfortunately, this is one of those wonders of the chemical age for which there really is no workable substitute. Just about the only other way to waterproof cottons, wools, and nylons is to put plastic slipcovers over your furniture or wear a plastic or rubber slicker when it rains.

Water Softener (Laundry)

> **Safety Rating: ALL WATER SOFTENERS MAY BE HARMFUL IF SWALLOWED. PRODUCTS CONTAINING SODIUM CARBONATE (A CORROSIVE) MAY BE EXTREMELY HARMFUL. CALL POISON CONTROL CENTER IMMEDIATELY FOR APPROPRIATE ANTIDOTE PROCEDURE.**

What's in it: The active ingredients in laundry water softeners are chemicals that interact with the minerals in "hard" water so as to keep them from forming a soap- or detergent-and-mineral scum that clings to your clothes. The commonest softeners are sodium carbonate (also known as washing soda or sal soda) and sodium hexametaphosphate, an alkali. There may also be an anticaking agent (sodium sulfate) in the package. Fragrances are optional.

How it works: A sodium carbonate softener, like ARM & HAMMER WASHING SODA (Church & Dwight Co.), combines with the minerals to form an insoluble compound that simply drops to the bottom of the tub, away from your wash. In other words, this kind of softener precipitates the minerals out of the water, which is why it is known as a "precipitating softener." It won't remove minerals already deposited on your clothes, so you should always add a sodium carbonate softener to the wash at the beginning of the cycle and make sure that it's dissolved before you add soap or detergent.

A sodium hexametaphosphate softener like CALGON (Beecham) can be added during the rinse cycle. That's because sodium hexametaphosphate softens water by keeping the minerals in solution, whirling around in the water away from your wash, and by dissolving away mineral scum left over from earlier washings. An obvious consumer corollary is that you don't have to read the list of ingredients in a water softener to know what's in it; you can tell just from reading the directions.

What it can do to you: Sodium carbonate is a caustic, strong enough to be used to flush out sluggish drains. It can burn your skin and eyes on contact and, if swallowed, can burn the inside of your mouth, your throat, and your stomach. How damaging it is depends on how concentrated it is.

Sodium hexametaphosphate is not corrosive, but it is an irritant that can be damaging to skin and to mucous membranes, such as your eyes.

As little as one fifth of an ounce of a product containing sodium carbonate may be lethal for a small child (22 pounds/10 kilograms). The probable lethal dose for a product containing sodium hexametaphosphate is similar to that of any other detergent product, which means that it may start as low as one fifth of an ounce for a small child.

What's better, safer, or cheaper: A store-brand washing soda (sodium carbonate) is almost certainly your most economical buy, but it's a waste of money to add any water softener if you don't really need to. Many common detergents already have water softeners in them. You'll find sodium carbonate in ALL, ARM & HAMMER, BOLD, CHEER, DASH, GAIN, OXYDOL, PUREX, RINSO, and TIDE. You may be able to solve your laundry problems simply by switching to one of these. One thing's for sure: Just looking at your clothes won't tell you whether or not you need a softener. Dingy wash may simply need a bleach or a different detergent.

To test your water for hardness, take two cups of hot water from the tap and pour them into a quart jar. Then add a teaspoonful of detergent and shake like mad. If you get good suds that last for a few minutes, forget the softener. The water is fine. But if the water doesn't get sudsy when you shake it, or if the bubbles break up fast, softeners may be the answer. How much will you need? Figure that out this way: Add about one half teaspoonful of softener to a gallon of hot water from the tap. Take two cupfuls of that softened water, pour them into the quart jar, add the detergent, and shake. Sudsy? Fine. You need a half teaspoonful of softener for each gallon of water in the washing machine.

If you don't get the suds you want, repeat the test, adding one half teaspoonful more softener each time, until you get the kind of foam you like. At that point, multiply the half teaspoonful of softener by the gallonage of your washing machine. That's how much softener you need per washload.

Some people, like me, find this kind of kitchen chemistry great fun. If you don't, and if you live in an area where the water is so hard that your clothes crackle when you take them out of the washing machine, you may have thought of investing in a mechanical water softener, which removes minerals by filtering them out. Simple and neat. But mechanical filters can be expensive, up to three hundred dollars and more to install, plus an additional five dollars or so for chemicals each month. And a mechanical filter takes the minerals out of all the water in your house—the drinking water as well as the washing water. The water from your tap may end up tasting flat.

Wax.

See Floor Polish (for Synthetic Floor Coverings); Furniture Polish; Wood Polish.

Wax Remover/Stripper.

See Floor-Polish Remover.

White Glue

What's in it: Adhesives like ELMER'S GLUE-ALL (Borden Chemical), ROSS WHITE GLUE (Ross Chemical), and WELDWOOD WHITE GLUE (U.S. Plywood-Champion Papers) are resin emulsions. They may also contain a plasticizer waterproofer such as dibutyl phthalate.

How it works: The emulsions are thermoplastic, which means that they harden when cooled or exposed to room temperatures which help to evaporate the emulsifiers and solvents that keep them liquid in the bottle.

What it can do to you: Because the plasticizers are toxic, the probable lethal dose of white glue for a small child (22 pounds/10 kilograms) is slightly less than an ounce, about a quarter of the contents of a four-ounce bottle.

What's better, safer, or cheaper: These glues are about the least expensive way to create a temporary bond for paper, wood, or fabrics, but if the glue is meant to be used by very young children, you might save some money by showing the child how to mix up a flour-and-water paste. Not only is it safe and cheap, but it's fun, too.

Window Cleaner.

See **Glass Cleaner; Glass Wax.**

Wood Filler

What's in it: I always thought that "plastic wood" was the generic term for wood filler, but it isn't. PLASTIC WOOD is actually the trademarked name for the wood filler made by Boyle-Midway. But it's easy to see how you could get the idea that it's a generic name: PLASTIC WOOD is the only brand of wood filler I could find in the hardware stores around my house. There are other brands available, though, such as DURATITE WOOD DOUGH (DAP). All are similar in composition. The basic ingredients are nitrocellulose (nitrate plus cellulose, the material that makes up the walls of plant cells) and wood flour (sawdust). These fibers are combined with a number of solvents (ketones, toluene, and alcohol), plus plasticizers to give you the plasticity that allows you to push the filler into holes and dents in wood surfaces. Dyes to match various wood tones are optional.

How it works: As the solvents evaporate, the fibers and plasticizers harden into a woodlike filler that can be sanded, stained, or painted. Since its surface is different from wood, however, color stains may not come out the same shade on the filler as on the wood. Painting really is the best way to deal with wood filler patches, but if you're determined to stain, you'll want to test first. When you fill the hole in the wood surface, put a few small lumps of filler on a piece of cardboard or heavy paper and let them harden. When everything's dry, test the stain on the lumps of filler. *Don't* test on the actual patch. Once you've put stain on filler, it's almost impossible—maybe it *is* impossible—to get it off. Experiment until you get a color that matches the wood surface.

What it can do to you: Wood filler is a deceptive product. It looks so much like a simple clay or putty that it's often hard to believe how hazardous it can be. For starters, nitrocellulose is both flammable and explosive. The solvents in the filler are flammable, too. Obviously, it's not the sort of thing to use around an open flame, and you shouldn't smoke while using it.

The vapors from the filler may, if inhaled, produce a kind of euphoria, as well as headaches and general disorientation. Skin contact is irritating; in severe cases, it can produce blisters. If swallowed, wood fillers are seriously toxic because they contain toluene. The probable lethal dose for a small child (22 pounds/10 kilograms) may be less than a teaspoonful.

What's better, safer, or cheaper: Wood putty (see Putty in alphabetical products listing) can be substituted for a plasticized wood filler. Since it doesn't contain any of the solvents found in the wood filler, it is safer, but it doesn't perform as well because it lacks the plasticizers that give the wood filler its strength.

Wood Paneling Adhesive.

See Contact Cement.

Wood Paneling Cleaner.

See Wood Polish.

Wood Polish

Safety Rating: IF SWALLOWED, PRODUCTS CONTAINING PETROLEUM DISTILLATES MAY BE EXTREMELY HARMFUL. CALL POISON CONTROL CENTER IMMEDIATELY FOR APPROPRIATE ANTIDOTE PROCEDURE.

What's in it: All polishes meant for use on wood that has not been protected with varnish, resin, or a plastic coating are based on petroleum distillate solvents such as mineral spirits or naphtha. (Products containing more than 10 percent petroleum distillates must be packaged in child-resistant containers.) The basic difference between liquid polish and paste wood polish is the amount of solids—waxes and resins—

162

in the mix. Paste polishes are as much as 25 percent wax (paraffin, microcrystalline, or carnauba wax), while liquids rarely contain more than 10 percent. Less than 5 percent is more common.

The simplest polishes, such as WILBERT'S LEMON OIL (Wilbert), may contain nothing more than a petroleum distillate plus fragrance (the lemon oil), or, like PARKER'S LEMON OIL (C. W. Parker), mineral oil plus color and fragrance. More complex products, like BRUCE PASTE WAX (Armour-Dial), KLEAR WOOD FLOOR WAX (S. C. Johnson & Son), or WOOD PREEN (Kiwi Polish Co.), all paste waxes, contain a variety of natural and/or synthetic waxes and/or resins in a petroleum solvent base. Polyethylene, a plastic, is sometimes added for strength, shine, and water resistance.

"Scratch-cover" polishes like OLD ENGLISH (Boyle-Midway) have all that plus staining oils. Products like PANEL AWARD (U.S. Plywood), meant especially for wood paneling, are made up of exactly the same ingredients as other multiple-ingredient wood polishes.

In truth, all wood polishes are practically interchangeable. You can use them on floors or furniture or cabinets with equally fine results, although some may be more convenient than others for specific jobs. A liquid polish, for example, may be easier to work with when you're doing the floors, and it will certainly be better than a paste on intricately carved pieces, but a paste may be more efficient on flat furniture surfaces.

How it works: The petroleum distillates in wood polishes are there to serve as a solvent base for the other ingredients and to help remove dirt and grime when you polish floors and furniture. As an added benefit, they'll help remove excess polish left over from previous waxings; you'll hardly ever have to use a wax remover on your floors.

Note: There's no water in wood polishes, because water damages wood. An all-purpose water-based furniture polish like PLEDGE or FAVOR can't give your wood pieces the kind of tender loving care they get from a solvent-based polish. You *can* use the all-purpose products on wood that has been coated with urethane, though, because what you're polishing there isn't wood at all; it's a plastic urethane surface.

When the solvents evaporate, a thin layer of waxes, resins, or plastic remains. A self-polishing product like KLEAR will glow softly at this point. You'll have to buff an ordinary polish like WOOD PREEN to make it shine. Either way, your wood surfaces will benefit from periodic buffing to bring up the polish glow.

What it can do to you: If swallowed, wood polishes containing petroleum distillate solvents can cause a burning sensation in the mouth, throat, or stomach. They can also make anyone who swallows them drowsy. The probable lethal dose for a small child (22 pounds/10 kilograms) may be less than an ounce, but in many cases the child may recover with no symptoms other than those described above. The exception is when a petroleum distillate is aspirated into the lungs. Even a minuscule amount can cause a lethal form of chemical pneumonia, which is why many experts still insist that it is dangerous to force a child who has swallowed a petroleum distillate to vomit. Others, however, believe that it is most important to get the polish out of the stomach.

Furniture polishes are irritating to the skin, and the vapors can cause symptoms similar to alcohol intoxication. If inhaled in sufficient concentrations, they may make your head hurt, make you feel nauseated or restless or confused, and, in really high concentrations, cause convulsions and coma.

What's better, safer, or cheaper: Old-fashioned, homemade furniture polishes (usually a mixture of linseed oil and beeswax) fail on all three points. They're no better than the commercial polishes, most of which are very good indeed. They're certainly not safer, since you have to heat the mixture to melt the beeswax, and linseed oil is extremely flammable. Life being what it is, they're no longer any cheaper either.

Among the commercial products, you will find price variations by brand. Choose the one that works best for you at the lowest price. Once you've chosen your polish, restraint is the better part of economy. Use as little polish as you can. It'll save you money, and it'll make the wood you're polishing look better. Too much polish on wood floors or furniture can make the surface tacky and gummy, and no matter how hard you buff, you'll never get a decent shine.

Wood Putty.

See Putty.

Wood Stain

What's in it: Penetrating wood stains such as MINWAX (Minwax Co.) usually contain a petroleum distillate solvent (mineral spirits), resinous varnishes, and an aniline dye (coal tar dye). They may also contain sealers, ingredients that prevent natural dyes in the wood from rising through the coating to discolor the surface.

How it works: The solvents in the stain enhance the dye's ability to penetrate the wood. The resins, which go in right along with the color, harden and strengthen raw wood as they dry. They don't actually make the surface waterproof in the sense that it will resist staining if you set a wet glass on it, but they do make the wood feel heavier and more solid to the touch and help to prevent warping by filling internal spaces with varnish and stain.

What it can do to you: Wood stains present multiple problems. First, the stains and their vapors are combustible and should never be used around an open flame. Next, the fumes can be narcotic if you inhale them in high concentrations in a room without adequate ventilation. Breathe in too much, and you may feel confused, even stuporous. Third, both the solvents and the dyes can be absorbed through intact skin. Aniline dyes may be carcinogenic, so you should always wear rubber gloves when working with one of these stains.

If swallowed, wood stains are extremely dangerous. The aspiration of even minute amounts of petroleum distillates into the lungs can cause a potentially fatal form of chemical pneumonia, and trying to predict probable lethal doses is futile. Petroleum distillate ingestion cases must be dealt with one by one. The best course is to store your stains in a place safe enough to guarantee that the small child in your house never turns out to be one of those cases.

What's better, safer, or cheaper: All penetrating stains from reputable companies are similar in composition, and their prices are fairly uniform, too. When you come down to it, your only meaningful choice is likely to be the color or shade you want to impart to your wood.

Glossary of Ingredients
and Label Terms

Most of the chemicals found in household products have more than one chemical or trade name. Therefore, I have tried to list in this glossary as many common names as possible for each ingredient, and I have cross-referenced all synonyms and trade names to make it easier for you to identify the ingredients you find on product labels. I have also included a number of generic terms, such as *emulsifier* and *surfactant,* because these words often appear on package labels either as modifiers of chemical terms or as substitutes for them.

As with the products in which they are found, the fact that some of these ingredients may be allergenic, irritating, or poisonous to some people or in some specific situations does not necessarily mean that they will always be allergenic, irritating, or poisonous to everyone in all situations.

A

ACETATE ELASTOMER. See *Elastomer.*

ACETATE RESIN EMULSION. An emulsion used to give strength and flexibility to such products as spackling compound.

ACETIC ACID. A clear, colorless liquid with a penetrating odor. If inhaled, acetic acid is irritating to the lungs. Its fumes are also irritating to the eyes, and, if swallowed, it can corrode the mouth and throat. It is commonly found in adhesive cements, solvents, and resins.

ACETONE. Acetone is a solvent used in paintbrush cleaners, adhesive cements, glues, varnishes, and lacquers, as well as in nail polishes and nail polish removers. It is flammable and moderately toxic. If swallowed, it can cause restlessness, vomiting, collapse, and stupor. The lethal dose may be an ounce or more for an adult, one fifth of an ounce or more for a small child.

3-(*alpha*-ACETONYLBENZYL)-4-HYDROXYCOUMARIN. A hydroxycoumarin compound with anticoagulant properties. Also known by the trade name Warfarin, it is used in rat poisons to cause death by internal hemorrhaging.

3-(*alpha*-ACETONYL-4-CHLOROBENZYL)-4-HYDROXYCOUMARIN. A hydroxycoumarin compound used as an anticoagulant in rat poisons to cause death by internal hemorrhaging. A trade name for this ingredient is Coumachlor.

ACID DYE. A coloring agent, also known as an azo dye, that is used in fabric dyes. Acid dyes are bright and resist fading when washed. There is some evidence that they may be absorbed through the skin.

ACRYLATE. See *Acrylic resin.*

ACRYLIC COPOLYMER. See *Acrylic resin; Polymer.*

ACRYLIC ELASTOMER. A rubberlike synthetic found in latex paints. See also *Elastomer.*

169

ACRYLIC ESTER. See *Acrylic resin.*

ACRYLIC MONOMER. See *Acrylic resin.*

ACRYLIC POLYMER. See *Acrylic resin; Polymer.*

ACRYLIC RESIN. Any one of a number of synthetic materials that are thermoplastic, that is, solid at ordinary room temperatures but soft when warmed. These resins are used as thickeners in paints. They can be irritating to the skin.

ACTIVE INGREDIENT. A substance that enables a product to do what it is supposed to, for example, the pigment in a paint or the insecticide in a bug spray. Active ingredients may or may not be more toxic than the inactive or inert ingredients found along with them in a product. The terms "active" and "inert" apply strictly to a particular ingredient's function in a product, not to any of its other properties.

ALCOHOL. A synonym for *ethyl alcohol.*

ALIPHATIC HYDROCARBON. Any one of a group of hydrocarbons whose molecules are arranged in straight or branched chains, in contrast to aromatic hydrocarbons, whose molecules are arranged in closed rings. Examples of aliphatic hydrocarbons are methane, butane, kerosine, and paraffin. See also Hydrocarbon and individual entries for above examples.

ALIPHATIC THIOCYANATE. One of a group of chemicals that are sources of cyanide. The compound is used in insecticides. Three examples of aliphatic thiocyanates are Lethane 384 (also known as beta-butoxy-beta-thiocyanodiethyl ether), Lethane 60, and Thanite (also known as isobornyl thiocyanoacetate).

ALKALI. Alkalis are naturally occurring substances that may be strongly caustic. Potash is an alkali; so are most detergent ingredients used in cleaners.

ALKANOLAMINE. An ammonia derivative which, when combined with fatty acids, forms soaps and foaming cleaners.

ALKYD RESIN. A type of resin used primarily in paints and coatings to give strength and water-resistance to the finished surface.

ALKYL AMMONIUM BROMIDE. A cationic surfactant used as a germicide and sanitizer. Between one teaspoonful and one ounce may be fatal for an adult.

ALKYL AMMONIUM CHLORATE. A cleaner and a disinfectant.

ALKYL AMMONIUM CHLORIDE. A cationic surfactant used as a germicide and sanitizer. Between one teaspoonful and one ounce may be fatal for an adult.

ALKYL ARYL AMMONIUM CHLORIDE. A generic name for a large group of cationic surfactants, which are used as germicides to give detergent products sanitizing characteristics. See also Quaternary ammonium compound.

ALKYL ARYL SODIUM SULFATE. A moderately toxic anionic surfactant used in laundry products.

ALKYL ARYL SODIUM SULFONATE. A class of anionic surfactants used in detergent products. They are irritating to the skin and can cause vomiting and gastric upset if swallowed.

170

ALKYL ARYL SULFONATE. A synthetic anionic surfactant commonly used in abrasive cleaners. It is made of at least 40 percent sodium alkyl aryl sulfonate, 2 percent moisture, 1 percent oil, and 57 percent or less sodium sulfate. If swallowed, an ounce or more may be fatal for an adult (the lethal dose for a small child may be one fifth of an ounce or more), and prolonged skin contact can be irritating.

ALKYL DIMETHYL BENZYL AMMONIUM CHLORIDE. A cationic surfactant used as a germicide and sanitizer in disinfectants or cleaners such as bathroom tub and tile cleaner.

ALKYL ETHOXYLATE SULFATE. An anionic surfactant used in household detergent products.

ALKYLPHENYL POLYETHOXYETHANOL. A nonionic surfactant that is used both as a surfactant and as an emulsifier. It is moderately toxic and can cause gastric irritation, diarrhea, and bloating if swallowed.

ALKYL SODIUM ISOTHIONATE. An anionic surfactant and detergent with very low toxicity. The lethal dose for an adult may be one pint or more; for a small child it may be two to five ounces.

ALKYL SODIUM SULFATE. One of a class of anionic surfactants used in cleaning and laundry products. (Sodium lauryl sulfate is an alkyl sodium sulfate.) Alkyl sodium sulfates are moderately toxic. They may be irritating to the skin and, if swallowed, can cause gastric distress, including diarrhea and bloating. Oral doses of one ounce or more may be fatal for an adult.

ALKYL SODIUM SULFONATE. One of a class of anionic surfactants whose toxicity is similar to that of alkyl sodium sulfates.

ALKYL SULFATE. A detergent found in dishwashing liquids.

d-trans-**ALLETHRIN.** A synthetic pyrethrin, used as an insecticide. It can cause allergic reactions in people sensitive to chrysanthemums, but it is relatively nontoxic for human beings. See *Pyrethrin*.

ALLYL ISOTHIOCYANATE. Imitation mustard oil. This is a violent irritant, used in some dog and cat repellents.

ALUMINUM MAGNESIUM SILICATE. A form of clay composed of particles of aluminum silicate combined with small amounts of magnesium silicate. It is very absorbent and is usually found in cat-box litter.

ALUMINUM SILICATE. Small particles of aluminum salt naturally occurring in the earth's crust. Used as an anticaking agent in cosmetics and in some household cleaning powders.

AMIDE. An organic or inorganic compound chemically related to ammonia. Amides are usually found in detergents.

AMINE. One of a group of ammonia derivatives used as solvents, detergents, plasticizers, and catalysts. Triethanolamine and diethanolamine are examples of amines.

AMINE CURING AGENT. The "hardener" that is sold along with an epoxy resin in epoxy glues. Combining the curing agent with the resin causes the mixture to harden and bond surfaces (make them stick together). Amines are ammonia derivatives.

AMINE OXIDE. An ammonia derivative; a detergent.

AMINO METHYL PROPANEDIOL. A crystalline substance that dissolves in water or alcohol and holds moisture, used as a humectant and an emulsifier in leather dressings, polishes, and cleaning compounds. It is moderately toxic (the lethal dose may be one ounce or more for an adult, one fifth of an ounce or more for a small child).

2-AMINO-2-METHYL-1,3-PROPANEDIOL. A synonym for *amino methyl propanediol*.

2-AMINO-2-METHYL-1-PROPANOL. A thick, viscous liquid, used as an emulsifier in floor, auto, and stove polishes.

AMMONIA. A sharp-smelling, colorless gas used medically as smelling salts. It is found in solution in household products, and the word "ammonia" on the label indicates that either ammonia water or ammonium hydroxide is contained within. Ammonia water, also known as spirit of hartshorn, is a solution containing 10 percent ammonia; ammonium hydroxide contains 28 to 29 percent ammonia. Products containing either one will carry a poison warning label, but ammonia's toxicity is unpredictable. People have been known to swallow as much as three or four ounces of household ammonia without showing any ill effects. In addition to household ammonia, ammonia solutions are commonly found in metal cleaners and polishes, porcelain cleaners, and general-purpose, heavy-duty household detergent cleaners.

AMMONIA WATER. See *Ammonia*.

AMMONIUM CHLORATE. A bleaching and disinfectant agent sometimes found in liquid toilet bowl cleaners.

AMMONIUM CHLORIDE. A naturally occurring ammonia salt used as a bleaching agent in some cleaning powders. Ammonium chloride may be irritating to the skin. If swallowed in large amounts, it can cause nausea, vomiting, systemic ammonia poisoning, or death.

AMMONIUM HYDROXIDE. See *Ammonia*.

AMYL ACETATE. A flammable, colorless liquid that smells and tastes something like pears and is also known as isoamyl acetate, as banana oil, and as pear oil. Derived from amyl alcohol, it is a solvent and fragrance used in shoe polish, waterproof varnishes, adhesive cements, and metallic paints. It is also used in dry-cleaning fluids and wax removers, and its vapors may be irritating. If inhaled directly, the vapors can cause central nervous system depression and nausea. Products containing amyl acetate should always be used in a room with adequate ventilation.

AMYL ALCOHOL. A colorless liquid that smells something like camphor. It is a solvent used in paint and wax removers, and its fumes may be irritating to the eyes, nose, and throat and may cause headache, dizziness, and drowsiness. Oral doses larger than one ounce may be fatal for an adult, and amyl alcohol has proved lethal when applied to the skin of laboratory rabbits. Also known as pentanol.

ANILINE DYE.   A synthetic dye or coloring agent made from coal tar or petrochemicals.

ANIONIC SURFACTANT.   Any of a group of surface-active ingredients whose molecules are negatively charged. In hard water containing calcium, anionic surfactants tend to leave a "precipitate," a kind of scum that clings to the wash unless the laundry powder, liquid, or tablets contain builders to inactivate the calcium. All anionic surfactants, such as linear alkyl benzene sulfonate and sulfated castor oil, may be irritating to the skin. See also Surfactant.

ANTIMONY.   A metallic element that occurs naturally in stibnite ore found in Mexico, Peru, and Algeria. It may also be recovered from scrap metal containing lead. Antimony compounds, such as antimony chloride, antimony trichloride, and solutions of these, are used chiefly as coloring agents in furniture and shoe polishes. Antimony is highly toxic; seven drops or more may be fatal for an adult (the lethal dose for a small child can be as little as one drop).

ANTIMONY CHLORIDE.   See *Antimony.*

ANTIMONY TRICHLORIDE.   See *Antimony.*

ANTIOXIDANT.   An ingredient that when added to other ingredients (like fats) keeps them from combining with oxygen and deteriorating. A preservative.

AQUEOUS SOLUTION.   A solution in which the solvent is water. The standard abbreviation for an aqueous solution is "aq.," but it is usually written out in full on household-product labels, with the words "aqueous solution" followed by the ingredients that have been dissolved in water. A typical label for a starch substitute, for example, might read: "aqueous solution of nonionic synthetic resins, silicone resins, buffers, starch, surfactants, corrosion inhibitor, fragrance, and propellant."

AROMATIC CHEMICAL.   Any of a number of pleasant-smelling petroleum distillates used as fragrances in a variety of products, including air fresheners. Aromatic chemicals are poisonous and may be allergenic. They have preservative properties.

AROMATIC HYDROCARBON.   One of a group of hydrocarbons whose molecules are arranged in closed ring structures, as opposed to aliphatic hydrocarbons, whose molecules are arranged in straight or branched chains. Examples of aromatic hydrocarbons are benzene, toluene, and xylene. See also Halogenated aromatic hydrocarbon.

ARSENIC.   A chemical element that is extremely toxic. As little as seven drops of some arsenic compounds may cause death within forty-eight hours. In addition, arsenic is a cumulative poison, capable of causing death after small amounts are absorbed over a long period of time.

ARSENIC DISULFIDE.   A poisonous arsenic compound. Its deep-red crystals are used as a pigment in paints.

ARSENIC PENTOXIDE.   A poisonous arsenic compound used in metal adhesives and wood preservatives.

ARSENIC TRIOXIDE. A poisonous arsenic compound also known as "white arsenic." The primary material for the manufacture of all arsenic compounds. Used as a pesticide.

B

BANANA OIL. A synonym for *amyl acetate*.

BARIUM SULFATE. A heavy white powder derived from barite, a mineral found in the southwestern part of the United States. Barium sulfate, which is also known as baryte, is the source of the chemical element barium. It is the only nontoxic barium compound and is used as an opacifier in paints.

BARYTES. See *Barium sulfate*.

BAYGON. A trade name for *2-isopropoxyphenyl* N-*methylcarbamate*.

BEESWAX. A wax that is manufactured by bees. Used as an emulsifier in polishing waxes and in all kinds of thick lotion-type products, from household cleaners to cosmetics.

BENZALKONIUM CHLORIDE. A cationic surfactant and germicide used as a sanitizer. Oral doses larger than one teaspoonful may be lethal for an adult. See also Quaternary ammonium compound.

BENZENE. A solvent derived from coal that is especially useful for dissolving grease. Also known as benzol, carbon oil, or mineral naphtha. Used in paint removers, wax removers, and other degreasing cleaners, as well as in lacquers, insecticides, and pesticides. Like other solvents derived from coal or oil, benzene is flammable. Benzene is also highly toxic. It can cause severe dermatitis if it touches the skin. If swallowed, it can cause gastric upset, coma, and death. If inhaled, it can cause mental disorientation, convulsions, and depression. In addition, it has the power to depress the ability of bone marrow to produce new blood cells, and inhalation over a period of time may cause leukemia. Products containing 5 percent or more benzene (by weight) must be labeled "Danger. Vapor harmful. Poison" and must also carry the skull-and-crossbones poison symbol.

BENZETHONIUM CHLORIDE. A cationic surfactant and germicide used as a disinfectant and preservative. Between one teaspoonful and one ounce may be the lethal oral dose for an adult.

BENZOL. See *Benzene*.

o-BENZYL-*p*-CHLOROPHENOL. See *Chlorophene*.

2-BENZYL-4-CHLOROPHENOL. See *Chlorophene*.

BETA-BUTOXY-BETA THIOCYANODIETHYL ETHER. See *Lethane 384*.

BETA TRICHLOROETHANE. A synonym for *1,1,2-trichloroethane*.

BETULA OIL. A synonym for *methyl salicylate*.

BIPHENYL. A fungicide found in mildew preventives. Poisonous whether swallowed or absorbed through the skin.

BLEACH. An oxidizing agent, such as hydrogen peroxide, sodium perborate, or chlorine, that can remove the color from fabrics, wood, and paper products. It may remove stains by this bleaching action also.

BLUING. A dye that increases "whiteness" of fabrics. Also a product category.

BOILED LINSEED OIL. See *Linseed oil, boiled.*

BORAX. A hydrated (moisture-containing) form of *sodium borate.* Used as a mild detergent in laundry products.

BORIC ACID. A synonym for *sodium borate.*

BRIGHTENER. See *Fluorescent brightener.*

BUILDER. An additive used in detergent powders, liquids, and tablets to increase the power of natural or synthetic cleaners. The most common builders are phosphates and EDTA.

BUTANE. A highly flammable gas derived from petroleum, used as lighter fluid and as a propellant in aerosol products. Its fumes are narcotic if inhaled in high concentrations, and they can cause suffocation if inhaled.

n-BUTANOL. A synonym for n-*butyl alcohol.*

2-BUTOXY-2-THIOCYANODIETHYL ETHER. See *Lethane 384.*

n-BUTYL ACETATE. A colorless, flammable liquid with a characteristic "fruity" aroma, used as a solvent in paint removers, wax removers, and spot-cleaning fluids. Its fumes are narcotic in high concentrations and irritating to lungs, eyes, and mucous membranes when inhaled even at low concentrations.

BUTYL ACRYLATE. See *Acrylic resin.*

n-BUTYL ALCOHOL. A flammable liquid that dissolves fat and is used as a solvent in waxes, resins, shellac, and varnish. Butyl alcohol is irritating to mucous membranes and can cause contact dermatitis. If inhaled, its fumes can cause dizziness and drowsiness.

t-BUTYL ALCOHOL. A synonym for tert-*butyl alcohol.*

tert-BUTYL ALCOHOL. A solvent with a smell like camphor. Used as a solvent in paint removers and as a denaturant for ethyl alcohol. It is flammable and may be irritating to the skin and mucous membranes.

BUTYL CELLOSOLVE. A combustible solvent found in floor polish removers. See also 2-Ethoxyethanol.

C

CALCIUM CARBONATE. One of the most abundant of nature's inorganic substances. Calcium carbonate is a major component of rocks such as limestone and, in its purest state, is found as marble and chalk. When finely ground, it is known as whiting. It is virtually nontoxic.

CALCIUM HYDROXIDE. An alkali derived by adding moisture to calcium oxide. It is also known as milk of lime and "slaked" lime ("slaked" refers to the reaction of calcium oxide with water or moisture to form calcium hydroxide). While calcium oxide is corrosive, calcium hydroxide, which is the white powder used in patching cements, cement, and mortar, is not. If swallowed, it would cause gastric irritation but no significant damage.

CALCIUM HYPOCHLORITE. A bleach, found in a number of products, including mildew-stain removers.

CALCIUM OXIDE. The corrosive alkali from which calcium hydroxide is made. Also known as lime or quicklime. Found in some construction and adhesion cements.

CALCIUM SULFATE. A heavy gray-white powder also known as plaster of Paris. A chief component of household plastics and construction and adhesive cements. (Gypsum is a form of calcium sulfate.) If swallowed, calcium sulfate will cause gastric obstruction, because it hardens quickly after absorbing moisture. To delay the hardening process, anyone who has swallowed a product containing calcium sulfate is often given copious amounts of water or water mixed with gelatin.

2-CAMPHANONE. A synonym for *camphor.*

CAMPHOR. A flammable substance with a strong, penetrating odor, originally obtained from a tree found chiefly on Taiwan. In the United States today, camphor is generally made synthetically from pinene, a constituent of oil of turpentine. It is used in moth repellent and moth flakes and is highly toxic. Capable of being absorbed through the skin, it may cause nausea and vomiting. Because it is a central nervous system stimulant, it can cause convulsions if swallowed. Also known as 2-Camphanone.

CAMPHOR TAR. See *Naphthalene.*

CARBITOL. A solvent, also known as diethylene glycol monoethyl ether. It is moderately toxic if swallowed, but rarely irritating to the skin.

CARBOLIC ACID. A synonym for *phenol.*

CARBON DIOXIDE. A colorless, odorless, and generally noncombustible gas with a faintly biting taste, used as a propellant in aerosols. Carbon dioxide is usually nontoxic, although if inhaled in high concentrations it can cause shortness of breath, vomiting, and disorientation.

CARBON OIL. See *Benzene.*

CARBON TETRACHLORIDE. Once used in dry-cleaning and furniture-cleaning products. A heavy, colorless liquid known to cause cancer in animals and central nervous system depression in humans, carbon tetrachloride was banned from use in home products in 1971.

CARBOPOL. A synonym for *carboxypolymethylene.*

CARBOXYMETHYL CELLULOSE. A water-soluble derivative of cellulose that is used as an emulsifier, foaming agent, thickener, and stabilizer in household liquids. It is also used in these capacities in cosmetic products. Carboxymethyl cellulose, which is not absorbed by the body, may be used medically as a cathartic, which by its sheer bulk helps to move things along in the alimentary tract. Also known as cellulose gum.

CARBOXYPOLYMETHYLENE. A heavy white powder used as an emulsifier to keep oil-in-water mixtures from thinning out and separating. It is also known as carbopol.

CARNAUBA WAX. A nontoxic, hard, brittle wax from the leaves of a palm tree found primarily in Brazil. Used as a texturizer and stiffener in floor and furniture polishes and leather dressings. Because it is nontoxic, it is also used in chewy candies.

CARRAGEENAN. A thickener derived from seaweed. Used in household products as an emulsifier or stabilizer to create solid gel blocks, as in solid air fresheners.

CATALYST. An ingredient that initiates chemical change without being changed itself.

CATIONIC SURFACTANT. Any of a group of synthetic *surfactants* whose molecules are positively charged. Cationic surfactants, such as benzalkonium chloride, are primarily quaternary ammonium compounds. They are used as germicides and disinfectants. See also Surfactant.

CAUSTIC POTASH. See *Potassium hydroxide.*

CAUSTIC SODA. See *Sodium hydroxide.*

CDA ALCOHOL. See *Denatured alcohol.*

CELITE. A trade name for *diatomaceous earth.*

CELLOSOLVE. See *2-Ethoxyethanol.*

CELLULOSE. A nontoxic fibrous material that is a component of plant cell walls. It is used as the base for a number of fillers, such as cellulose acetate butyrate, which is used in such household products as glues, cements, and putties.

CELLULOSE ACETATE. A thickener containing cellulose that is used in such products as household glues and cements.

CELLULOSE ACETATE BUTYRATE. A filler material used in some household cements and glues. Derived from cellulose or wood fiber.

CELLULOSE GUM. A synonym for *carboxymethyl cellulose.*

CELLULOSE NITRATE. A synonym for *nitrocellulose.*

CERESIN. A wax that is a purified form of ozocerite.

CHELATING AGENT. See *Sequestrant.*

CHLORAMINE. A gas formed when ammonium hydroxide (an ammonia solution, household ammonia) is combined with sodium hydroxide (household chlorine bleach). Chloramines are irritating to the skin and mucous membranes, including the eyes and the respiratory tract, and are potentially lethal if inhaled in high concentrations.

CHLORINATED BENZENE. The active constituent in hexachlorobenzene. See also Hexachlorobenzene.

CHLORINATED HYDROCARBON. A synthetic product obtained by replacing one or more of the hydrogen atoms of a hydrocarbon with chlorine. Chlorinated hydrocarbons are used as solvents in cleaning fluids, insecticides (DDT is a chlorinated hydrocarbon), and fumigants. Most chlorinated hydrocarbons are toxic, poisons that collect in and may inactivate the kidneys and liver. Most have a characteristic sharp and penetrating odor, and some, like chloroform, are narcotic.

CHLORINE. A chemical element, used in the manufacture of a number of commercial products, including insecticides and plastics. Around the house, chlorine—which has the ability to bleach and to disinfect—is most commonly found in laundry products and disinfectants. The chlorine in these products is usually derived from the chlorine-source ingredient sodium hypochlorite.

CHLOROBENZENE. A halogenated aromatic hydrocarbon used as a dry-cleaning solvent.

1-CHLORO-2,3-EPOXYPROPANE. A synonym for *epichlorohydrin.*

CHLOROFLUOROCARBON. Any of a group of nonflammable, *propellant* gases, also known by the trade name Freon. Chlorofluorocarbons are central nervous system depressants and potential cardiac sensitizers if inhaled in high concentrations. Because they are considered hazardous to the ozone layer of the earth's atmosphere, chlorofluorocarbons have been banned from use in most aerosol products manufactured or sold after 1979.

CHLOROPHENE. A disinfectant and germicide found in liquid household cleaners in such compounds as *o*-benzyl-*p*-chlorophenol, 2-benzyl-4-chlorophenol, and ortho benzyl parachlorophenol. Products that contain 10 percent or more chlorophene are irritating to the skin. Chlorophene can also be absorbed through the skin, and when it was applied experimentally to the skin of laboratory rabbits it caused diarrhea, lassitude, collapse, and in some cases death.

CHROMATE SALT. One of a number of corrosive compounds, of which sodium chromate and potassium chromate are two examples. These substances can cause acidlike burns on contact with skin. If swallowed, they can cause violent gastroenteritis, followed by kidney and circulatory collapse.

CHROMIUM. A chemical element, chromium is a grayish metal derived from chromite ore, found in the earth's crust in South Africa, Russia, and the Philippines. Chromium compounds, such as chromium oxide green, are used as coloring agents in paints and pigments; in cosmetics, chromium oxides are used to color eyeshadows and mascaras. Inhalation of chromium dust is irritating; if swallowed, it can cause gastric irritation. Some people are allergic to chromium compounds. In addition, chromium oxide green is a suspected carcinogen that has caused cancer in rats when injected into the peritoneal cavity.

CHROMIUM OXIDE. See *Chromium.*

CINERIN I. The active ingredient in pyrethrins, which are insecticides derived from the ground-up dried flowers of certain types of chrysanthemums.

CITRIC ACID. An acid derived from citrus fruits and used as a cleaning agent in various kinds of metal polishes. It may also be used as a preservative in some cosmetic products.

CLARIFIER. A chemical that attracts small particles in clear liquids, such as detergent liquids (or shampoos), so as to keep the products from looking cloudy. Tetrasodium pyrophosphate is a clarifier.

COAL OIL. See *Kerosine.*

COAL TAR DYE. A more-or-less outmoded name for synthetic coloring agents, colors that have never existed in nature and are created by color chemists in the laboratory. Originally, the basic materials for these synthetic dyes were coal tar derivatives, which is why they became known as coal tar dyes. Today most synthetic colors are made from petrochemicals, ingredients derived from petroleum or natural gas. You can recognize a synthetic coloring agent made from these ingredients by its name. All colors whose names begin with letters— "FD&C" (food, drugs, and cosmetics), "D&X" (drugs and cosmetics), or "Ext. D&C" (external drugs and cosmetics)—are synthetics. Many of these colors have been shown to cause cancer when fed to, injected into, or applied to the skin of laboratory animals.

COLOR BRIGHTENER. See *Fluorescent brightener; Bluing.*

COUMACHLOR. A trade name for *3-(alpha-Acetonyl-4-chlorobenzyl)-4-hydroxycoumarin.*

COUMAFURYL. A hydroxycoumarin compound also known as Fumarin. Used in rat poisons.

CRESOL. Any of a group of colorless, yellow, brown, or pinkish liquids obtained from coal tar. Cresols have a sharp smell, rather like that of a *disinfectant.* The fumes are irritating if inhaled. If swallowed, cresols can cause circulatory collapse and death; the same effects may occur if they are absorbed through the skin. Cresols are used as disinfectants.

CRESYLIC ACID. See *Cresol.*

CRESYLOL. See *Cresol.*

CUBE EXTRACT. An insecticide derived from powdered Derris root and used in houseplant insecticides.

CYANIDE. One of the most powerful poisons known. As part of the compounds hydrogen cyanide and sodium cyanide, it is found in rat poisons. Prussic acid is another name for hydrogen cyanide.

CYANOACRYLATE. A liquid plastic used in "instant" glues. When applied to certain nonporous surfaces, the cyanoacrylate molecules intermix with the molecules of the surface to form a tight and lasting bond. Also known as cyanoacrylate monomer.

CYANOACRYLATE MONOMER. See *Cyanoacrylate.*

CYANURIC ACID. See *Trichloroisocyanuric acid.*

D

DDT. The first popular commercial organophosphate insecticide, now banned in most areas. The initials stand for dichloro-diphenyl-trichloro-ethane.

DDVP. A synonym for O,O-*dimethyl O-(2,2-dichlorovinyl) phosphate.*

DENATURANT. See *Denatured alcohol.*

DENATURED ALCOHOL. Ordinary (ethyl) alcohol to which a substance, such as camphor, castor oil, or acetone, has been added so as to make the alcohol unfit for consumption as a beverage. Denaturants, the chemicals used to produce this effect, not only make ethyl alcohol taste and smell bad but sometimes make it significantly more toxic. Some denatured alcohols are more toxic than others. A completely denatured alcohol (CDA) contains methanol, which is highly poisonous. Specially denatured alcohols (SDA or SD alcohol), such as tert-butyl alcohol, are less dangerous. Denatured alcohols are used as solvents in a variety of products.

DEOBASE. A trade name for *deodorized kerosine.*

DEODORIZED KEROSINE. A solvent. Although this highly purified form of kerosine no longer smells like kerosine, it is still as poisonous as plain kerosine. One ounce or more may be fatal to an adult if swallowed.

DETERGENT. Strictly speaking, a detergent is a cleaner, either natural or synthetic. Common usage, however, has come to define detergents as synthetic, nonfat cleaners that usually work as well in cold, hard water as they do in warm, soft water. Soaps, which are natural, fatty products, will not work in cold water. Detergents are "surface-active"; they reduce the surface tension between dissimilar liquids or surfaces. (Surface-active detergents are also known as surfactants or wetting agents.) Therefore, they can soften and emulsify oil or grease stains on clothing and make it easier to remove such stains in the laundry. Some detergents may be poisonous if swallowed. See also Surfactant; Anionic surfactant; Cationic surfactant; Nonionic surfactant.

DEXTRIN. A nontoxic vegetable gum used in putties and some caulks.

DIATOMACEOUS EARTH. A bulky, light powder, white to light gray or beige in color, that is used as a clarifier or absorbent and as a filler and very fine abrasive in metal polishes and as a filler in paint. Chronic inhalation of diatomaceous earth can cause silicosis, a serious lung disorder. Diatomaceous earth is said to be composed of the skeletons of petrified microscopic marine creatures, which is why it is sometimes called "fossil flour." It is also known as infusorial earth.

DIAZINON. A synonym for O,O-*diethyl O-(2-isopropyl-4-methyl-6-pyrimidyl) phosphorothionate.*

s-(1,2-DICARBETHOXYETHYL)-O,O-DIMETHYL DITHIOPHOSPHATE. See *Malathion.*

p-DICHLOROBENZENE.   An insecticide used in moth flakes and mothballs, and a disinfectant used in toilet bowl blocks. It is the least toxic of the ingredients used in moth repellents; nevertheless, its vapors can irritate skin, eyes, and throat, and prolonged exposure to high concentrations of *p*-dichlorobenzene can cause dizziness, weakness, weight loss, and liver damage. In addition, it is a suspected carcinogen. Also known as paradichlorobenzene, paramoth, and parazene.

DICHLOROMETHANE.   See *Methylene chloride.*

DICHLORVOS.   A synonym for O,O-*dimethyl O-(2,2-dichlorovinyl) phosphate.*

DIETHANOLAMINE.   An emulsifier and solvent that may be irritating to the skin. See also Amine.

DIETHYLENE GLYCOL.   A colorless liquid with a sharp, sweetish taste but no discernible odor. It absorbs water and is therefore used to keep pastes, cosmetics, and inks for ball-point pens from drying out. Diethylene glycol is moderately toxic. If swallowed, one ounce or more can cause kidney or liver damage or death. Products containing 10 percent or more diethylene glycol (by weight) must carry the words "Warning. Harmful if swallowed."

O,O-DIETHYL   O-(2-ISOPROPYL-4-METHYL-6-PYRIMIDYL)   PHOSPHOROTHION-ATE.   An insecticide, also known as Diazinon, that may be fatal if swallowed or absorbed through the skin.

O,O-DIMETHYL   O-(2,2-DICHLOROVINYL)   PHOSPHATE.   An insecticide also known as DDVP, Dichlorvos, or Vapona. Rarely toxic to humans except those suffering from liver disease, because it is rapidly inactivated by the enzymes in a healthy mammalian liver.

DIMETHYL KETONE.   See *Acetone.*

DIPENTENE.   A solvent with a pleasant lemony odor used in waxes, polishes, and paint driers. It is found in essential oils such as oils of lemon, orange, dill, and bergamot and is obtained by distilling either these oils or wood turpentine. It is a mild local irritant and skin sensitizer and is combustible.

DIPHENADIONE.   An indanedione compound used in rat poisons. Also known as 2-diphenylacetyl-1,3-indanedione.

2-DIPHENYLACETYL-1,3-INDANEDIONE.   See *Diphenadione.*

DIRECT DYE.   A water-soluble coloring agent used in fabric dyes. Direct dyes are a type of acid dye and can be easily absorbed by cotton, rayon, and other materials made from cellulose-type fibers. They work when warmed.

DISINFECTANT.   An ingredient or product that slows the growth of organisms on a surface. Phenyphenol is a disinfectant; so is chlorine bleach.

DISPERSANT.   An ingredient used to keep small particles of solid material suspended in a liquid.

DISPERSE DYE.   A coloring agent used in fabric dyes. It is a coal tar dye that may cause allergic reactions and can sometimes irritate the skin.

DOWCIDE 1.   A phenol compound used as a germicide and disinfectant. See also Phenylphenol.

DRIER. An ingredient which hastens oxidation and thus the drying of liquid mixtures, such as paint.

DUTCH LIQUID. A synonym for *ethylene dichloride.*

E

EDC. A synonym for *ethylene dichloride.*

EDTA. A synonym for *ethylenediaminetetraacetic acid.*

ELASTOMER. One of a group of rubberlike synthetics that are used to make latex paints strong, durable, and water-resistant. Some examples are acetate elastomer, acrylic elastomer, styrene butadiene elastomer, and neoprene elastomer.

EMULSIFIER. See *Emulsion.*

EMULSION. A mixture of usually unmixable liquids, such as oil and water. An emulsifier (for example, ethanolamine) keeps the ingredients in an emulsion from separating.

ENZYME. Enzymes are catalysts that initiate chemical actions. They are used in laundry detergents to help remove stains. Since the enzymes in these products are derived from proteolytic bacteria (organisms that have the ability to decompose proteins), they are most useful in washing away protein stains, like those made by blood or meat.

EPICHLOROHYDRIN. A colorless, flammable liquid that smells like chloroform. It is used as a solvent in varnishes, paints, and nail polishes. Epichlorohydrin is a strong skin sensitizer. Its vapors are irritating to the eyes and to mucous membranes. It has caused tumors when injected under the skin of laboratory rats, and, if swallowed, less than one ounce may be fatal for an adult. Also known as 1-chloro-2,3-epoxypropane.

EPOXY RESIN. A resin used in epoxy glues. It is nontoxic. (The amine curing agent, or hardener, which mixes with the resin to form the adhesive, is poisonous if swallowed.)

ESSENCE OF MIRBANE. A synonym for *nitrobenzene.*

ESSENTIAL OIL. One of a number of nonfatty oils derived from plants. Essential oils, such as geraniol or eucalyptol, have the taste and smell of the original plant. They are sometimes called volatile oils because they evaporate quickly. Most are poisonous in the pure state (in some cases, as little as seven drops can be fatal). Essential oils are used to perfume household products, as well as cosmetics and (in diluted form) foods. They are also used as germicides and preservatives, since they have the ability to destroy bacteria.

ETHANEDIOIC ACID. A synonym for *oxalic acid.*

ETHANEDIOL. A synonym for *ethylene glycol.*

182

ETHANOL. A synonym for *ethyl alcohol.*

ETHER. One of a group of organic compounds created either by removing the water from alcohols (glycol ether, for example, is derived from ethylene glycol) or by adding water to olefins. Most ethers are liquids, and many are very flammable. They are used as solvents and plasticizers. ("Ether" as an anesthetic is actually ethyl ether, made from ethanol, or ethyl alcohol.)

2-ETHOXYETHANOL. Also known as cellosolve. A combustible solvent used in floor and furniture polish, varnish remover, and wallpaper remover, as well as nail polishes. A colorless and odorless liquid, 2-ethoxyethanol will pass through intact skin and can cause depression of the central nervous system and kidney damage. If swallowed, one ounce or more may be fatal for an adult. Butyl cellosolve is a more toxic form of this solvent.

ETHOXYLATED ALKYL ALCOHOL. A nonionic surfactant used as a detergent and solvent in household cleaners.

ETHOXYLATED LINEAR ALCOHOL. A detergent used in toilet bowl cleaners.

ETHYL ACETATE. A clear liquid, with a fruity odor and a pleasant taste, that is obtained by slowly distilling acetic acid, ethyl alcohol, and sulfuric acid. It is a very flammable solvent used in varnishes, lacquers, and some model cements. Its vapors are irritating, and prolonged inhalation can produce depression of the central nervous system, as well as kidney and liver damage. If swallowed, an ounce or more may be fatal for an adult.

ETHYL ACRYLATE. An *acrylic resin.*

ETHYL ALCOHOL. Ordinary or grain alcohol, often simply called "alcohol." A solvent in paint and wax removers, it is also an antiseptic and preservative. If swallowed, it produces gastrointestinal irritation, central nervous system depression, and (if sufficient amounts are ingested) coma and death.

ETHYL AMYL KETONE. A flammable solvent derived from cellulose. See also Ketone.

ETHYL CELLULOSE. A plastic used to give strength and water-resistance to paints and coatings.

ETHYLENE. An olefin from which many plastics and elastomers are derived.

ETHYLENE CHLORIDE. A synonym for *ethylene dichloride.*

ETHYLENEDIAMINETETRAACETIC ACID. A water-softening agent and sequestrant added to detergent products so as to inactivate the minerals (such as calcium) in hard water. More commonly known as EDTA.

ETHYLENE DICHLORIDE. A flammable, poisonous solvent with a pleasant odor and a sweet taste. Also known as Dutch liquid, ethylene chloride, or EDC. Its vapors are irritating and can cause central nervous system disorders, as well as stomach cramps and dizziness. It is used in paint removers, dry-cleaning fluids, and plastic glues. If swallowed, one ounce or more may be fatal to an adult.

ETHYLENE GLYCOL. A colorless, syrupy alcohol with a sweet taste that is used as a humectant in antifreeze and brake fluids, as well as in inks and ink pads. Its vapors are irritating, and, if swallowed, ethylene glycol can cause vomiting, convulsions, coma, kidney damage, and death. Products containing 10 percent or more (by weight) must contain the words "Warning. Harmful or fatal if swallowed." Also known as ethanediol.

ETHYLENE GLYCOL ALKYL ETHER.   A solvent that is found in wax and acrylic removers, among other products. Ethylene glycol ethers are produced by removing the water from ethylene glycols.

ETHYLENE GLYCOL DISTEARATE.   A practically nontoxic, white, waxy nonionic surfactant used to make liquid detergents and dishwashing liquids opaque white.

ETHYLENE TETRACHLORIDE.   A synonym for *tetrachloroethylene.*

F

FATTY ACID.   A nontoxic liquid or solid organic acid such as capric acid, lauric acid, myristic acid, oleaic acid, and stearic acid. When combined with alkanolamines, they make soap.

FELDSPAR.   Any of a group of inorganic minerals that are found in nearly all crystalline rocks. Feldspar is ground up to act as a mild abrasive in abrasive cleaners such as Bon Ami.

FILLER.   Any ingredient used to bulk up or extend powders, pastes, or thick liquids. Sodium chloride, for example, can be used as a filler in fabric dyes (up to 98 percent). Talc may be used as a filler in cosmetic powders and make-up bases; clay in abrasive scouring powders.

FLAXSEED OIL.   A synonym for *linseed oil.*

FLUORESCENT BRIGHTENER.   A dye, such as fluorescein, that is made from anthracene, an oil extracted from coal. Fluorescent brighteners are added to cleaning products (including laundry detergents and dishwashing liquids) to make things look "whiter than white." See also Bluing.

FORMALDEHYDE.   A colorless gas produced by the oxidation of methyl alcohol. Dissolved in water, it is known as formaldehyde solution, Formalin, or Formol and used as a disinfectant, germicide, fungicide, and perservative in a variety of products, including cosmetics. It is found in wick-type room deodorizers, plastic menders, glues, and starch products. Formaldehyde is a formidable allergen and allergic sensitizer. Its vapors are irritating to mucous membranes, and, if swallowed, it can cause gastric pain, internal bleeding, dizziness, coma, and death. One ounce of formaldehyde has been known to produce death within two hours. Paraformaldehyde is a polymerized form of parmaldehyde.

FORMALIN.   A trade name for *formaldehyde.*

FORMIC ACID.   A poisonous liquid that smells bad and is irritating to the skin and eyes.

FORMOL.   See *Formaldehyde.*

184

FOSSIL FLOUR. A synonym for *diatomaceous earth*.

FRAGRANCE. An ingredient, such as an essential oil, which gives a pleasing scent to a product.

FREON. See *Chlorofluorocarbon*.

FUMARIN. A trade name for *coumafuryl*.

FUMIGANT. An ingredient or product that kills insects when released into the air.

FUNGICIDE. An ingredient or product that kills or retards the growth of fungi and molds. Biphenyl is a fungicide used in mildew preventives.

G

GERMICIDE. An ingredient which, like a disinfectant, kills or retards the growth of microorganisms such as bacteria, viruses, and molds.

GLYCERIN. A humectant that keeps products like mucilage glues from drying out.

GLYCOL. A thick, syrupy alcohol which acts as a humectant, holding moisture in such products as floor waxes.

GLYCOL ETHER. A flammable liquid, used as a solvent in various cleaning products. Derived by removing the water from (dehydrating) ethylene glycol.

GLYCOLIC ACID. A synonym for *hydroxyacetic acid*.

GUM ARABIC. A sticky water-soluble substance, obtained from a tropical tree, used in ordinary glues.

GUM CAMPHOR. A synonym for *camphor*.

GUM ROSIN. See *Rosin*.

GUM TURPENTINE. See *Turpentine*.

GYPSUM. A form of calcium sulfate that tends to harden after absorbing water. If swallowed, it can cause intestinal obstructions. Gypsum is used in the manufacture of cements and plasters.

H

HALOCARBON. An organic compound to which a halogen has been added. Examples of halocarbons are such propellants as chlorofluorocarbons and chlorinated hydrocarbons.

HALOGEN. The five chemical elements astatine, bromine, chlorine, fluorine, and iodine. Each may be combined with organic compounds to produce halocarbons.

HALOGENATED ALIPHATIC HYDROCARBON. An aliphatic hydrocarbon to which a halogen has been added. Examples are propylene dichloride, an ingredient in soil fumigants, and epichlorohydrin, a widely used liquid solvent.

HALOGENATED AROMATIC HYDROCARBON. An aromatic hydrocarbon to which a halogen has been added. Examples are chlorobenzene, a solvent used in dry cleaning, and hexachlorobenzene, a solvent and fumigant.

HEXACHLOROBENZENE. A halogenated aromatic hydrocarbon used as a solvent in antifreeze solutions and as a fumigant. A poison that, if swallowed, can cause skin lesions, weight loss, and wasting of the skeletal muscles. Also known as perchlorobenzene.

HEXAMETAPHOSPHATE. A phosphate salt used in laundry detergents. If swallowed, it can cause severe gastroenteritis, including vomiting, diarrhea, and possible strictures (scar-tissue obstructions) in the esophagus.

HEXANE. A colorless, flammable liquid with a faint odor. It evaporates quickly and is used as a solvent in rubber cement and glues. The fumes are irritating to the respiratory tract, and they can be narcotic in high concentrations.

HUMECTANT. An ingredient that absorbs and holds moisture so as to keep thick liquids from drying out.

HYDROCARBON. Any gas, liquid or solid, composed of carbon and hydrogen molecules. Hydrocarbons differ from one another according to the number and arrangement of these molecules, and are derived from coal, petroleum (which is a mixture of individual hydrocarbons), or vegetation. They are used as fuels and solvents. Most hydrocarbons are both flammable and poisonous; their fumes are irritating. Examples of hydrocarbons are methane gas and benzene. See also Aliphatic hydrocarbon; Aromatic hydrocarbon; Chlorinated hydrocarbon; Halogenated aliphatic hydrocarbon; Halogenated aromatic hydrocarbon.

HYDROCHLORIC ACID. Also known as muriatic acid. A yellowish solution of hydrogen chloride in water, hydrochloric acid is used in metal cleaners and polishes and toilet bowl cleaners. It is corrosive; a concentrated solution may cause severe skin burns and, if splashed into the eye, blindness. If inhaled, hydrochloric acid fumes may cause choking and inflammation of the respiratory tract. Products containing 10 percent or more hydrochloric acid (by weight) must be labeled "Poison."

HYDROGEN CHLORIDE. A gas formed by combining hydrogen and chlorine. Hydrochloric acid is a solution of hydrogen chloride and water.

HYDROGEN CYANIDE. See *Cyanide.*

HYDROGEN PEROXIDE. An oxidant, bleach, and germicide that is caustic in high concentrations (a 90 percent hydrogen peroxide solution is used as rocket fuel) but essentially harmless in the 3 percent solution sold over the counter as a first-aid preparation. It is sometimes found in metal cleaners.

HYDROXYACETIC ACID. A hydrophilic, or "water-loving," ingredient which absorbs and holds moisture. It is also known as glycolic acid. It may be found in wallpaper removers.

186

HYDROXYCOUMARIN COMPOUND. A compound based on coumarin, an ingredient that interrupts the production of vitamin K (which helps blood clot). Hydroxycoumarin compounds are used in rat poisons. They cause death by internal hemorrhage. Examples include Coumachlor and Warfarin.

2-HYDROXYETHYL-*n*-OCTYL SULFIDE. An insecticide that is less toxic for human beings than most. Also known as MGK 874.

I

INACTIVE INGREDIENT. From the manufacturers' point of view, inactive ingredients are the fillers, solvents, and vehicles that play supporting roles in products. In contrast, the active ingredients are those that actually carry out the function a product is supposed to perform. However, an ingredient labeled "inactive" is not necessarily innocuous; the term definitely does not indicate that an ingredient is guaranteed safe or nonpoisonous. For example, kerosine, which is both flammable and poisonous, is the inactive ingredient in some pest sprays. The clearest illustration of the commercial differentiation between active and inactive ingredients can be found on the labels on paint cans, where the pigments (or coloring agents) are clearly distinguished from the vehicles (or inactive ingredients).

INDANEDIONE COMPOUND. A compound that produces hemorrhaging, as a hydroxycoumarin compound does. Indanedione compounds are more toxic, however. It takes less to produce a fatal effect. Examples of indanedione compounds are Diphenadione and Valone, both of which are used in rat poisons.

INERT INGREDIENTS. Ingredients that normally do not react chemically with other substances. Water is the most common inert solvent. Talc and silica are common inert fillers.

INFUSORIAL EARTH. A synonym for *diatomaceous earth*.

INSECTICIDE. An ingredient or product used to kill insects.

IODOPHOR. Any combination of iodine and detergent used as a disinfectant in household cleaners.

IRON OXIDE. A natural or synthetic form of iron combined with oxygen. Iron oxides are used as coloring agents in various forms of cosmetics.

ISOAMYL ACETATE. See *Amyl acetate*.

ISOBORNYL THIOCYANOACETATE. An aliphatic thiocyanate that serves as a source of cyanide in insecticide compounds. See Thanite.

ISOPROPANOL. A synonym for *isopropyl alcohol*.

2-ISOPROPOXYPHENYL N-METHYLCARBAMATE. A highly toxic roach killer. As little as a taste may be fatal for both adults and children. Also known as Propoxur, Baygon, and Unden.

ISOPROPYL ALCOHOL. A colorless, highly flammable liquid with a bitter taste that is used as a denaturant for ethyl alcohol. It is also used as a solvent for gums and shellac, in jewelry cleaners, floor polishes, and furniture polishes. If swallowed, or if large quantities of the vapors are inhaled, isopropyl alcohol can cause flushing, headache, dizziness, and mental depression. Also referred to as isopropanol.

2-ISOVALERYL-1,3-INDANEDIONE.   An indanedione compound used as an anticoagulant in rat poisons, to cause death by internal hemorrhaging. Also known by the trade name Valone.

J

JAPAN WAX.   A fat or waxy material obtained from the fruit of *Rhus succedanea L.*, a plant indigenous to the Far East. Japan wax smells something like tallow and is used in the same kinds of products—furniture and floor waxes and polishes—in which you would expect to find beeswax. It is essentially nontoxic.

K

KAOLIN.   A clay (aluminum silicate) used as an anticaking agent or as a filler in a wide variety of products.

KEROSENE.   See *Kerosine*.

KEROSINE.   A petroleum distillate whose name (also spelled "kerosene") comes from the Greek word for wax. This pale yellow or white oily liquid is a solvent and degreasing agent used in furniture and floor polishes, paint removers, spot cleaners, dry-cleaning fluids, and wallpaper cleaners. It is poisonous; an ounce or more may be fatal if swallowed by an adult. Also known as Coal oil. See also Deodorized kerosine; Deobase.

KETONE.   One of a group of chemical solvents that work particularly well on materials derived from cellulose. Acetone, which is most familiar as a nail polish solvent or remover, is probably the best-known of the group.

L

LAC, LACCA.   The major constituent of shellac. See also Shellac.

LEAD.   A chemical element, lead is a heavy gray metal that is soft and easily molded. Lead compounds are used primarily as coloring agents in paints, but not in paints used for home interiors, since children who chew on peeling or chipped lead paint may develop lead poisoning. Lead compounds are sometimes also used as coloring agents in the hair dyes that are advertised as "color restorers"; the lead compounds build up in layers on the hair to make it look darker. Lead compounds may cause contact dermatitis and are poisonous whether swallowed or inhaled as dust. Lead is a cumulative poison, and small amounts ingested or inhaled over a long period of time can cause leg cramps, muscle weakness, numbness, and brain damage.

LEAD ARSENATE. A highly toxic insecticide.

LETHANE 60. An aliphatic thiocyanate, or cyanide-releasing insecticide.

LETHANE 384. An aliphatic thiocyanate, or cyanide-releasing insecticide, also known as beta-butoxy-beta thiocyanodiethyl ether or 2-butoxy-2-thiocyanodi-ethyl ether.

LIGROIN. See *Mineral spirits.*

LIME. A synonym for *calcium oxide.*

LINEAR ALKYL BENZENE SULFONATE. A biodegradable anionic surfactant synthesized from petroleum and used in household laundry detergents. It is practically harmless—only because, if swallowed, the surfactant promptly induces vomiting, after which there is almost nothing left in the stomach to be absorbed by the body.

LINSEED OIL. A yellowish liquid obtained by crushing flax seeds (linseed oil is also known as flaxseed oil). It has a characteristic odor, a bland or faintly disagreeable taste, and is both digestible and nutritious. Because it dries to a hard, water-resistant film, it is often used as a vehicle in paints and varnishes.

LINSEED OIL, BOILED. Boiled linseed oil is a very different ingredient from linseed oil. It has not actually been boiled, but has been thickened by having air blown through it. Unlike plain linseed oil, it may be toxic since lead, cobalt, manganese, and other toxic substances are often added to the oil. Boiled linseed oil is used in polishes.

LIQUID ROSIN. See *Tall oil.*

LYE. See *Potassium hydroxide; Sodium hydroxide.*

LYSOL. Outside the United States, "lysol" is the name for an extremely toxic and corrosive cresol and soap solution. In this country, however, "Lysol" is used as a trademark for a product line of Lysol brand household cleaners. None of these products contains the highly toxic ingredient cresol.

MAGNESIUM LAURYL SULFATE. An anionic detergent and surfactant used in laundry products. It is a possible skin irritant.

MAGNESIUM SILICATE. Small particles of naturally occurring rock found in cat-box litters as aluminum magnesium silicate.

MALATHION. Also known as *S*-(1,2-dicarbethoxyethyl)-*O,O*-dimethyl dithio-phosphate, malathion is a poison used in some houseplant insecticides and ordinary insecticides.

MALEIC ANHYDRIDE-STYRENE COPOLYMER. A plasticizer, used in aerosal foaming cleaners.

METHANE. An aliphatic hydrocarbon; a naturally occurring, bad-smelling, flammable gas.

METHANOL. A flammable, colorless or light-colored liquid that smells like alcohol. Originally obtained from the distillation of wood, methanol is now manufactured synthetically. It is used as a solvent in stove fuels, paint removers and paintbrush cleaners, and dry-cleaning fluids. It is also used as a denaturant—perhaps the chief denaturant—for ethyl alcohol, to make it unfit for consumption. Methanol (which is also known as methyl alcohol, wood spirits, or wood alcohol) is poisonous if swallowed; it may also be absorbed through the skin. Products containing more than 4 percent methanol (by weight) must carry the following label copy, in addition to the traditional skull-and-cross-bones poison symbol: "Danger. Poison. Vapor harmful. May be fatal or cause blindness if swallowed. Cannot be made nonpoisonous."

METHOXYCHLOR. See *1,1,1-Trichloro-2,2-bis(p-methoxyphenyl) ethane.*

METHOXY-DDT. See *1,1,1-Trichloro-2,2-bis(p-methoxyphenyl) ethane.*

METHYL ACETATE. A colorless liquid, with a pleasant or fragrant aroma, that is used as a solvent in glues, particularly fabric glues. It is flammable and the fumes are irritating to the respiratory tract and can be narcotic if inhaled in high concentrations.

METHYL ACRYLATE. See *Acrylic resin.*

METHYL ALCOHOL. A synonym for *methanol.*

METHYL BENZENE. A synonym for *toluene.*

METHYL CHLOROFORM. A synonym for *1,1,1-trichloroethane.*

METHYL CELLULOSE. A cellulose-based thickener. May be found in some paint strippers, among other products.

METHYLENE CHLORIDE. A colorless gas that can be compressed into a colorless liquid to be used as a solvent in paint removers. Its vapors are neither flammable nor explosive, but they are narcotic in high concentrations and can be particularly dangerous to persons who have had heart attacks or who are heavy smokers. Methylene chloride is sometimes used as an anesthetic; it is not absorbed through the skin. Also known as dichloromethane.

METHYL ETHYL KETONE. A solvent used in a variety of products. It may be irritating to the skin, and its vapors may be irritating to the eyes and mucous membranes.

METHYL NONYL KETONE. A solvent with penetrating fumes that are irritating to the skin and mucous membranes. Used in animal repellents.

METHYL POLYSILOXANE. A silicone compound used in water-repellent silicone sprays or liquids.

METHYL SALICYLATE. A fragrance, sanitizer, and deodorant obtained by distilling the crushed leaves of sweet birch, cassia, or wintergreen. Also known as oil of wintergreen or sweet birch oil, methyl salicylate is a strong skin and mucous membrane irritant and is poisonous if swallowed or absorbed through the skin. It can cause nausea, vomiting, convulsions, and death, and when injected under the skin of pregnant rabbits, it caused fetal deformities. Betula oil, extracted from the leaves of the white birch, is similar in its toxicity.

MGK 264. A synergist that increases the action of the poison or active ingredient in an insecticide.

MGK 874. See *2-Hydroxyethyl-n-octyl sulfide.*

MICROCRYSTALLINE WAX. A material derived from petroleum and made up of very small crystals. It is similar to paraffin wax but has a thicker, more viscous consistency and a greater ability to penetrate porous surfaces like wood. It is used in adhesives and in various kinds of polishes.

MILK OF LIME. See *Calcium hydroxide.*

MINERAL NAPHTHA. See *Benzene.*

MINERAL OIL. A colorless oily liquid that is tasteless, odorless, and edible. Used medically as a laxative, it may be used in household oils or as a cheap substitute for these products.

MINERAL SEAL OIL. A liquid hydrocarbon similar to mineral spirits or naphtha in its toxic effects. It is used in the dark and reddish shades of floor and furniture polishes.

MINERAL SPIRITS. A highly flammable naphtha, or mixture of liquid hydrocarbons, that is used as a solvent in paints and in floor and furniture polishes. A petroleum distillate, it is also known as petroleum spirits or ligroin. The word "mineral" is used to identify its origins in material found in the earth's crust (i.e., petroleum); the word "spirits" (which comes from the Latin word for "breath") is an unscientific term once generally applied to substances that are volatile, or evaporate quickly. Mineral spirits is flammable, its vapors are irritating, and it is poisonous if swallowed. Products containing 10 percent or more (by weight) must carry the label warning "Danger. Harmful if swallowed. If swallowed, do not induce vomiting. Call physician immediately." As with other petroleum distillates, there is some question about whether the directive not to induce vomiting is still correct poison-control practice.

MIRBANE. A synonym for *nitrobenzene.*

MONOPOTASSIUM PEROXY MONOSULFATE. A bleach and disinfectant.

MORPHOLINE. A highly alkaline emulsifier used, for example, in floor polishes. Both the liquid and its vapors are irritating to the skin and to the mucous membranes of eyes and throat. If swallowed, as little as one fifth of a teaspoonful may be fatal for a small child.

MURIATIC ACID. A synonym for *hydrochloric acid.*

N

NAPHTHA. Any one of several either coal-tar-based or petroleum-based mixtures of liquid hydrocarbons usually used as solvents. Examples include mineral spirits (also known as petroleum spirits or ligroin) and petroleum benzin (also known as petroleum ether). All naphthas are flammable, poisonous, and volatile.

NAPHTHALENE. Also known as naphthene. The primary constituent of coal tar. When purified for commercial use, it takes the form of white flakes and its coal tar odor is changed so that it smells like *camphor*. Naphthalene may be used as a moth repellent (although p-dichlorobenzene is used more frequently today) and as a deodorant in toilet bowl blocks. Its fumes are combustible, and it is poisonous whether swallowed, inhaled, or absorbed through the skin. Symptoms of naphthalene poisoning include nausea, vomiting, headaches, convulsions, and coma.

NAPHTHENE. A synonym for *naphthalene*.

NEOPRENE. See *Elastomer*.

NITRATE. A compound containing nitrogen. One example is nitrocellulose. Nitrates are usually explosive and flammable.

NITROBENZENE. A colorless or pale yellow oily liquid that smells like almonds. Also known as essence or oil of mirbane, it is used as a solvent in furniture, floor, and shoe polishes and is extremely toxic. If swallowed, as little as seven drops may be fatal to an adult, and its vapors are poisonous, too. Products containing nitrobenzene should never be allowed to fall on your clothes as you work, because the nitrobenzene can seep through the material to be absorbed in fatal amounts through your skin. Always wear impermeable gloves when using products containing this ingredient.

NITROCELLULOSE. A highly flammable mixture of nitrate and cellulose, the latter being the material found in the walls of plant cells. Also referred to as cellulose nitrate. Although it may be explosive as well as flammable, nitrocellulose is nontoxic. It is used to lend bulk to glues and fast-drying lacquers.

NITROGEN. A chemical element. An essential plant nutrient, nitrogen is usually found in plant foods.

NONIONIC SURFACTANT. Surface-active agents whose molecules are neither positively nor negatively charged. Nonionic surfactants such as ethylene glycol distearate are often used as opacifiers in liquid detergents. See also Surfactant.

O

OIL OF CITRONELLA. An essential oil used as a fragrance. It is irritating to the skin and may be used in dog and cat repellents.

OIL OF LEMONGRASS. An essential oil used as a fragrance in a variety of household products and cosmetics.

OIL OF MIRBANE. A synonym for *nitrobenzene*.

OIL OF TURPENTINE. See *Turpentine*.

OIL OF VITRIOL. A synonym for *sulfuric acid.*

OIL OF WINTERGREEN. A synonym for *methyl salicylate.*

OLEFIN. One of a major class of aliphatic hydrocarbons that includes ethylene, a flammable gas from which many plastics are derived, and butadiene, a flammable gas used in resins and synthetic rubbers.

OLEIC ACID. A nontoxic fatty acid, used in soaps and as a thickener in various lotion-type products, like floor polishes.

OLEORESIN CAPSICUM. Oil of an African chili. An irritant used in animal repellents.

OPACIFIER. An ingredient that makes clear liquids opaque. Ethylene glycol distearate, for example, is used to make dishwashing liquids an opaque white.

OPTICAL BRIGHTENER. See *Fluorescent brightener.*

ORGANOPHOSPHATE. A compound containing an organic ingredient plus a phosphate (an inorganic alkali). Malathion is an organophosphate insecticide; so is parathion.

ORTHO BENZYL PARACHLOROPHENOL. See *Chlorophene.*

ORTHOXENOL. See *Phenylphenol.*

OXALIC ACID. Colorless, corrosive crystals, also known as ethanedioic acid, that occur naturally in many plants and vegetables, including spinach and dieffenbachia. The latter has been dubbed "dumb cane" because when its leaves are chewed the oxalic acid contained in them causes the tongue to swell and the victim cannot speak; he is dumb. Oxalic acid can be manufactured by oxidizing sugars and starches. It is used as a corrosive cleaner and stain remover in metal polishes, floor and furniture polishes, paint and varnish removers, and rust and stain removers. If swallowed this poisonous substance may cause gastroenteritis, vomiting, diarrhea, and, in large doses, death. It is also corrosive to the skin and mucous membranes. Products containing concentrations of oxalic acid stronger than 10 percent must be labeled "Poison."

OZOCERITE. A waxlike substance composed of hydrocarbons and solid wastes of petroleum. When purified for use in household and other products, such as cosmetics, ozocerite is known as ceresin.

P

PARADICHLOROBENZENE. See p-*Dichlorobenzene.*

PARAFFIN. A flammable mixture of solid hydrocarbons derived from petroleum and used as a waterproofing agent in floor waxes and polishes and waxed paper. Because it cannot be absorbed by the body, it is nontoxic.

PARAFFIN WAX. See *Paraffin.*

PARAFORMALDEHYDE. A polymerized form of formaldehyde. See also Formaldehyde.

PARAMOTH. A trade name for p-*dichlorobenzene.*

PARATHION. A derivative of phosphoric acid originally developed as a nerve gas and later used as an insecticide. Severely toxic to human beings.

PARAZENE. A synonym for p-*dichlorobenzene.*

PEAR OIL. A synonym for *amyl acetate.*

PENTANOL. A synonym for *amyl alcohol.*

PERCHLOROBENZENE. See *Hexachlorobenzene.*

PERCHLOROETHYLENE. See *Tetrachloroethylene.*

PERFUME. A synonym for *fragrance.*

PERFUME OIL. A synonym for *fragrance* or *essential oil.*

PEROXIDE. See *Hydrogen peroxide.*

PEROXY BLEACH. A bleach based upon an oxygenating ingredient such as sodium perborate. Laundry bleaches labeled "all-fabric" are peroxy-based bleaches.

PESTICIDE. An ingredient or product used to destroy pests.

PETROLEUM BENZIN. A highly flammable, clear, and colorless petroleum distillate used as a solvent in floor and furniture polishes, dry-cleaning fluids, and some stove cleaners. Petroleum benzin, which evaporates quickly, is also known as petroleum ether. It is very toxic.

PETROLEUM DISTILLATE. A generic name for clear or colorless solvents obtained from the distillation of petroleum. Petroleum distillates are found in dry-cleaning fluids, liquid floor and furniture polishes, insecticides, and other household products. They are flammable and poisonous, and many are photosenzitizers, which means that contact with them can make the skin very sensitive to light. Examples of petroleum distillates are kerosine, mineral spirits, petroleum benzin, and Stoddard solvent. Products containing 10 percent or more (by weight) of any of these or any other petroleum distillates must be labeled "Danger. Harmful if swallowed. If swallowed, do not induce vomiting. Call physician immediately." The instructions not to induce vomiting were originally applied to cases of petroleum distillate poisoning because of the risk of breathing the distillates into the lungs during vomiting. Aspiration of distillates into the lungs can cause a potentially lethal form of chemical pneumonia. However, because these chemicals are so toxic, some poison control experts now feel that the most important objective is to get them out of the stomach before they can be absorbed into the body. Whether the label instructions on products containing petroleum distillates should be revised is currently being debated.

PETROLEUM ETHER. See *Petroleum benzin.*

PETROLEUM OIL. See *Mineral oil.*

PETROLEUM SOLVENT. See *Petroleum distillate.*

PETROLEUM SPIRITS. See *Mineral spirits.*

194

PHENOL. A caustic poison obtained either from coal tar or from benzene compounds. Phenol is used as a general disinfectant in toilet-bowl, floor, or general-purpose cleaners. It is poisonous whether swallowed or absorbed through the skin (over large areas). Swallowing even small amounts can cause nausea, vomiting, convulsions, coma, and death. Also known as carbolic acid.

PHENOLIC CASTOR OIL. A base for synthetic resins such as those used in varnishes.

PHENYLPHENOL. White, flaky crystals obtained from coal tar and used as a germicide and disinfectant. Phenylphenol is poisonous; if swallowed it may cause nausea, vomiting, circulatory collapse, convulsions, and coma. It is irritating to the skin but, unlike phenol, cannot be absorbed through normal, unbroken skin. Also known as orthoxenal. Dowcide 1 is a phenylphenol.

PHOSPHATE. One of a group of inorganic compounds commonly found in natural rock structures. Phosphates are the basic material from which phosphorus, an essential mineral nutrient for plants and animals, is derived. In household products, phosphates (usually tripolyphosphate and sodium tripolyphosphate) are used as builders, to intensify the stain-lifting action of detergents and surfactants in laundry detergents. When waste water containing these phosphates is discharged into sewer systems, however, the phosphates so enrich the waterways into which they flow that an overgrowth of algae can result, choking off fish and other aquatic animal life. In recognition of this hazard, phosphate detergents have been banned in many parts of the country. Medically, phosphate detergents may be irritating to the skin; if swallowed, they may cause vomiting and diarrhea.

PHOSPHORIC ACID. A corrosive mineral acid, used in rust removers.

PHOSPHORIC ACID, DILUTE. A colorless, odorless solution of phosphate in water or alcohol that is used as a cleaner and polisher in metal polishes. Strong concentrations are irritating to the skin and will damage porcelain. Dilute phosphoric acid is usually stored in stainless steel containers.

PHOSPHORUS. A chemical element that is an essential nutrient for plants. Phosphorus is found in houseplant foods.

PINENE. See *Camphor.*

PINE OIL. A colorless-to-pale-yellow combustible oil that smells somewhat like turpentine and is derived from pine trees. It is used as a solvent, disinfectant, and deodorant in household cleaners. Pine oil is irritating to the skin and mucous membranes and, if swallowed, can cause nausea, vomiting, and convulsions. It is also a possible allergen, and is sometimes known as yarmor.

PIPERONYL BUTOXIDE. A synergist, or booster, found in household and houseplant insecticides. It increases the toxicity of both.

PLASTER OF PARIS. A synonym for *calcium sulfate.*

PLASTICIZER. An ingredient that gives plastic coatings or films their flexibility and gloss.

POLYALKALINE GLYCOL. A moderately toxic nonionic detergent. If swallowed, one ounce or more may be a lethal dose for an adult.

POLYAMIDE. One of a class of polymers from which plastics, adhesives, and coatings such as paints are made. Some polyamides are natural (casein, the main protein in milk, is one example); some, like nylon or some form of resins, are synthetic.

POLYAMIDE RESIN. A plastic, used in epoxy adhesives.

POLYETHOXY POLYPROPOXY ETHANOL-IODINE COMPLEX. An iodophor, used as a disinfectant in household disinfectant/deodorizing cleaners.

POLYETHYLENE. A plastic, often included in furniture polishes for body, shine, and water resistance.

POLYETHYLENE GLYCOL. See *Ethylene glycol.*

POLYHYDRIC ALCOHOL. A plasticlike coating agent.

POLYMER. A chemical compound whose molecules are formed by a chemical reaction in which two or more small molecules are combined into one large molecule. (The literal definition of polymer is "of many parts.") The molecules in a polymer are usually arranged in long chains, which gives the polymer strength and elasticity. Plastics are polymers; so are some fibers, rubber, and, of course, human tissues. See also Resin.

POLYSTYRENE RESIN. A resin used as a base in some household cements and glues. Polystyrenes are polymers that harden when exposed to room temperature.

POLYURETHANE. A plastic polymer used in coatings.

POLYVINYL ACETATE. A rubberlike synthetic ingredient usually found in latex paints. It is used to give strength and elasticity to the paint.

POLYVINYL ADHESIVE. A thermoplastic (heat-sensitive) plastic such as polyvinyl acetate, used as an adhesive.

POLYVINYL PLASTIC. An ingredient that gives strength to such products as spackling compounds. Polyvinyls are polymers which harden when exposed to room temperatures.

POTASH. A generic name for the potassium salts found in plant foods. (Potassium is an essential nutrient for plants.)

POTASSIUM. A chemical element that is an essential nutrient for plants. Potassium is found in houseplant foods, usually listed as potash.

POTASSIUM CHLORATE. A white or colorless powder that is both flammable and explosive, commonly used in match heads. If swallowed, potassium chlorate is irritating to the gastrointestinal tract, causing nausea and vomiting. It can also cause kidney and blood disorders; one teaspoonful or more may be fatal to an adult.

POTASSIUM CHLORIDE. A buffer that controls the acid/alkali balance; sometimes found in detergents, including dishwashing liquids.

POTASSIUM CHROMATE. See *Chromate salt.*

POTASSIUM DICHROMATE. Bright orange-red crystals, used as protective pigment in antirust and anticorrosion products. Potassium dichromate is a corrosive poison; ingestion of as little as one fifth of a teaspoonful may be fatal for an adult. It can corrode the skin, too, and long-term exposure (such as people working with potassium dichromate in industrial situations might experience) can lead to skin ulcers or, if the dust is inhaled, to perforation of the nasal septum.

POTASSIUM HYDROXIDE. A white corrosive powder, also known as lye; or caustic potash, that is used in cleaning agents, detergents, paint and varnish removers, and drainpipe cleaners. If swallowed, potassium hydroxide causes violent pain and severe burning of the throat and esophagus. If these injuries are not immediately fatal, the victim may recover—only to develop strictures (scar tissue formations) of the esophagus, which can prevent swallowing and breathing and must be treated surgically. Products containing potassium hydroxide must be packed in child-proof containers. See also Sodium hydroxide.

POTCRATE. See *Potassium chlorate.*

PRESERVATIVE. An ingredient that keeps other ingredients in a product from deteriorating. Many preservatives have germicidal properties and may be used to keep bacteria from proliferating in the product once the container has been opened.

1,2-PROPANEDIOL. A synonym for *propylene glycol.*

PROPANONE. See *Acetone.*

PROPELLANT. A gas that is introduced into sealed containers (aerosols) to push liquid-, lotion-, or cream-type products out of the container. See Butane; Carbon dioxide; Chlorofluorocarbon.

PROPOXUR. A synonym for *2-isopropoxyphenyl N-methylcarbamate.*

PROPYLENE GLYCOL. A clear, colorless, syrupy liquid with a faintly bitter taste, which sometimes substitutes for ethylene glycol as a solvent or moisture-absorbing humectant in a wide variety of lotion-type products. Also known as 1,2-propanediol.

PRUSSIC ACID. A synonym for *hydrogen cyanide.*

PYRETHRIN. Insecticide drawn from ground-up flowers of a chrysanthemum, *Chrysanthemum cinerariaefolium.* Pyrethrins, which are used in all kinds of bug killers, are not very toxic to human beings, but they may be severe allergens to anyone sensitive to pollens.

Q

QUATERNARY AMMONIUM COMPOUND. A cationic surfactant, synthetically derived from ammonium chloride, that is widely valued for its ability to sanitize, deodorize, and clean. Quaternary ammonium compounds are used in all kinds of detergent products, from diaper cleaners to general household disinfectant cleaners. Depending upon the dose and the concentration, all these compounds can be toxic. If they are concentrated, they can be severely irritating to the skin and mucous membranes, and swallowing them may be fatal. The probable lethal dose for an adult is one teaspoonful or more. Two examples of quaternary ammonium compounds are alkyl aryl ammonium chloride and benzalkonium chloride (the latter is significantly less toxic than most quaternary ammonium compounds).

QUICKLIME.   A synonym for *calcium oxide.*

N-2-QUINOXALYL-SULFANILAMIDE.   A synonym for *sulfaquinoxaline.*

R

RED SQUILL.   A natural poison drawn from the inner scales of the bulb of the *Scilla maritima.* Used in rat poisons, it causes violent convulsions and severe vomiting. Red squill is lethal to rats because their bodies lack the ability to regurgitate the contents of their stomachs. It is unlikely to be lethal to human beings and household pets such as dogs and cats because all these would quickly vomit it up.

RESIN.   A water-resistant substance that occurs naturally in many trees and shrubs. Resins are sticky and soft when warm, and hard and brittle when cool. They can be dissolved either in alcohol or in petroleum distillates such as kerosine or benzene, and they are used in varnishes and adhesives. Resinlike substances, called polymers, are manufactured synthetically. These plastics and fibers have some of the properties of resins (they're soft and pliable when warm, and hard and strong when cool), but they are not called resins, because that term refers only to the natural substance. See also Acrylic resin.

RESMETHRIN.   A synthetic derivative of natural pyrethrins that is used as an insecticide. It is generally even less toxic to humans than the natural pyrethrins.

ROSIN.   The residue that remains after the essential oils have been distilled away from pine resins. Gum rosin is produced by distilling crude turpentine gum; wood rosin is the product obtained by distilling pine stumps. Both rosins are water-resistant and assumed to be nontoxic. Rosins are used in adhesives and as the sticky element on flypaper. (Flypaper covered with rosin but not sprayed with an insecticide is nontoxic.)

ROTENONE.   An insecticide drawn from dried and powdered *Derris* or *Lonchocarpus* (cube) roots and used in houseplant insecticides. It is rarely lethal for human beings, because if it is swallowed it causes immediate vomiting.

S

SAL SODA.   A synonym for *sodium carbonate.*

SALT.   A synonym for *sodium chloride.*

SANITIZER. An ingredient such as benzalkonium chloride, that eliminates germs and makes a surface cleaner and more sanitary. Germicides are sanitizers.

SD ALCOHOL. See *Denatured alcohol.*

SEQUESTRANT. An ingredient that combines with specific metals in a solution, inactivating them so that they do not affect the action of other ingredients or products in the solution. For example, phosphates are sequestrants that are used in detergent products to soften hard wash water by binding calcium so that it does not cling to clothes as a dirty-looking scum, thus inactivating the cleaning action of a detergent ingredient such as sodium lauryl sulfate. Sequestrants are sometimes known as chelating agents.

SHELLAC. The resinous excretion of an insect that lives on the kusum tree in India. The natural product, a whitish powder, is dissolved in methanol, or wood alcohol (which makes it poisonous), to form a sticky solution that dries to form a hard, transparent finish. Sometimes an arsenic compound is added to give color to the shellac solutions.

SILICA. Sand. Silica is used as a filler in many household products.

SILICA GEL. A solid, porous material made from silica that absorbs moisture. It is used in roach killers. When a roach walks through the silica gel, the gel adheres to its body and absorbs the moisture in it so that the insect actually "dries" to death.

SILICATE. See *Sodium metasilicate; Sodium polysilicate; Sodium silicate.*

SILICON. The second most abundant chemical element on earth (the first is oxygen), composing about 27.6 percent of the earth's crust, where it is found in a variety of rock substances such as quartz, sand, sandstone, feldspar, and kaolinite. A source of silicones, which are used in waterproofing products.

SILICON DIOXIDE. An abrasive used in metal cleaners.

SILICONE. One of a number of waterproofing and bonding agents derived from siloxanes, compounds of silicon and oxygen. Silicones may occur as fluids (silicon oils), rubbers, or resins and are used in a wide variety of products including lubricants, adhesive and caulking compounds, paints, enamels and varnishes, and water repellents for fabrics and clothes. Perhaps the most famous silicone product is "Silly Putty," the children's toy that can be bounced, stretched, broken, or shattered without being damaged.

SLAKED LIME. See *Calcium hydroxide.*

SOAP. Humankind's basic "natural" cleaner, a simple mixture of fats (animal or vegetable) and alkalis, such as *lye*. Modern soaps also contain humectants (moisture absorbing ingredients), usually glycerol, a syrupy *alcohol*. In general, simple soaps are harmless. Laundry soaps, which contain more alkalis than face or bath soaps do, are more irritating to the skin. Unlike synthetic detergents, soaps are likely to leave an alkali film on clothes and skin, which is why old-fashioned soap shampoos were always followed with an acid (lemon or vinegar) rinse to dissolve and remove the alkali soap "scum" they left behind.

SODA ASH. A synonym for *sodium carbonate.*

SODA LYE. See *Sodium hydroxide.*

SODIUM ACID SULFATE. A synonym for *sodium bisulfate.*

SODIUM ALKYL ARYL SULFATE. A synonym for *alkyl aryl sodium sulfate.*

SODIUM ALKYL SULFATE. A synonym for *alkyl sodium sulfate.*

SODIUM ARSENATE. A highly toxic (60 percent arsenic) insecticide.

SODIUM BISULFATE. A strongly corrosive mineral acid used in crystalline toilet bowl cleaners as a cleaner and disinfectant. Also known as sodium acid sulfate.

SODIUM BORATE. An anhydrous (moistureless) form of borax that is available as crystals, granules, or powder. A mild alkali, sodium borate is used as a detergent in a variety of cleansers. It is moderately toxic when inhaled, absorbed through broken skin, or swallowed. If ingested, the probable lethal dose for an adult may be one ounce or more; for a small child, however, one sixth of an ounce or more may be fatal. Sodium borate is also known as boric acid.

SODIUM CARBONATE. An alkali used in laundry bleach powders, laundry detergents, and water softeners to soften water and increase the cleaning power of the detergent. It can be corrosive in strong concentrations. One form of sodium carbonate is also known as washing soda, sal soda, or soda ash.

SODIUM CHLORIDE. Ordinary table salt. Sodium chloride is used in fabric dyes to increase the absorption of dye by the fibers. It is poisonous if swallowed in large quantities.

SODIUM CHROMATE. See *Chromate salt.*

SODIUM CITRATE. White, odorless crystals or powder with a slightly salty taste. Used as a water softener and detergent.

SODIUM CYANIDE. See *Cyanide.*

SODIUM DICHLORO-S-TRIAZINETRONE SULFONATE. A synonym for *trichloroisocyanuric acid.*

SODIUM DODECYLBENZENESULFONATE. An anionic surfactant of the alkyl aryl sodium sulfonate group. It may be irritating to the skin and, if swallowed, can cause vomiting.

SODIUM EDETATE. A synonym for *sodium salt of ethylenediaminetetraacetic acid.*

SODIUM FLUORIDE. Sodium fluoride is a safe and effective decay preventive when added to water supplies in a low concentration of one part sodium fluoride to one million parts water. High concentrations of sodium fluoride, however, are toxic to humans, animals, and insects. As little as one sixth of an ounce of pure sodium fluoride has caused human death; when ingested in high concentrations, it may also cause nausea, vomiting, gastroenteritis, convulsions, and respiratory or kidney failure. It is used in insecticides at concentrations that may exceed 180,000 parts per million.

SODIUM FLUOSILICATE. A corrosive, abrasive compound used in metal cleaners.

SODIUM HEXAMETAPHOSPHATE. A dispersant that helps to keep calcium, magnesium, and iron salts in solution in the wash water so that these minerals won't adhere as scum to the clothes. It is used as a water softener and as a detergent.

SODIUM HYDROXIDE. A white, corrosive alkaline powder also known as caustic soda, soda lye, lye, and sodium hydrate. There is no way to pin down a specific lethal dose for this poisonous alkali, because its toxicity is directly related to its concentration. Powder drain cleaners (or granules) may be 100 percent sodium hydroxide, while liquid drain cleaners contain a less concentrated form of the ingredient. Any product containing a concentration of sodium hydroxide higher than 10 percent, however, must be labeled "Poison" and must be packed in a "child-proof" container. See also Potassium hydroxide.

SODIUM HYPOCHLORITE. White crystals; a source of chlorine, a bleach and disinfectant in dishwashing liquids and laundry detergents. Sodium hypochlorite is irritating to the skin, and to the respiratory tract if inhaled. If swallowed, it can cause burns and perforation of the esophagus and stomach.

SODIUM LAURYL SULFATE. One of a group of anionic surfactants described by the generic name alkyl sodium sulfates. It may cause skin irritation and, if swallowed, may cause mild gastric upset, including diarrhea and bloating.

SODIUM LINEAR ALKYL BENZENE SULFONATE. See *Linear alkyl benzene sulfonate*.

SODIUM METASILICATE. An alkali used in laundry and dishwashing detergents, as well as in aluminum cleaners. Crystals are obtained by fusing sand and soda ash at temperatures up to 1150 degrees Fahrenheit. Sodium metasilicate is corrosive to skin, eyes, and all mucous membranes. In fact, it may well be the most corrosive element in ordinary household laundry and dishwashing products.

SODIUM NITRATE. Also known as black powder or saltpeter. The colorless or transparent crystals are found in a number of products, including crystal drain cleaner (in which sodium nitrate functions as a corrosion inhibitor) and gunpowder. Sodium nitrate is also used as a food preservative (predominantly in meat products, such as bologna, bacon, hot dogs) and is under government suspicion as a possible carcinogen. Most sodium nitrate is mined in Chile.

SODIUM ORTHOSILICATE. An anticaking agent similar to sodium silicate.

SODIUM PERBORATE. A strongly alkaline white, odorless powder that tastes slightly salty. This bleach is commonly found in abrasive cleaners, laundry and dishwashing detergents, powder bleaches, and coffeepot cleaners (it cleans metal well). It is a systemic poison that can damage eyes and the central nervous system if absorbed through mucous membranes or broken or irritated skin and can cause vomiting and diarrhea if swallowed. As little as one teaspoonful may be fatal for an adult.

SODIUM PHOSPHATE. A phosphate that is used in various detergents to increase cleansing action. It is mildly irritating to the skin and mucous membranes and, if swallowed, can cause purging. In fact, it is used medically as a cathartic.

SODIUM POLYSILICATE. An anticaking ingredient in powdered detergents.

SODIUM PYROPHOSPHATE. See *Tetrasodium pyrophosphate.*

SODIUM SALT OF ETHYLENEDIAMINETETRAACETIC ACID. A sequestrant that is used to attract free-floating microscopic metal particles in various liquid detergent products. Also known as sodium edetate, ethylenedinitrilo tetra-acetic acid (tetrasodium salt), tetrasodium ethylenediamine triacetate, and tetrasodium salt of EDTA, it is used medically in cases of metal poisoning to detoxify lead and other heavy metals and to increase their excretion from the body.

SODIUM SESQUICARBONATE. An alkali produced from sodium carbonate and sodium bicarbonate and used in laundry soaps and powder bleaches. It may be corrosive if swallowed in sufficient concentrations and can be irritating to the skin and mucous membranes. It is also a possible allergen.

SODIUM SILICATE. Used as an anticaking agent in detergents and soaps. It is irritating to skin and mucous membranes and, if swallowed, can cause vomiting and diarrhea. Because its colorless-to-gray-white crystals can be dissolved in water, producing an alkaline solution, sodium silicate is also known as water glass and soluble glass.

SODIUM SILICOFLUORIDE. A synonym for *sodium fluosilicate.*

SODIUM STEARATE. An emulsifier and soap found in, among other products, liquid detergents.

SODIUM SULFATE. An anhydrous (moistureless) form of sulfuric acid, found in nature in the minerals mirabilite and thenardite, which are mined in the western United States. The crystalline powder is used as an anticaking agent in soaps and detergents (see Alkyl aryl sulfonate). Taken internally, sodium sulfate draws water to the bowels, so it has medicinal uses as a purgative.

SODIUM TETRABORATE. See *Sodium borate.*

SODIUM TRIPOLYPHOSPHATE. Alkaline crystals used to intensify the action of detergents and cleaners of all kinds. Also known as STPP. If swallowed, sodium tripolyphosphate can cause serious gastric upset; it is also irritating to the skin and mucous membranes. See also Phosphate.

SODIUM XYLENE SULFONATE. A solvent, cleaner, and disinfectant derived from petroleum. See also Xylene.

SOLUBLE GLASS. See *Sodium silicate.*

SOLVENT. A liquid that dissolves other ingredients. The most common solvents are water, ethyl alcohol, and the hydrocarbons, such as benzene and toluene.

STABILIZER. An ingredient that keeps an emulsion well-mixed and creamy.

STARCH. A carbohydrate polymer that occurs naturally in a wide variety of plants, including corn, tapioca, rice, and potatoes. When mixed with warm water, starch forms a stiff gel (cold water will merely turn it into hard lumps) that can give body to fabrics if applied after laundering. Starch, which is also known as smylum, is virtually nontoxic.

STODDARD SOLVENT. A petroleum distillate used as a solvent in dry-cleaning fluids. Products containing 10 percent or more Stoddard solvent (which is also known as white spirits) must be labeled "Danger. Harmful or fatal if swallowed. If swallowed do not induce vomiting. Call physician immediately."

STPP. A synonym for *sodium tripolyphosphate.*

STYRENE BUTADIENE ELASTOMER. A rubberlike synthetic used to give elasticity and strength to latex paints.

STYRENE COPOLYMER. A synthetic, resinlike substance. See also Resin; Polymer.

SULFAMIC ACID. A cleaning agent used in metal cleaners. Irritating to the skin and the mucous membranes.

SULFAQUINOXALINE. An ingredient that inhibits the growth of the intestinal bacteria which produce vitamin K, the vitamin that enables the blood to clot. Sulfaquinoxaline is usually added to rat poisons containing hydroxycoumarin compounds, so as to increase the ability to kill the rats by producing internal hemorrhaging. Also referred to as *N*-2-quinoxalyl-sulfanilamide.

SULFATED CASTOR OIL. Castor oil treated with sulfuric acid. It is an anionic surfactant that is used in dyeing fabrics to produce brighter colors. It is also used in cosmetics as a color remover that strips metallic hair dyes from the hair. If swallowed, sulfated castor oil is moderately toxic; an ounce or more may be fatal for an adult. Also known as turkey-red oil or sulfonated castor oil.

SULFONATED CASTOR OIL. See *Sulfated castor oil.*

SULFOTEPP. A synonym for *tetraethyl dithiopyrophosphate.*

SULFUR. A chemical element that makes up about 0.05 percent of the earth's crust. It is found—mainly as sulfides and sulfates—in the American Southwest, in Sicily, and in the Middle East. Sulfur is used mostly on match heads and in metal and glass cements. It can be irritating to the skin, the eyes, and the mucous membranes. If inhaled, the dust is irritating to the respiratory tract, but sulfur is practically nontoxic if swallowed.

SULFURIC ACID. A clear or colorless, odorless oily liquid that is highly corrosive. Sulfuric acid is used in pipe and drain cleaners, which require "special" or "child-proof" packaging. If inhaled in high concentrations, the vapors can be damaging to the respiratory tract.

SURFACTANT. Surfactants lower the surface tension of liquids, allowing them to spread out more quickly (as window cleaner on a window) or to penetrate fabrics more quickly (as in fabric softeners) or to lift off other liquids (as in a detergent product's "lifting off" grease stains). All detergents are surfactants or surface-active agents; whether or not a surfactant is classified as a detergent depends on how it is used, that is, in what kind of product and for what purpose. See also Anionic surfactant; Cationic surfactant; Nonionic surfactant.

SYMCLOSENE. A synonym for *trichloroisocyanuric acid.*

SYNERGIST. An ingredient that boosts the effect of another ingredient. For example, MGK 264 and piperonyl butoxide are synergists used in insecticides to boost the power of the primary bug killer.

T

TALLEOL. A synonym for *tall oil.*

TALL OIL. "Tall" is the Swedish word for pine; this dark brown liquid is a by-product of the pine wood and pulp industries. It smells something like burnt rosin and is used in paints, resins, and leather polishes. It is a mild skin irritant and a possible allergic sensitizer.

TALLOL. A synonym for *tall oil.*

TARTARIC ACID. An acid that occurs naturally in many fruits, including grapes. Tartaric acid is the base from which cream of tartar is made; the acid may also be used in commercial products, as in metal or jewelry cleaners.

TERPINEOL. A thick, colorless liquid composed of three of the major constituents of pine oil (which is about 75 percent terpineol). Terpineol has a faint odor of lilacs and is used both as a fragrance and an antiseptic. It can be irritating to eyes and mucous membranes and, if swallowed, can cause central nervous system depression as well as gastric hemorrhaging. An ounce or more may be fatal for an adult.

TETRACHLOROETHYLENE. A colorless, nonflammable liquid used as a solvent in metal cleaners and dry-cleaning fluids. Its vapors are narcotic in high concentrations. Because it can dissolve fat, tetrachloroethylene can be irritating to the skin. If swallowed, one ounce or more may be fatal for an adult. Also referred to as ethylene tetrachloride.

TETRAETHYL DITHIOPYROPHOSPHATE. One of the (if not *the*) most toxic of the insecticides used in household bug killers. As little as a taste may be fatal for either child or adult. It is also poisonous if absorbed through the skin. Also known as sulfotepp.

TETRASODIUM ETHYLENEDIAMINETRIACETATE. A synonym for *sodium salt of ethylenediaminetetraacetic acid.*

TETRASODIUM PYROPHOSPHATE. An alkaline, crystalline substance that acts as a sequestrant, a clarifier, and a water softener and is used in cleaning products and one-fluid ink eradicators. It is irritating to the skin and mucous membranes and, if swallowed, can cause nausea, vomiting, and diarrhea. Oral doses of one ounce (and sometimes less) may be fatal for an adult. Also referred to as TSPP.

TETRASODIUM SALT OF EDTA. See *Sodium salt of ethylenediaminetetraacetic acid.*

THANITE. An aliphatic thiocyanate, or cyanide-releasing insecticide containing isobornyl thiocyanocetate.

THIOCARBAMIDE. A synonym for *thiourea.*

THIOUREA. A derivative of ammonia used in metal (particularly silver) cleaners. It is relatively nontoxic.

204

TITANIUM DIOXIDE. A white powder that occurs naturally in the following mineral ores: brookite, ilmenite, octahedrite, perovskite, and rutile. It is used as a white color or opacifier in enamels, paints, and shoe polishes. If inhaled in high concentrations, the powder can be irritating to the lungs, but titanium dioxide is virtually harmless otherwise. Quantities as great as one pound have been consumed without ill effect.

TOLUENE. A colorless, flammable, and poisonous petroleum distillate used as a solvent in glue, cement, paintbrush cleaners, paint removers, and dry-cleaning fluids. Toluene is a source of both benzene and phenol. If inhaled in high concentrations, it is narcotic and capable of causing both depression of the central nervous system and psychological aberrations. If swallowed, it can cause mild anemias; an oral dose of one teaspoonful or more may be fatal for an adult. Products containing 10 percent or more toluene (by weight) must be labeled "Danger. Harmful if swallowed. If swallowed, do not induce vomiting. Call physician immediately. Vapor harmful." Also known as toluol.

TOLUOL. A synonym for *toluene*.

TRI. A synonym for *trichloroethylene*.

TRICHLORAN. See *Trichloroethylene*.

alpha-TRICHLOROETHANE. A synonym for *1,1,1-trichloroethane*.

1,1,1-TRICHLOROETHANE. A degreasing solvent widely used in dry-cleaning fluids and typewriter cleaners. Nonflammable and only mildly irritating to the skin, it can be absorbed through the lungs but is harmful only in high concentrations. The lethal oral dose for an adult may be one ounce or more.

1,1,2-TRICHLOROETHANE. A solvent that is used in some cleaning fluids. It can be absorbed into the body through the lungs, through intact skin, and, if swallowed, through the gastrointestinal tract. It is a stronger central nervous system depressant than chloroform, and oral doses as small as one teaspoonful may be fatal for an adult. Also known as vinyl trichloride.

TETRASODIUM PYROPHOSPHATE. A clarifier, used to keep liquids from clouding.

TRICHLOROETHYLENE. A heavy, colorless liquid solvent that smells something like chloroform. It is used in waxes, resins, oils, paints, and varnish, as well as dry-cleaning fluids and rug cleaners. Trichloroethylene is nonflammable, but moderate inhalation can cause a kind of inebriation and, in heavy concentrations, it is narcotic in effect. It can be absorbed through the skin, and as little as one teaspoonful may be a lethal oral dose for an adult. Finally, it is a proven animal carcinogen. Trichloroethylene is also referred to as trichloran, trilene, and TRI.

TRICHLOROISOCYANURIC ACID. A chlorinated form of cyanuric acid, used as a source of chlorine (bleach) in various household cleaners such as scouring powders and laundry bleach tablets. It is irritating to the eyes and to abraded or injured skin. If swallowed, it is corrosive to the stomach lining (one ounce or more may be fatal for an adult), and inhaling the dust can cause spasms of the air passages.

1,1,1-TRICHLORO-2,2-*bis*(*p*-METHOXYPHENYL) ETHANE.   An *insecticide* similar to *DDT* but only 10 percent as lethal if swallowed by human beings. It is also known as methoxychlor or methoxy-DDT.

TRIPOLYPHOSPHATE.   An alkali, also known as sodium tripolyphosphate, found in many detergent products. Like other alkalis found in household detergents, it can cause gastric upset if swallowed in quantity.

TRISODIUM CITRATE.   See *Sodium citrate.*

TRISODIUM PHOSPHATE.   Colorless or white alkaline crystals used in all-purpose powder cleaners and as a water softener in laundry products. Trisodium phosphate is corrosive and caustic to the skin. How harmful it is if swallowed or absorbed through the skin depends on how concentrated it is. Also referred to as TSP.

TSP.   A synonym for *trisodium phosphate.*

TSPP.   A synonym for *tetrasodium pyrophosphate.*

TURKEY-RED OIL.   A synonym for *sulfated castor oil.*

TURPENTINE.   A hydrocarbon solvent obtained by distilling yellow, sticky exudate from the bark of pine trees (gum turpentine) or from pine stumps (wood turpentine). Chemically, the name "turpentine" also refers to oil or spirit of turpentine, an essential oil of the pine tree. Turpentine is flammable and poisonous. As little as one ounce may be a lethal oral dose for an adult. It can be absorbed through the skin and has caused tumors when applied to the skin of laboratory mice. Turpentine is used in waxes, shoe polishes, leather and furniture polishes, and as a paint thinner and paint remover. Products containing 10 percent or more (by weight) must be labeled "Danger. Harmful or fatal if swallowed."

TURPENTINE GUM.   See *Turpentine.*

U

ULTRAMARINE.   See *Ultramarine blue.*

ULTRAMARINE BLUE.   A pigment prepared from powdered lapis lazuli which occurs naturally in the earth's crust. It is used as a coloring and brightening agent in liquid and powder laundry bluing products. It may also be produced synthetically as a pigment containing a mixture of kaolin, soda ash, sulfur, and charcoal.

UNDEN.   A trade name for *2-isopropoxyphenyl* N-*methylcarbamate.*

UREA.   A germicide and preservative derived from ammonia and carbon dioxide. Urea also occurs as a natural component of urine.

V

VALONE. A trade name for *2-isovaleryl-1,3-indanedione.*

VAPONA. A trade name for O,O-*dimethyl* O-*(2,2-dichlorovinyl) phosphate.*

VEHICLE. A liquid base, such as a solvent. See also *Inactive ingredient.*

VINYL TRICHLORIDE. A synonym for *1,1,2-trichloroethane.*

VOLCANIC ASH. An abrasive that is used in scouring cleaners.

W

WARFARIN. A trade name for *3-(alpha-acetonylbenzyl)-4-hydroxycoumarin.*

WASHING SODA. A synonym for *sodium carbonate.*

WATER GLASS. A synonym for *sodium silicate.*

WATER SOFTENER. An ingredient added to detergent products to keep minerals from forming a scum on laundry. Some water softeners, such as sodium carbonate (washing soda), work by precipitating calcium and magnesium out of the water. Others, such as the phosphates, work by keeping the minerals in suspension so that they cannot cling to clothes or linens.

WAX. A thermoplastic solid, which is soft and pliable when warm, and hard and brittle when cool. Waxes may be derived from animals (beeswax), minerals (ozocerite/ceresin), or hydrocarbons (paraffin wax). They are used in shoe, furniture, and floor polishes, waxed papers, and, of course, candles. Waxes are generally nontoxic.

WETTING AGENTS. See *Detergent.*

WHITENER. See *Fluorescent brightener; Bluing.*

WHITE SPIRITS. A synonym for *Stoddard solvent.*

WHITING. A finely pulverized form of calcium carbonate, or chalk. Despite its name, whiting does not serve as a coloring agent; rather, it is used as a filler in plastics and rubbers and in putty. It is virtually nontoxic.

WINTERGREEN; WINTERGREEN OIL. A synonym for *methyl salicylate.*

WOOD ALCOHOL. A synonym for *methanol.*

WOOD FLOUR. Powdered sawdust, used as a filler in some putties and other filling products.

WOOD ROSIN. See *Rosin.*

WOOD SPIRITS. A synonym for *methanol.*

WOOD TURPENTINE. See *Turpentine.*

X

XYLENE. A flammable, colorless petroleum distillate with a characteristic odor. Xylene is obtained from coal tar and gas, although its name comes from the Greek word for wood *(xylos)*. It is used as a solvent in paintbrush cleaners, and, because it dissolves fat, it is irritating to the skin. It is also highly toxic, and if ingested as little as one teaspoonful can be fatal for an adult. Its vapors may be narcotic in high concentrations. Products containing more than 10 percent xylene (by weight) must be labeled "Danger. Harmful or fatal if swallowed. If swallowed, do not induce vomiting. Call physician immediately."

Y

YARMOR. A synonym for *pine oil*.

Z

ZEIN. The major protein in corn. Used as a thickener in adhesives and shellac substitutes.

ZINC ARSENATE. An insecticide whose lethal action is due to the arsenic.

ZINC ARSENITE. An insecticide whose toxicity is due to the arsenic.

ZINC CHROMATE (VI) HYDROXIDE. A fine yellow powder used as a pigment or coloring agent in paints and varnishes.

ZINC META-ARSENITE. See *Zinc arsenate*.

ZINC OXIDE. A substance obtained from the mineral zincite. Its fumes may be toxic, but it does not appear to be poisonous if ingested in powder form. Zinc oxide is used instead of lead as a white pigment in paints.

ZINC WHITE. A synonym for *zinc oxide*.

Writing Complaint Letters

Most of the time, the products we buy do what they are supposed to.

Once in a while, though, something goes wrong. Either the product doesn't work, or it actually does some damage—to your clothes, your furniture, or you. That's the point at which you will want to write an effective complaint letter.

Will the manufacturer listen? Some manufacturers will. Some won't. Unfortunately, you cannot tell in advance whether your letter will elicit results. The only way to find out is to write.

That's exactly what I did when I was doing the research for this book. I had specific questions about a number of different products, and I sent my requests for information either to "President" or "Research Director." I got answers from the following companies: Airwick, American Cyanamid, Amway, Armour-Dial, Beecham, Bissell, Borden, Clorox (which also sent along a nifty little booklet on how to write complaint letters), CPC, DAP, Dow, Drackett, DuPont, Independence Chemical, S. C. Johnson & Son, Krazy Glue, Knomark, Lehn & Fink, Miller-Morton, NIP-CO, Noxell, Sherwin-Williams, Testor, 3M, Topco, Union Carbide, and West Chemical.

On the other hand, a number of companies never did find the time to answer. This does not mean that Balkamp, Boyle-Midway, Nutcher Polish, Carbona, Glamourene, Gorham, Hartz Mountain, Lever Brothers, Procter and Gamble, Purex, Texize, U.S. Plywood, and Wilbert's do not make excellent products. But it does say something about the quality of their consumer relations.

Perhaps the biggest surprise of my letter-writing campaign was the fact that some consumers' advocates are not much more responsive. Heaven knows that if there is a consumer's sacred cow in this country, it is Consumers Union. Yet my experience was that *Consumer Reports*, the Consumers Union magazine, simply would not take the time to answer serious questions about some of its product ratings. This was all the more surprising in view of *Consumer Reports'* well-taken displeasure with manufacturers or other companies that do not wish to take the time to answer questions relating to *Consumer Reports* articles.

Complaints about complaint letters aside, though, it does make sense to follow a few simple rules in writing letters to large corporations so as to make yours the kind of letter that gets answered.

Start by writing a letter which is legible enough to be read. If you don't have access to a typewriter, print your letter in clear, block letters.

Be sure to put your name and address on the letter itself, as well as on the envelope, so that if the envelope and letter get separated, you can still receive an answer. You may also want to include your telephone number since some companies now call consumers directly with an answer.

State your complaint clearly; don't beat around the bush. Nobody is perfect, and even giant corporations make mistakes. If you let a company know that something isn't working, there is always the chance the people there will appreciate the chance to set things right.

Be precise: Tell them the exact name of the product about which you are complaining, including the size of the package and the number which you find stamped or embossed on the bottom. That way, they can pin down the trouble to one particular batch of the product; in really serious cases, it may enable the company to recall an entire batch.

It is not a bad idea to let the company know exactly what you want them to do about the problem you had with their product. Will an apology do? Do you want a replacement? A coupon? Reimbursement for damage done to your belongings? The more information you supply, the more likely you are to get what you want.

Finally, if someone was injured by the product—even though the product was used correctly—you may be faced with a situation in which it is difficult for you to be realistic and calm. Make the effort. If necessary, get professional help in writing your letter. The clearer, calmer, and more direct you are, the better your chances of reaching a satisfactory resolution of the problem.

The following is a list of the major manufacturers of household products with their mailing addresses:

AIRKEM see Airwick

AIRWICK INDUSTRIES, INC.
380 North Street
Teterboro, New Jersey 07608

AMERICAN CYANAMID COMPANY
Consumer Products Division
Berdan Avenue
Wayne, New Jersey 07470

AMERICAN HOME PRODUCTS
CORP.
685 Third Avenue
New York, New York 10017

AMWAY CORP.
7575 East Fulton Road
Ada, Michigan 49301

A & P
90 Delaware Avenue
Paterson, New Jersey 07503

ARMOUR-DIAL, INC.
100 South Wacker Drive
Chicago, Illinois 60680

BALKAMP, INC.
2601 South Holt Road
P.O. Box 41008
Indianapolis, Indiana 46241

BEATRICE FOODS CO.
120 South LaSalle Street
Chicago, Illinois 60603

BEECHAM PRODUCTS
P.O. Box 1467
Pittsburgh, Pennsylvania 15230

BEST FOODS
1437 West Morris Street
Indianapolis, Indiana 46206

BISSELL, INC.
Grand Rapids, Michigan 49501

BORDEN CHEMICAL
see BORDEN, INC.

BORDEN, INC.
277 Park Avenue
New York, New York 10017

BOYLE-MIDWAY
South Avenue and Hale Street
Cranford, New Jersey 07016

BRONDOW, INC.
1075 Central Park Avenue
Scarsdale, New York 10583

BUTCHER POLISH CO.
Bartlett Street
Marlborough, Massachusetts 01752

CARBONA PRODUCTS CO.
30–50 Greenpoint Avenue
Long Island City, New York 11101

CLIMALENE CO.
1022 Ninth Street S.W.
Canton, Ohio 44701

CHURCH & DWIGHT CO., INC.
20 Kingsbridge Road
Piscataway, New Jersey 08854

THE CLOROX COMPANY
P.O. Box 24305
Oakland, California 94623

COLGATE-PALMOLIVE CO.
300 Park Avenue
New York, New York 10022

DAP, INC.
P.O. Box 277
Dayton, Ohio 45401

d-CON CO., INC.
90 Park Avenue
New York, New York 10018

DEVCON CORP.
Danvers, Massachusetts 01923

DOW CHEMICAL
Midland, Michigan 48640

DRACKETT CO.
5020 Spring Grove Avenue
Cincinnati, Ohio 45232

E. I. DUPONT DE NEMOURS & CO.
Wilmington, Delaware 19898

EASTMAN CHEMICALS
343 State Street
Rochester, New York 14650

ECONOMICS LABORATORY, INC.
Osborn Building
St. Paul, Minnesota 55102

ELECTROLUX CORP.
235 East 42 Street
New York, New York 10017

E-Z-EST PRODUCTS CO., INC.
2528 Adeline Street
Oakland, California 94607

FAULTLESS STARCH CO.
1025 West 8 Street
Kansas City, Missouri 64101

GENERAL CABLE CORP.
500 West Putnam Avenue
Greenwich, Connecticut 06830

GLAMORENE PRODUCTS CORP.
175 Entin Road
Clifton, New Jersey 07014

J. GODDARD & SON
see S. C. JOHNSON & SON, INC.

GORHAM
333 Adelaide Avenue
Providence, Rhode Island 02907

L. S. GREEN ASSOCIATES
162 West 56 Street
New York, New York 10019

W. J. HAGERTY & SONS, LTD., INC.
1503 Prairie Avenue
P.O. Box 1496
South Bend, Indiana 46624

HARTZ MOUNTAIN CORP.
700 South Fourth Street
Harrison, New Jersey 07029

J. I. HOLCOMB
4401 Cold Springs Road
Indianapolis, Indiana 46208

INDEPENDENCE CHEMICAL
COMPANY
North Railroad and Essex Street
Gloucester City, New Jersey 08030

JOHNSON WAX
see S. C. JOHNSON & SON, INC.

S. C. JOHNSON & SON, INC.
1525 Howe Street
Racine, Wisconsin 53403

KIWI POLISH CO.
2 High Street
Pottstown, Pennsylvania 19464

KNOMARK, INC.
132–20 Merrick Boulevard
Jamaica, New York 11434

KRAZY GLUE
53 West 23 Street
New York, New York 10011

LEHN & FINK PRODUCTS CO.
225 Summit Avenue
Montvale, New Jersey 07645

LEVER BROTHERS
390 Park Avenue
New York, New York 10022

LEWAL INDUSTRIES, INC.
1841 Central Park Avenue
Yonkers, New York 10710

LEWIS RESEARCH
LABORATORIES
75 Oak Street
Norwood, New Jersey 07648

MILES LABORATORIES, INC.
Elkhart, Indiana 46514

MINWAX CO., INC.
75 Oak Street
Clifton, New Jersey 07014

MIRRO ALUMINUM CO.
Manitowoc, Wisconsin 55404

NIP-CO MANUFACTURING, INC.
Route 28
Glenford, New York 12433

NOXELL CORP.
11050 York Road
Baltimore, Maryland 21203

PATTERSON LABORATORIES, INC.
11930 Pleasant Avenue
Detroit, Michigan 48217

PLANTABBS CORP.
Timonium, Maryland 21093

PLANT MARVEL LABORATORIES
624 West 119 Street
Chicago, Illinois 60628

PROCTER & GAMBLE CO.
301 East 6 Street
Cincinnati, Ohio 45202

PUREX CORP., LTD.
24600 South Main Street
Carson, California 90744

REEFER-GALLER, INC.
see Colgate-Palmolive

I. ROKEACH & SONS, INC.
560 Sylvan Avenue
Englewood Cliffs, New Jersey 07632

ROSS CHEMICAL
8485 Melville Street
Detroit, Michigan 48209

SAVOGRAN CO.
P.O. Box 130
Norwood, Massachusetts 06062

SCHULTZ CO.
11730 Northline
Maryland Heights
St. Louis, Missouri 63042

SCOTT'S LIQUID GOLD, INC.
4880 Havana Street
Denver, Colorado 80239

SHERWIN-WILLIAMS
101 Prospect Avenue N.W.
Cleveland, Ohio 44115

STAR BRONZE CO.
Alliance, Ohio 44601

STIM-U-PLANT LABORATORIES, INC.
2077 Parkwood Avenue
Columbus, Ohio 43219

SUNBEAM APPLIANCE
5430 West Roosevelt Road
Chicago, Illinois 60609

TESTOR CORP.
630 Buckbee Street
Rockford, Illinois 61101

TEXIZE CHEMICAL CO.
P.O. Box 368
Greenville, South Carolina 29602

TOPCO ASSOCIATES, INC.
7711 Gross Point Road
Skokie, Illinois 60076

3M COMPANY
3M Center
St. Paul, Minnesota 55101

TRAUM, DAVID CO., INC.
85 Tenth Avenue
New York, New York 10011

UNCLE SAM CHEMICAL CO., INC.
573–577 West 131 Street
New York, New York 10027

UNION CARBIDE
270 Park Avenue
New York, New York 10017

UNITED GILSONITE LABORATORIES
Scranton, Pennsylvania 18501

U.S. BORAX & CHEMICAL CORP.
3075 Wilshire Boulevard
Los Angeles, California 90010

U.S. PLYWOOD-CHAMPION INTERNATIONAL
1 Landmark Square
Stamford, Connecticut 06921

WAVERLY MINERAL PRODUCTS
3018 Market Street
Philadelphia, Pennsylvania 19104

WEST CHEMICAL PRODUCTS,
INC.
42–16 West Street
Long Island City, New York 11101

WHITE LABORATORIES, INC.
c/o Schering Corp.
Bloomfield, New Jersey 07003

WHITE ROSE FOOD CORP.
150 Price Parkway
Farmingdale, New York 11735

WILBERT PRODUCTS CO., INC.
805 East 139 Street
Bronx, New York 10454

J. A. WRIGHT & CO.
Keene, New Hampshire 03431

Directory of Poison Control Centers

Wherever you are, there is a poison control center within calling distance. The centers listed below are all open 24 hours a day; in an emergency, they can answer your questions or direct you to a center nearer your home.

Alabama
Poison Control Center
Children's Hospital
1601 6th Avenue South
Birmingham, Alabama 35233
(205) 933-4050

Alaska
Poison Control Center
Providence Hospital
3200 Providence Drive
Anchorage, Alaska 99504
(907) 274-6535

Arizona
Poison Control Center
Arizona Health Sciences
    Center
University of Arizona
Tucson, Arizona 85721
(602) 626-6016

Arkansas
Poison Control Center
University of Arkansas Medical
    Center
4301 W. Markham Street
Little Rock, Arkansas 72201
(501) 661-6161

California
Poison Control Center
Thomas J. Fleming Memorial
    Center
Children's Hospital of Los
    Angeles
Los Angeles, California 90054
(213) 664-2121

Poison Control Center
County Health Department
135 Polk Street
San Francisco, California 94102
(415) 431-2800

Colorado
Rocky Mountain Poison Center
Denver General Hospital
West 8 Street & Cherokee Street
Denver, Colorado 80204
(303) 629-1123

Connecticut
Poison Control Center
Yale–New Haven Hospital
789 Howard Avenue
New Haven, Connecticut
    06504
(203) 436-1960

Delaware

Poison Information Service
501 West 14 Street
Wilmington, Delaware 19899
(302) 655-3389

District of Columbia

Poison Control Center
Children's Hospital National
  Medical Center
111 Michigan Avenue N.W.
Washington, D.C. 20010
(202) 745-2000

Florida

Poison Control Center
Jackson Memorial Hospital
1611 N.W. 12th Avenue
Miami, Florida 33136
(305) 325-6799

Poison Control Center
St. Vincent's Hospital
Barrs Street & St. John's Avenue
Jacksonville, Florida 32204
(904) 389-7751

Georgia

Poison Control Center
Grady Memorial Hospital
80 Butler Street S.E.
Atlanta, Georgia 30303
(404) 588-4400

Hawaii

Poison Control Center
Kauikeolani Children's
  Hospital
226 Kuakini Street
Honolulu, Hawaii 96817
(808) 537-1831

Idaho

Poison Control Center
St. Alphonsus Hospital
1065 North Curtis Road
Boise, Idaho 83704
(208) 376-1211

Illinois

Rush-Presbyterian/St. Luke's
  Poison Center
Rush-Presbyterian/St. Luke's
  Medical Center
Chicago, Illinois 60612
(312) 942-5969

Indiana

Poison Control Center
Wishard Memorial Hospital
1001 West 10th Street
Indianapolis, Indiana 46202
(317) 630-7251

Iowa

Poison Control Center
Iowa Methodist Hospital
1200 Pleasant Street
Des Moines, Iowa 50308
(515) 283-6212

Kansas

Poison Control Center
University of Kansas Medical
  Center
39th and Rainbow Boulevard
Kansas City, Kansas 66103
(913) 588-6633

Kentucky

Drug Information Center
University of Kentucky Medical
  Center
Lexington, Kentucky 40506
(606) 233-5320

Louisiana

Poison Control Center
Charity Hospital
1532 Tulane Avenue
New Orleans, Louisiana 71040
(504) 568-2311

Maine

Maine Medical Center
Emergency Division
22 Bramhall Street
Portland, Maine 04102
(207) 871-2381

Massachusetts

Boston Poison Information
Center
300 Longwood Avenue
Boston, Massachusetts 02115
(617) 232-2120

Michigan

Poison Control Center
Children's Hospital of Michigan
3901 Bauebien
Detroit, Michigan 48201
(313) 494-5711

Minnesota

Hennepin Poison Center
Hennepin County Medical Center
701 Park Avenue
Minneapolis, Minnesota 55414
(612) 347-3141

Mississippi

Poison Control Center
University Medical Center
2500 North State Street
Jackson, Mississippi 39216
(601) 354-7660

Missouri

St. Louis Poison Center
Cardinal Glennon Children's
Hospital
1465 South Grand Avenue
St. Louis, Missouri 63104
(314) 772-5200

Montana

Poison Control Center
St. Vincent's Hospital
2915 12th Avenue North
Billings, Montana 59103
(406) 657-7762

Nebraska

Poison Control Center
Children's Memorial Hospital
44th and Dewey Streets
Omaha, Nebraska 68105
(402) 553-5400

Nevada

Poison Control Center
Southern Nevada Memorial
Hospital
1800 West Charleston Boulevard
Las Vegas, Nevada 89102
(702) 385-1277

New Hampshire

Poison Control Center
Mary Hitchcock Hospital
2 Maynard Street
Hanover, New Hampshire 03755
(603) 643-4000

New Jersey

Poison Control Center
Newark Beth Israel Medical
Center
201 Lyons Avenue
Newark, New Jersey 07112
(201) 726-7242

Poison Control Center
Helene Fuld Medical Center
750 Brunswick Avenue
Trenton, New Jersey 08607
(609) 396-10077

New Mexico

New Mexico Poison Drug
Information and Medical Crisis
Center
University of New Mexico
Albuquerque, New Mexico
87131
(505) 843-2551

New York

Western New York Poison Center
Children's Hospital of Buffalo
219 Bryant Street
Buffalo, New York 14222
(716) 878-7000

New York City Poison Control
New York City Department of
Health
Bureau of Laboratories
455 First Avenue
New York, New York 10016
(212) 340-4494

North Carolina

Poison Control Center
Duke University Medical Center
Durham, North Carolina 27710
(919) 684-8111

North Dakota

Poison Control Center
Bismarck Hospital
300 North 7th Street
Bismarck, North Dakota 58501
(701) 223-4357

Ohio

Poison Control Center
Academy of Medicine
10525 Carnegie Avenue
Cleveland, Ohio 44106
(216) 231-4455

Oklahoma

Poison Control Center
Oklahoma Children's Memorial
Hospital
940 Northeast 13th
Oklahoma City, Oklahoma 73126
(405) 271-5454

Oregon

Oregon Poison Control and Drug
Information Center
University of Oregon
Health Sciences Center
3181 S.W. Sam Jackson Park
Road
Portland, Oregon 97201
(503) 225-8500

Pennsylvania

Pittsburgh Poison Center
Children's Hospital of Pittsburgh
125 DeSoto Street
Pittsburgh, Pennsylvania 15213
(412) 681-6669

Rhode Island

Poison Control Center
Department of Health
Providence, Rhode Island 02908
(401) 277-2401

South Carolina

Poison & Drug Information
Center
College of Pharmacy
University of South Carolina
Columbia, South Carolina 29208
(803) 765-7359

South Dakota

West River Poison Center
Rapid City Regional Hospital East
Rapid City, South Dakota 57701
(605) 343-3333

Tennessee

Midsouth Poison Center
University of Tennessee
College of Pharmacy
874 Union Avenue
Memphis, Tennessee 38163
(901) 528-6048

Texas

Poison Control Center
W. I. Cook Children's Hospital
1212 West Lancaster
Fort Worth, Texas 76102
(817) 336-5521

Southeast Texas Poison Control
Center
8th and Mechanic Streets
Galveston, Texas 77550
(713) 765-3332

Utah

Intermountain Regional Poison
Control Center
50 North Medical Drive
Salt Lake City, Utah 84132
(801) 581-2151

Virginia

Virginia Poison Center
Virginia Commonwealth
University
Richmond, Virginia 23298
(804) 786-9123

Washington

Poison Center
Children's Orthopedic Hospital
  and Medical Center
4800 Sandpoint Way, N.E.
Seattle, Washington 98105
(206) 634-5252

West Virginia

Poison Control Center
Charleston Area Medical Center
  Memorial Division
Washington and Chestnut
  Streets
Charleston, West Virginia 25304
(304) 348-4211

Wisconsin

Milwaukee Poison Center
Milwaukee Children's
  Hospital
1700 West Wisconsin
Milwaukee, Wisconsin
  53233
(414) 931-4053

Wyoming

Wyoming Poison Center
DePaul Hospital
2600 East 18th Street
Cheyenne, Wyoming 82001
(307) 635-9256

Sources

Books

The Clinical Toxicology of Commercial Products, ed. Gosselin, Hodge, Smith, and Gleason (Baltimore: Williams and Wilkins, 1977).

A Consumer's Dictionary of Cosmetic Ingredients, Ruth Winter (New York: Crown, 1974).

A Consumer's Dictionary of Food Additives, Ruth Winter (New York: Crown, 1978).

The Encyclopedia of Household Hints and Dollar Stretchers, Michael Gore (New York: Hanover House, 1957).

The Glossary of Chemical Terms, Clifford Hampel and Gessner Hawley (New York: Van Nostrand Reinhold Co., 1976).

The Hazards of Medication, Eric Martin (Philadelphia: J. B. Lippincott Co., 1977).

The Household Encyclopedia, N. H. Mager & S. K. Mager (New York: Pocket Books, 1975).

How to Clean Everything, Alma Chestnut Moore (New York: Simon and Schuster, 1968).

Kitchen Wisdom, Frieda Arkin (New York: Holt, Rinehart, and Winston, 1977).

The Merck Index, ed. Martha Windholz (Rahway, N.J.: Merck & Co., 1976).

The Merck Manual, ed. Robert Berkow (Rahway, N.J.: Merck & Co., 1977).

The Physicians' Desk Reference (Oradell, N.J.: Medical Economics, 1979).

The Registry of Toxic Effects of Chemical Substances (Cincinnati: National Institute for Occupational Safety and Health, 1977).

Booklets and pamphlets

Abbott Laboratories (Consumer Products Division): "Antidote Information and Instruction."

American Medical Association: "General First Aid Measures" (chart).

————: "Home Accidents Aren't Accidental," 1971.

Bristol-Myers: "Consumer Guide to Product Information," ed. Bess Myerson, 1977.

Clairol, Inc.: "Composition of Clairol Products with Special Reference to First Aid Measures," 1972.

Clorox Company: "Your Right to Write."

National Paint and Coatings Association: "The Household Paint Selector," 1975.

National Poison Center Network: "Enjoy Your Plants, but Protect Your Family."

New York City Poison Control Center: "Household Items of Low Toxiciy."

Soap and Detergent Association (Scientific and Technical Report No. 52): "Cleaning Products and Their Accidental Ingestion," October 1976.

U.S. Consumer Products Safety Commission:
Fact Sheet #14: "Lead Paint Poisoning," January 1978.
Fact Sheet #21: "Poisonous Household Products," March 1975.
Fact Sheet #23: "Flammable Liquids," June 1975.
Fact Sheet #33: "Aerosols," August 1974.
Fact Sheet #46: "Poison Prevention Packaging," May 1976.
Fact Sheet #55: "The Federal Hazardous Substances Act," May 1975.
Fact Sheet #67: "Oven Cleaners," May 1975.
Fact Sheet #72: "Drain Cleaners," October 1975.
Technical Fact Sheet #4: "Regulations under the Hazardous Substances Act," November 1975.

U.S. Environmental Protection Agency: "Protecting Our Environment," March 1977.

Articles

"Aid for lead paint removal," *The New York Times,* March 6, 1979.

"All-purpose cleaners," *Consumer Reports,* February 1979.

"A new scouring cream: better than cleanser?" *Consumer Reports,* July 1978.

"Antidote labels on many toxic products ineffective, experts say," *Los Angeles Times,* July 23, 1978.

"Beware of Warning Labels," Jack Anderson, *New York News,* July 18, 1978.

"Beware the Label," Sue Berkman, *The New York News Sunday Magazine,* August 1, 1977.

"Caulking Compounds," *Consumers' Research Magazine,* September 1977.

"Checkout Time at the Roach Motel," Scot Haller, *New York* Magazine, July 9–16, 1979

"Chemicals in search of a solution," Richard Lyons, *The New York Times,* December 25, 1977.

"Common Household Poisons," Teat, Stramoski, and Green, *U.S. Pharmacist,* March 1979.

"Dishwasher Detergents and Two Rinsing Aids," *Consumers' Research Magazine*, August 1977.

"Dishwasher Detergents (Machine)," *Consumers' Research Buying Guide*, 1978.

"Diswashing Detergents," *Consumers' Research Magazine*, April 1977.

"Don't crack up over leather furniture," Lois Libien and Margaret Strong, *The New York News*, January 1, 1978.

"Drain Cleaners," *Consumers' Research Buying Guide*, 1978.

"Exterior Caulking Compounds," *Consumer Reports*, September 1978.

"Floor Waxes and Finishes," *Consumers' Research Buying Guide*, 1978.

"Foam caulk requires a deft hand to apply," *Consumer Reports*, April 1979.

"General purpose cleaners," *Consumers' Research Buying Guide*, 1978.

"General purpose household cleaners," *Consumers' Research Magazine*, May 1977.

"Hazards in Arts and Crafts," *Consumers' Research Magazine*, July 1977.

"Home water repellent treatment for fabrics," *Consumers' Research Magazine*, February 1977.

"Household Cements," *Consumers' Research Magazine*, September 1977.

"Household Insecticides," *Consumer Reports*, June 1979.

"How to identify the poisonous plants that can hurt your pets," Guy Hodge, *The Humane Society News*, Spring 1977.

"Latex Interior Paints," *Consumer Reports*, February 1978.

"Laundry detergents," Consumers' Research Buying Guide, 1978.

"Long-lived detergents," *The New York Times*, March 13, 1979.

"Michigan to sue 3 detergent marketers," *Advertising Age*, January 9, 1978.

"The Nontoxic Ingestion," H. C. Mofenson and J. Grensher, *Pediatric Clinics of North America*, August 1970.

"Personal Health," Jane Brody, *The New York Times*, March 22, 1978.

"Program cuts adult resistance to child resistant caps," *National Association of Retail Druggists Journal*, September 1978.

"Psst! Aerosol Alternatives," *Newsweek*, May 9, 1977.

"Scouring cleansers," *Consumers' Research Magazine*, July 1977.

"Scouring Products: powders and pads," *Consumer Reports*, March 1978.

"Seven basics of upholstery spot removal," Lois Libien and Margaret Strong, *The New York News*, January 29, 1978.

"Silver care products," *Consumer Reports*, February 1978.

"Soft cleaner warning out," *The New York News*, February 10, 1978.

"Spackling compounds," *Consumer Reports*, May 1979.

"Spray-on, wipe-off cleaners," *Consumers' Research Magazine,* February 1974.

"Three more prewash preparations," *Consumers' Research Magazine,* February 1977.

"Toilet bowl cleaners, *Consumers' Research Buying Guide,* 1978.

"Warning on paint removers," *Health Digest,* May 1978.

"What to do in a poison emergency," *Consumer Reports,* January 1978.

"When in doubt, just add a little salt," Lois Libien and Margaret Strong, *The New York News,* September 25, 1977.

"Youthful solvent sniffers are warned," T. R. Van Dellen, *The New York News,* May 27, 1976.

Miscellaneous

Government Printing Office: The Code of Federal Regulations, Title 16 (Consumer Product Safety Commission, as of January 1977).

————: A Compilation of Laws Administered by the U.S. Consumer Product Safety Commission.

State of New York, Senate-Assembly bill S. 8668, A. 11490, March 20, 1978, "An act to amend the public health law, in relation to regulating the distribution, sale, or transportation of hazardous substances."

Statement by Michael A. Brown, Executive Director, U.S. Consumer Product Safety Commission, before the House Committee on Interstate and Foreign Commerce, Subcommittee on Oversight and Investigation, Children's Hospital, Los Angeles, July 21, 1978.

Statement by Congressman Henry A. Waxman before the House Committee on Interstate and Foreign Commerce, Subcommittee on Oversight and Investigation, Children's Hospital, Los Angeles, July 21, 1978.

Brand-Names Index